U.S. MARINES IN IRAQ, 2003 COMBAT SERVICE SUPPORT DURING OPERATION IRAQI FREEDOM

U.S. Marines in the Global War on Terrorism

by
Lieutenant Colonel Melissa D. Mihocko
U.S. Marine Corps Reserve

History Division
United States Marine Corps
Washington, D.C.
2011

Foreword

The story of combat service support during Operation Iraqi Freedom–I is one that could have been easily overlooked by history, except what would have been lost is more than a simple tale of Marines performing exceptionally during a time of war. Lost would have been a recollection of historical firsts, an account of extraordinary vision and insight from some of the Marine Corps' top leaders, and a chronicle of miracles performed in the heat of battle by individuals who rarely receive the glory and praise of their front-line combat counterparts. This monograph tells the story of the Marines and sailors from 1st Force Service Support Group and 2d Force Service Support Group, whose combined efforts helped pave the way for the Marine Corps' success during Operation Iraqi Freedom–I.

The author, Lieutenant Colonel Melissa D. Mihocko, is a supply officer who has served as a field historian with the History Division since 2002. Before this service, LtCol Mihocko was assigned to 4th Civil Affairs Group and deployed twice to the Balkans and once during a MEU's Mediterranean deployment. In 2003, just months after joining the detachment, she mobilized and deployed as a field historian in support of Operation Iraqi Freedom. Between February and May of that year, LtCol Mihocko was assigned to 1st Force Service Support Group and traveled to Kuwait and Iraq to collect more than 130 oral history interviews, along with documents, artifacts, and photos. More important, however, she gained a firsthand look at the Marines Corps' combat service support in action. Following her deployment, she remained on active duty and mobilized again to work on this monograph.

Dr. Charles P. Neimeyer
Director of Marine Corps History

Preface

It is never easy to honor and recognize Marines and sailors for simply doing their jobs, even when those jobs are performed in an exemplary manner. And when those jobs span a wide spectrum of distinct combat support specialties, they are often overshadowed by the stories of frontline combat troops. Combat service support Marines are not the traditional "trigger-pullers;" they are the ones who help pave the path for successful Marine Corps operations. They are the ones pushing fuel through a hose across 60 miles of battlefield, building bridges under fire to allow the infantry to fight through to Baghdad, supplying ammunition throughout the night to support a barrage of U.S. artillery fire, turning wrenches in sweltering heat to ensure vehicles and equipment are combat ready, purifying water from a polluted canal, and providing rations to sustain combat troops.

Behind the historical firsts and monumental feats stand leaders and individuals who exercised a level of innovation and ingenuity that merit both recognition and praise. The goal of this monograph is to honor those combat service support Marines and sailors who selflessly performed their jobs, and doing so in such an extraordinary manner, ensured the success of the Marine Corps during Operation Iraqi Freedom–I. This monograph represents an operational history developed from a collection of oral history interviews and perspectives on the ground from a wide range of resources. It is not an official history, but rather a segment of a story that will be written and told for many years to come of Marine Corps operations during the Global War on Terrorism. This monograph covers the combat service support operations during Operation Iraqi Freedom–I between November 2002 and October 2003. The main characters are 1st and 2d Force Service Support Groups (FSSGs), and in its eight chapters, the manuscript tells a story of reorganization, preparation, and execution.

For me, this project began in early 2003, when I was assigned as a field historian to 1st Force Service Support Group. As a fairly inexperienced field historian, I quickly realized that my assignment depended less on formal training and advanced history degrees than it did on my own adaptability, flexibility, and capacity to listen. I interviewed Marines and sailors from lance corporal to commanding general, and each interview was different. Some would answer the question at hand and only the question at hand, offering no further details unless specifically asked. Others would respond to the question and continue to elaborate freely, often moving into new topics. Each interview though—including those collected by my colleagues from other logistics units—provided a piece of the overall story. Each personal account added texture and color to the narrative pieced together from command chronologies, unit reports, and operational summaries. After demobilizing and letting the proverbial dust settle, I was fortunate to have the opportunity to write the History Division's monograph on combat service support during OIF-I. Thus began my long journey of mobilizations, research, writing, editing, more research, and more writing. During the past five years since my last demobilization, I have continued writing and editing, with tremendous help throughout the review and editing process.

There are so many individuals without whom I'd never have been able to complete this monograph. First and foremost, I would like to thank my fellow Marines in the Marine Corps History Division Individual Mobilization Augmentee (IMA) Detachment, who allowed me the opportunity, not only to join the IMA unit, but to go forward and collect history in the field: retired Colonel Nicholas Reynolds, a real mentor to me, both in his brilliant writing and his humble leadership style; retired Colonel David Watters, who recruited me into the History Division and was a constant source of motivation; Colonel Michael Visconage, whose sense of humor and Starbuck's frappaccino from the air wing went a long way in dry sweltering desert heat; retired Colonel Reed Bonadonna, who captured the soul of Task Force Tarawa's struggles and heartache through his interviews and historian's journal; and Chief Warrant Officer–3 William Hutson, an intelligent and humble individual who conducted interviews with Marines from 2d Marine Logistics Command, thereby providing the building blocks to their story as part of this monograph.

My experience with 1st Force Service Support Group was marked with support, cooperation, and enthusiasm for my mission as a field historian. Now-retired Major General Edward Usher allowed me access to his staff, his battalions, and his organization as a whole, clearly articulating the challenges they faced at every phase of the fight. Notably, Major General Darrell Moore, retired Colonel John Sweeney, Major General Tracy (Mork) Garrett, all battalion commanding officers, and group staff were instrumental in my collection efforts. Colonel Adrian Burke, a veteran of the first Gulf War, was a key architect in the reorganization of 1st FSSG to its battlefield configuration, and he also took over command of CSSB-12 just prior to the start of the war. He provided a great deal of insight into 1st FSSG's transformation. Colonel Niel Nelson, commander of an engineer battalion who accomplished significant bridging feats during OIF-I, provided key information during the research and writing phase of this project. LtCol John Cassady, the mortuary affairs officer-in-charge, afforded me the opportunity to witness firsthand the care and reverence he and his Marines took in processing each and every fallen Marine. I'd like to thank the liaison officers of 1st FSSG, Lieutenant Colonel (retired) Valerie Thomas, Lieutenant Colonel Paul Miller, and Lieutenant Colonel (retired) Tom Leonard, who helped me maintain my sanity in the desert. I would also like to thank Master Sergeant (retired) Edward Kniery, combat cameraman, who deployed with me and captured the majority of photographs in this monograph.

During my second period of mobilization, I was afforded the opportunity to work offsite, and I'd like to extend my appreciation to Lieutenant Colonel Patrick Kirchner and his staff at MACS-24 in Virginia Beach, Virginia for graciously providing me with office space and administrative support while I researched and wrote the initial draft of this manuscript. In the early editing phase, several individuals generously lent their time to review and edit numerous drafts of my manuscript: Colonel Nathan Lowrey, Colonel Kurtis Wheeler, Lieutenant Colonel Valerie Jackson, and Gunnery Sergeant Brad Wineman. At the Marine Corps History Division, I would like to express my appreciation to several individuals, without whom this monograph would never have happened: the late Colonel John W. Ripley, the former director of the History Division; Dr. Charles P. Neimeyer, the current director; and Charles Melson, the division's chief historian. I would also like to thank the outstanding editing and design staff led by Kenneth Williams, to include Wanda Renfrow, Jim Caiella, and W. Stephen Hill, as well as Annette Amerman in the reference section. I owe them a debt of gratitude for the time and care they took in ensuring the monograph's accuracy, readability, and graphic design.

Lastly, I would like to thank my husband, Dave, who himself deployed with I MEF during OIF–I and twice since then. He has continued to support and encourage me throughout this entire process.

There are those who may not agree with the story exactly as I have told it; they may remember things differently because their perspective was different. Despite my utmost desire to provide an accurate and comprehensive historical account, the sheer complexity of the situation makes it unlikely that every perspective will be adequately represented in this monograph. However, it is undeniable that the Marines and sailors who served with 1st and 2d FSSGs during this period served honorably and performed miraculously. My hope is that this monograph will simply tell their story, and in doing so, capture the innovation and ingenuity, not only of the leaders and the planners, but the individual Marine at every level, who has earned a place in Marine Corps history.

Melissa D. Mihocko
Lieutenant Colonel, U.S. Marine Corps Reserve
Quantico, Virginia

Table of Contents

Foreword iii
Preface v
Table of Contents vii
Map ix
Chapter 1   Setting the Stage for War 1
Chapter 2   Arrival in Theater 19
Chapter 3   Opening Days of the War (17-22 March 2003) 39
Chapter 4   Battling for An-Nasiriyah and Beyond (23-26 March 2003) 53
Chapter 5   Northern Support Areas (27 March-3 April 2003) 69
Chapter 6   Taking Baghdad and Tikrit (4-22 April 2003) 79
Chapter 7   Security and Stabilization Operations 93
Chapter 8   The Special Purpose MAGTF 101
Epilogue 107
Notes 109
Appendix A   Chronology of Significant Events 115
Appendix B   Command and Staff List 119
Appendix C   Unit List 123
Appendix D   Glossary of Terms and Abbreviations 125
Appendix E   Presidential Unit Citation 131
Appendix F   Navy Unit Commendation 133
Index 135

Chapter 1

Setting the Stage for War

"Recently, General [Tommy] Franks, (Combatant Commander, Central Command) visited with the staff of the I Marine Expeditionary Force (I MEF). After the standard brief and discussions, General Franks asked the MEF staff what the biggest success for the MEF was during OIF [Operation Iraqi Freedom]. Much praise was given to the successful use of combined arms, close air support, and those warfighting functions that one would assume are the ingredients for success on the battlefield. When it was Lieutenant General [James T.] Conway's (Commanding General, I MEF) turn to provide his insight, he said one word . . . 'LOGISTICS'!"[1]

In June 2002, President George W. Bush introduced a new defense doctrine based on the concept of preemption. In his first commencement address following the attacks on 11 September 2001, President Bush described his vision for the war against terrorism and beyond in a speech to cadets at the U.S. Military Academy at West Point, New York. He stated, "Our security will require all Americans to be forward-looking and resolute, to be ready for preemptive action when necessary to defend our liberty and to defend our lives."[2] In the fall of that year, after President Bush challenged the United Nations to enforce its own resolutions against Iraq, Congress authorized an attack on that country, and the United States moved one step closer to war. In late December, President Bush approved the deployment of U.S. troops to the Persian Gulf region, and by March 2003, approximately 200,000 American servicemen and women were stationed there in support of Operation Iraqi Freedom (OIF).

For the Marine Corps' part, OIF not only called for the largest deployment of Marine forces since Operations Desert Shield and Desert Storm, but it also required they move rapidly over unprecedented distances. Without a doubt, the Marine Corps' success was largely dependent on combat service support. Although often overshadowed in the history books by stories of air and ground combat, the logistical aspect of warfare, often described as the range of tasks necessary to man, arm, fuel, fix, and move a force, played a major role during OIF. In addition to facing many traditional obstacles to providing logistics support, 1st and 2d Force Service Support Groups (FSSGs), which are highlighted in this monograph, were also required to develop innovative solutions to new challenges and frequently redefine the familiar concepts, processes, and organizational structures during Operation Iraqi Freedom.

Rethinking Combat Service Support Operations

The basic role of an FSSG is to provide logistical support for a Marine expeditionary force while in garrison, employed by itself, or as part of a traditional Marine air-ground task force (MAGTF) operation. During Operations Desert Shield and Desert Storm, Brigadier General James A. Brabham, commanding general of 1st Force Service Support Group (1st FSSG), drew from his experiences involving direct and general support missions in Vietnam to suggest a reorganization of both the 1st and 2d FSSGs for wartime operations.[3] The resulting "general support" and "direct support" group concepts were endorsed by the I Marine Expeditionary Force (I MEF) commanding general, Lieutenant General Walter E. Boomer; however, he wanted the changes implemented through a single FSSG with one commander. To accommodate this request, the two FSSGs combined into a single group, and General Brabham, who was senior to Brigadier General Charles C. Krulak, the commanding general of 2d FSSG, assumed command.[4]

The new organization was extremely successful, and following the Persian Gulf War, many articles were published discussing the role of the FSSG during Operations Desert Shield and Desert Storm. Although there was an initial push to implement permanent organizational changes based on the lessons learned in the desert, inertia was lost as time passed, and few changes actually occurred.[5] The FSSGs each resumed their former garrison configurations, and for more than a decade, they pursued traditional peacetime roles.

Fortunately, logistics planners in both FSSGs continued to think about the future of combat service

BGen Edward G. Usher III, Commanding General 1st FSSG, speaks to Marines prior to the start of the war.
Courtesy of CSSB-10

support operations. Recapturing concepts developed by Generals Brabham and Krulak, they used them as the genesis for defining the functional relationship between 1st FSSG and 2d FSSG during Operation Iraqi Freedom; 1st FSSG would provide direct support and 2d FSSG would provide general support. There were, however, two distinct differences from Operations Desert Shield and Desert Storm. First, each FSSG retained its own command identity. Second, while 1st FSSG served under I MEF, 2d FSSG deployed into theater as the Marine Logistics Command (MLC), a subordinate element of Marine Forces Central Command (MarCent). As the service component representative, MarCent was responsible for ensuring that Marine forces were employed appropriately in Central Command's theater of operations and that they received necessary administrative and logistical support.

Restructuring the 1st Force Service Support Group

While planning for Operation Iraqi Freedom, Brigadier General Edward G. Usher, commanding general of 1st Force Service Support Group, faced a number of challenges: great distances across the battlefield, a shortened timeline, extensive lines of communication from operational level logistics to the FSSG's most forward units, potentially severe weather, and unpredictable enemy forces. The biggest obstacle in 1st FSSG's path to success, however, was the basic nature of its organizational structure.[6]

While operating in a peacetime garrison environment, 1st FSSG had always emphasized efficiency over effectiveness, having focused primarily on providing cost-effective logistics support. The battalions were organized by function: headquarters and service, supply, maintenance, engineer support, transportation, medical, and dental. General Usher understood that this functional structure would not work in wartime, and that he needed to task organize his command to support I MEF's mission on the battlefield. Although this was similar to the problem faced by the FSSGs during the Persian Gulf War, this time around, General Usher's goal was not only to reorganize, but also to minimize the amount of restructuring that would have to occur once in theater. Ultimately, he wanted to avoid the difficulties and challenges that General Brabham encountered while organizing in theater, and therefore planned the reorganization to take place prior to deployment.[7] Lieutenant Colonel Adrian W. Burke, 1st FSSG future operations officer, understood the significance of General Usher's intent to solidify the organization as early as possible, and he emphasized the importance of developing habitual relationships between the supporting and supported commanders.

> One of the things that cause things to survive or work well on the battlefield is relationships. Relationships can solve 8/10ths of all your problems. Commanders know each others' limitations and capabilities. They have friendships with each other; they work and train together through various exercises before they go into combat together. You can't buy that anywhere, and if you have ad hoc organizations that form up on the battlefield, all of the depth of respect and trust and instinct that those commanders develop with each other, is not there.[8]

For General Usher, a third-generation Marine who had previously commanded a Marine expeditionary unit service support group and a transportation support battalion, the idea of reorganizing the FSSG into combat service support elements emerged two years earlier when I MEF began planning for contingency

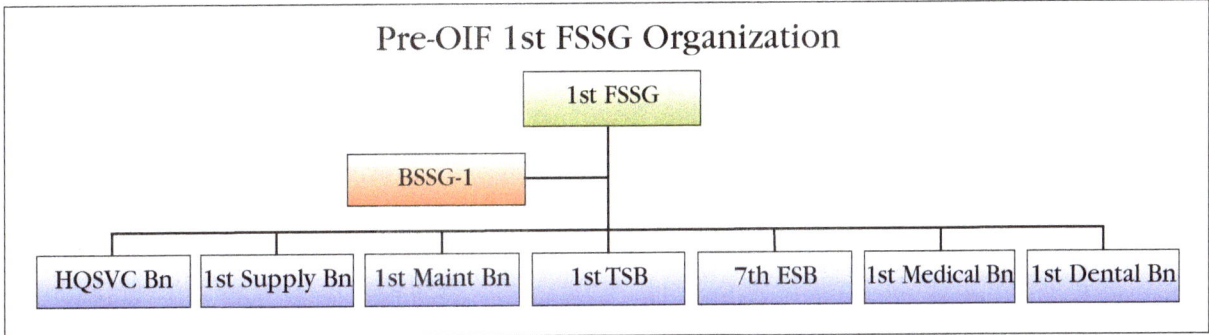

In garrison, 1st FSSG consisted of seven functional battalions and a brigade service support group (BSSG).

operations in Iraq. Shortly after 9/11, operational planning teams consisting of key staff officers within the FSSG, liaison officers from adjacent commands and attachments, and subject matter experts gathered to plan for the eventual U.S. response to the terrorist attacks. General Usher realized that to fulfill the full range of combat service support responsibilities and enter the theater as an integrated operational command, a solid commitment from all of his commanders was paramount.[9] What developed during the next 19 months reflected extensive planning and coordination on the part of the FSSG staff and the battalion commanders.

A garrison organization of functional battalions was once again transformed into a structure based on an operational template reflecting the need to provide both direct and general support combat service support to I MEF's ground combat element, 1st Marine Division. An emphasis was placed on the mobility of the direct support units, as well as the ability for the larger general support units to move in echelon across the battlefield. With augmentation from both 2d and 4th FSSGs, as well as the U.S. Army, other areas also underwent change. During initial mission analysis, planners determined that the FSSG's most critical asset was its distribution capability and as a result, formed the Transportation Support Group. Commanded by Colonel David G. Reist, the group was three battalions deep and included various transportation, bulk fuel, and maintenance elements. En-

With augmentation from both 2d and 4th FSSGs, as well as the U.S. Army, 1st FSSG reorganized its functional battalions into task-organized units for OIF.

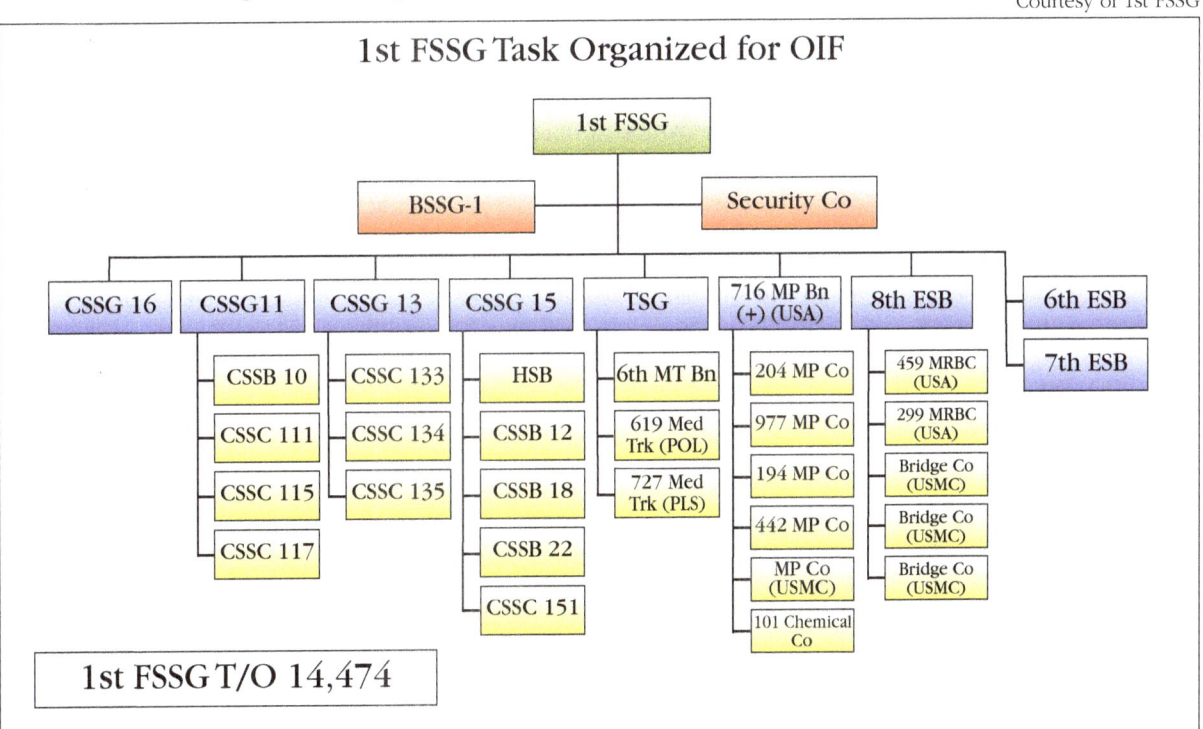

gineering missions were segregated and assigned to three engineer support battalions, largely mirroring their original formation. Medical support underwent several innovative changes, resulting in a number of firsts in both organization and implementation. Military police and motor transport were each critical in nature, but short in numbers. As a result, new units augmented 1st FSSG's organic capabilities in these areas. Colonel Darrell L. Moore, 1st FSSG's chief of staff, called it "the largest FSSG ever assembled during wartime."[10] Without question, this newly reorganized FSSG was a considerable force, carefully tailored to sustain combat operations during Operation Iraqi Freedom.

Direct and General Support

The core of 1st FSSG's warfighting organization was Combat Service Support Group 11 (CSSG-11). Commanded by Colonel John J. Pomfret, CSSG-11 provided direct combat service support to approximately 22,000 Marines in the 1st Marine Division. While the concept of direct support was not new, the units employed during the Persian Gulf War were smaller and less mobile than CSSG-11. During Operation Iraqi Freedom, the group actually maneuvered across the battlefield, moving in conjunction with elements of 1st Marine Division.[11]

During the planning phase, General Usher and his deputy commander, Colonel John L. Sweeney Jr., who himself had served in 1st FSSG during Operations Desert Shield and Desert Storm, recognized several areas in need of improvement and implemented a plan that emphasized enhancements in transportation availability and relationship building. Combat service support commanders and ground combat commanders initiated planning well in advance of the war and began joint training as early as July 2002. As a result, there was a greater amount of trust between the division and FSSG.[12] Lieutenant Colonel John J. Broadmeadow, the 1st Marine Division logistics officer stated,

> With foresight and innovativeness, 1st FSSG developed an agile, capable, and wholly unique combat service support (CSS) structure to interface with the division and I MEF. This structure did more than support our high-tempo operations. It made the regimental combat team S-4s the linchpins of logistics for the division . . . and provided a critical link between division and the FSSGs and MLC sources of supply. Within this framework, division had the first fully embedded CSS capability in recent history.[13]

The headquarters element of CSSG-11 maintained command and control of the group while a combat service support battalion (CSSB) and three combat service support companies (CSSCs) executed the daily operations. The three combat service support companies, approximately 230 Marines each, supported the three regimental combat teams in the 1st Marine Division. Required to hold two days of supplies, they provided medical, supply, maintenance, motor transport, fuel, water, food, and command and control support.[14] Combat Service Support Company 111 (CSSC-111), commanded by Captain Grant R. Shottenkirk, sailed over on amphibious shipping, in support of Regimental Combat Team 1 (RCT-1), while both Combat Service Support Company 115 (CSSC-115), commanded by Captain Suzan F. Thompson, and Combat Service Support Company 117 (CSSC-117), commanded by Captain Andrew J. Bergen, flew into theater with Regimental Combat Team 5 (RCT-5) and Regimental Combat Team 7 (RCT-7). The CSSCs formed from the three transport companies of 1st Transportation Support Battalion and traveled directly in trace, if not right alongside the fast-moving regimental combat teams. In essence, these companies were the forward edge of combat service support. Operationally controlled by 1st FSSG, the companies were tactically controlled by their respective regimental combat teams for reasons of practicality.

Commanded by Lieutenant Colonel Robert K. Weinkle Jr., Combat Service Support Battalion 10 (CSSB-10) consisted of approximately 947 Marines. Its mission was to provide direct support to 1st Marine Division units aside from the three regimental combat teams, such as 11th Marine Regiment, as well as general support to the three companies in CSSG-11.[15] With a more robust capability than the companies, CSSB-10 carried three to five days worth of supply, and together with CSSG-11, established several repair and replenishment points as forces moved up the battlefield.[16] This often put them close to, if not on, the frontlines. The battalion strategically placed its repair and replenishment points to best support the ground combat forces while also setting the stage for the establishment of more permanent follow-on support areas.

In garrison, Lieutenant Colonel Weinkle commanded Combat Service Support Group 1 at Twentynine Palms, California. In December 2002, he had the daunting task of building a battalion from scratch. Training and integration were difficult from the start, because the majority of his Marines, including most of his company commanders, were located at Camp Pendleton, California, while his core staff was at

Courtesy of CSSB-10

LtCol Robert K. Weinkle, a logistics officer commissioned in 1985, commanded CSSG-1 based in Twentynine Palms, CA, before it reorganized into CSSB-10.

Twentynine Palms. The Marines, who possessed various military occupational specialties, came from each existing FSSG battalion and included augments from both the Marine Corps Reserves and the U.S. Army who had to be trained and integrated within a short pre-deployment workup period.[17]

For General Usher, implementation of the direct support combat elements was critical to the FSSG's ability to support 1st Marine Division and I MEF as they maneuvered across the battlefield. He described the challenges of combat service support as analogous to a game of chess. "You've got to think ahead four or five moves, because when the division needs ammunition/fuel resupply, it's too late for us to then get trucks on the road. Therefore, situational awareness and flexibility to make changes on the fly have allowed for some smart decision making."[18]

While CSSG-11 supported 1st Marine Division, Combat Service Support Battalion 13 (CSSB-13) was created to provide direct combat service support to the 3d Marine Aircraft Wing (3d MAW). Often confused with the Marine wing support groups, which provide, among other things, engineers to build runways and airfields, CSSB-13 was the air wing's ground combat service support element, providing not only supply and maintenance support, but also postal, disbursing, exchange, and legal services. CSSB-13's headquarters was made up entirely of the headquarters personnel from 4th Landing Support Battalion (4th LSB), 4th FSSG.* Based out of Fort Lewis, Washington, 4th LSB, a reserve battalion, was commanded by Lieutenant Colonel Michael D. Malone, an attorney by training and a certified public accountant and business executive by trade.

When headquarters and service company at 4th LSB was activated in February 2003, Colonel Malone assumed command of CSSB-13 and three diverse companies. Combat Service Support Company 133 (CSSC-133) was largely composed of Marines from Combat Service Support Detachment 16, an aviation support element in Yuma, Arizona. Combat Service Support Company 134 (CSSC-134) was formed from an intermediate maintenance element out of Miramar, California. Combat Service Support Company 135 (CSSC-135) was an ad hoc unit comprised mostly of reserve Marines from the headquarters and service and alpha companies of 4th LSB. Although the mix-

---

* During OIF, other elements of 4th LSB deployed to various ports and airfields throughout the United States to prepare and transport personnel and equipment to war. In total, 700 of the 1,200 Marines and sailors in LtCol Malone's reserve battalion were called to active duty during Operation Iraqi Freedom.

USMC Photo

Col Bruce E. Bissett, commanding officer of CSSG-15, deployed in support of both Desert Shield/Desert Storm and Somalia as the XO and then CO of MSSG-15.

ing of regular companies and reserve Marines under a reserve command was uncommon, integration within the battalion was seamless. The inclusion of reserve Marines, who comprised one-third of the battalion's personnel, was a key factor in CSSB-13's success.[19]

Operationally, CSSC-133 and CSSC-134 were assigned to provide support on the two air bases in Kuwait: al-Jaber, where the headquarters of CSSB-13 was also located, and Ali al-Salem. CSSC-135 deployed to Iraq to support Marine wing support squadrons that were constructing forward operating bases and forward arming and refueling points. In an interview with the command historian, Colonel Malone commented on the geographical dispersion of his companies across the battlefield and how it was similar to the dispersion of his reserve companies in garrison, which are as far apart as Fort Lewis, Washington and Puerto Rico. In actuality, during Operation Iraqi Freedom, the various elements of his battalion were closer.[20]

While CSSG-11 was at the core of 1st FSSG's direct support capability, Combat Service Support Group 15 (CSSG-15) was at the center of the FSSG's general support effort. CSSG-15 provided an entry point for CSSG-11 and CSSB-13 to access the larger logistics operations. Colonel Bruce E. Bissett, commanding officer of 1st Supply Battalion, 1st FSSG, took charge of CSSG-15 and formed his staff from the headquarters of his garrison battalion. A 28-year Marine veteran, Colonel Bissett had spent ten of the last 14 years with 1st FSSG, to include a previous assignment as the group's operations officer.[21] As a result, he was very familiar with the intricacies of the FSSG's transformation from a garrison to a warfighting organization, the lessons learned during Operations Desert Shield and Desert Storm, and the importance of CSSG-15's general support mission. Holding a doctrinal five to seven days of supply, CSSG-15's primary mission was to push supplies forward to strategic points on the battlefield, where they could be readily accessible to I MEF ground units.[22]*

CSSG-15's general support mission required the establishment of several combat service support areas in the vicinity of 3d Marine Aircraft Wing forward operating bases. Two subordinate general support battalions carried out this mission. Combat Service Support Battalions 12 (CSSB-12) and 18 (CSSB-18) were transformed from two 1st FSSG garrison battalions—the 1st Maintenance Battalion and the Headquarters and Service Battalion—into task organized combat service support organizations. The battalion commanders, Lieutenant Colonel Kathleen M. Murney and Lieutenant Colonel Thomas N. Collins, assumed their new roles as the workhorses of 1st FSSG's general support mission. Leapfrogging across the battlefield, these general support battalions established the combat service support areas–also known as logistics support areas–and utilized both push and pull techniques to provide I MEF forces with sustained logistical support.

Another subordinate element within CSSG-15 was Combat Service Support Company 151 (CSSC-151). Smaller in size than the two combat service support battalions, its mission was to provide inorganic logistics support to the I MEF command element and its headquarters group. Commanded by Lieutenant Colonel Robert W. Higbee,** CSSC-151 provided rations, water, fuel, ammunition, and repair parts, and

---

* CSSG-15 was assigned numerous auxiliary missions to include limited vehicle evacuation and recovery, the establishment of salvage points, and the development of temporary enemy prisoner of war holding facilities.

** Although CSSC-151 was a company-sized element with just under 130 Marines and sailors, it was determined that the commanding officer should be a lieutenant colonel due to the nature of its close relationship with I MEF. (LtCol Robert W. Higbee, USMC intvw, 7Mar03, USMC [Oral HistColl], Quantico, VA.)

acted as I MEF's conduit to the higher maintenance echelons.[23]

Also subordinate to CSSG-15 was Combat Service Support Battalion 22 (CSSB-22), commanded by Lieutenant Colonel Thomas N. Goben. While CSSG-11 supported 1st Marine Division, CSSB-22 provided direct combat service support to Task Force Tarawa, comprised of a Marine expeditionary brigade (MEB) headquarters and Regimental Combat Team 2 (RCT-2). Although the total number of personnel fluctuated throughout the war, Task Force Tarawa initially deployed with just over 7,000 Marines and sailors.[24] While Task Force Tarawa and CSSB-22 were part of the II Marine Expeditionary Force, based at Camp Lejeune, North Carolina, during Operation Iraqi Freedom, they fell under the operational command of I MEF. Like the other combat service support units in 1st FSSG, CSSB-22 was specifically formed for OIF. Unlike the functional battalions in 1st FSSG, however, CSSB-22 had already been task-organized as a Marine expeditionary unit service support group (MSSG).*

With only 12 days to reorganize his staff into a deployable combat service support battalion, Colonel Goben faced a number of challenges within his new mission to support Task Force Tarawa. For one, the MSSG had been designed to support a battalion landing team, a unit considerably smaller than the regimental combat team serving with Task Force Tarawa. One of the major changes he made to accommodate the larger force was to increase his transportation assets by doubling the number of vehicles and drivers. His medical capability also grew from a small detachment to a shock trauma platoon.* In other areas, such as maintenance, engineering, communications, and supply, Colonel Goben lost resources; with less robust capabilities in these areas, he had to rely on additional support from CSSB-12, CSSB-18, 1st FSSG, and Task Force Tarawa.[25]

Distribution: The Critical Key to Success

Speed, distance, environment, and weather all challenged the FSSG's ability to distribute supplies across the battlefield. Early in the planning process, at one of General Usher's "Council of Colonels"** meetings, it was agreed that smooth and uninterrupted distribution was the key to ensuring 1st FSSG's success. The council recognized that if distribution failed, all other areas of combat service support would also be ineffective, and it made several organizational changes to maximize the FSSG's distribution capabilities. In December of 2002, one such change involved the transformation of the 1st Transportation Support Battalion (1st TSB) into a larger transportation support group (TSG).[26]

Colonel David G. Reist, the original commanding officer of 1st TSB, remained in charge and was responsible for restructuring his unit to meet the massive transportation requirements of I MEF. The peacetime structure of 1st TSB included seven companies: headquarters and service, three truck, support, landing support, and maintenance. Before leaving Camp Pendleton, four of these companies migrated to CSSG-11. Alpha, Bravo, and Charlie Companies formed the core of the three mobile combat service support companies in direct support of the three regimental combat teams in 1st Marine Division, while the majority of Support Company transferred to CSSB-10. This left Colonel Reist with Headquarters and Service, Landing Support, and Maintenance Companies.[27]

Anticipating the challenges of moving large convoys through open desert, as well as the threat of enemy attacks on soft targets such as trucks carrying fuel or supplies, the headquarters element of the Maintenance Company was sectioned off to form a new company specifically focused on convoy control and security. Convoy Control Company provided additional security personnel and vehicles to all convoys; they also conducted mission planning for convoy security, routes, fires, and estimates of time and

---

* In October 2002, LtCol Goben assumed command of MEU Service Support Group 22 (MSSG-22). The combat service support arm of the deploying Marine air-ground task force (MAGTF), 22 Marine Expeditionary Unit (22d MEU), MSSG-22 was scheduled for a routine six-month deployment. When it was determined in January 2003 that all elements of the 22d MEU would integrate and deploy as part of TF Tarawa, LtCol Goben's 231 Marines were initially redesignated as Combat Service Support Company 222 (CSSC-222). On 9 January 2003, CSSC-222 boarded the USS *Saipan* (LHA 2) and sailed from Camp Lejeune, North Carolina, a week later. While making the four-week-long transit to the Persian Gulf, LtCol Goben's Marines focused on nuclear, biological, and chemical responsiveness training, weapons familiarization, immediate action drills, and basic Arabic phrases. During the ship's transit across the Arabian Gulf, LtCol Goben experienced yet another change: although CSSC-222's organization mirrored that of the three CSSCs supporting 1st Marine Division's regimental combat teams, the commanding general, 1st FSSG redesignated them as CSS Battalion 22, largely because its commanding officer was a lieutenant colonel. When CSSB-22 arrived in theater in mid-February, the battalion was reassigned under 1st FSSG. (Combat Service Support Battalion 22 ComdC, 1Jan03–30Jun03; LtCol Thomas N. Goben, USMC intvw, 27Apr03, USMC [Oral HistColl], Quantico, VA.)

---

* Shock trauma platoons are discussed in the "Medical Support" section of this chapter.
** The Council of Colonels was a periodic meeting that Gen Usher held with his colonels in 1st FSSG to gain insight and conduct planning on a particular topic.

Shown here as a brigadier general, Col David G. Reist, commanding officer of 1st Transportation Support Group, had previously served two company command and one battalion command tours with landing support battalions, as well as with 3d Marine Division and Marine Barracks, Washington, DC.

distance. In essence, the new company planned for the "mechanics" of the convoys, allowing the vehicle operators to focus solely on their task at hand: driving.[28]

Having lost his three line companies and the bulk of his transportation assets, Colonel Reist needed augmentation from another unit to perform the multitude of distribution missions required during Operation Iraqi Freedom. In late January, he received this from 6th Motor Transport Battalion (6th MTBn), a reserve unit commanded by Lieutenant Colonel Patrick J. Hermesmann and headquartered out of Redbank, New Jersey. Bringing over 300 vehicles and several hundred drivers, 6th MTBn mobilized quickly and became the core of the TSG's distribution capability.* One challenge the battalion faced was that the equipment the Marines had been training on was outdated. Because the Marine Corps had fielded the new seven-ton medium tactical vehicle replacement, all reserve Marines had to be retrained and relicensed.[29]

Another attachment to the TSG was the U.S. Army's 319th Petroleum, Oil, and Lubricants Company. A great asset to Colonel Reist, it more than doubled his fuel distribution capability. At full capacity, these soldiers could transport 300,000 gallons of fuel in a single lift. This proved to be invaluable during combat operations, as both ground and air forces covered distances unmatched in any previous operation.[30]

One key factor contributing to 1st FSSG's effective distribution during combat operations was the tasking procedures established between 1st FSSG and TSG. Early in the planning process, a logistics movement control center (LMCC) was established to coordinate the FSSG's transportation assets in garrison. It was expected that the three engineer battalions would require the bulk of available transportation assets, and the scope of the engineering support missions had grown beyond the capabilities of its engineer support element (ESE) within in the operations section.[31] As a result, the LMCC combined with the ESE to form the logistics movement and engineering coordination center (LMECC), which was co-located with the TSG to afford better integration and coordination of operations. In this configuration, LMECC was the staff agent and the transportation support group was the executing agent. Lieutenant Colonel Jorge Ascunce, officer-in-charge of the LMECC, described the importance of this relationship:

> The distribution mission, the success or failure of that, the ability to have the right stuff at the right place at the right time, is what makes or breaks the FSSG's mission. What General Usher was trying to do with the creation of the Transportation Support Group and the focus of the LMECC was to have that central, localized pool of assets, resources, and staff coordination, to be best managed . . . this center of gravity.[32]

The mission of the LMECC, which included just over 100 Marines and sailors, was to coordinate and control the movement of all I MEF assets. Their focus was on the three engineer support battalions, the unit movement coordination centers, and an air movement coordination element. Although Colonel Ascunce had initially questioned the decision to focus on the engineering missions, he later acknowledged that integrating these efforts had been crucial, as the three battalions were key to the successful movement of the ground forces, and the FSSG's distribution capability directly affected the sustainment of the bat-

---
* 6th Motor Transport Battalion had been mobilized during Operations Desert Shield and Desert Storm, earning the title "Baghdad Express."

talions' missions.[33] Additional elements in the LMECC were communications assets, an intelligence section, and a small medical evacuation team.

The Engineer Battalions

To the planners of Operation Iraqi Freedom, the three main engineering missions were obvious: bulk liquids, general engineering (including construction, mobility, and counter-mobility), and bridging. It was also clear that no one battalion could handle all three functions, thus unlike the other combat service support functions, which were task organized to provide a comprehensive support approach to ground forces, engineering missions were distinguished and assigned at the battalion level. While battalions such as headquarters and service, supply, and maintenance were divided and redistributed in smaller segments to various 1st FSSG task-organized units, 6th, 7th, and 8th Engineer Support Battalions (ESBs) generally maintained unit integrity and were assigned a specific mission that capitalized on their special skills and expertise. As General Usher explained during an interview with the command historian, "the discreet tasks just manifest themselves in the planning process and mission analysis, and . . . to do it any other way, I would think would be very confusing for an ESB commander to try and plan against."[34]

The 6th Engineer Support Battalion (6th ESB), a reserve unit from Portland, Oregon, was assigned the bulk liquids mission. Commanded by Lieutenant Colonel Roger R. Machut, the battalion was responsible for the unique implementation of the hose-reel system. The hose reel, one of the 1st FSSG's greatest success stories from the war, was comprised of segments of six-inch-diameter rubber hose, manually connected and laid in the sand, through which engineers would pump millions of gallons of fuel. This concept, which had never been implemented in greater than 10-mile lengths, originated with 7th Engineer Support Battalion (7th ESB) at Camp Pendleton, California, but was assigned to 6th ESB, which had four companies dedicated to handling bulk liquids and possessed the highest number of trained Marines in this field.[35] As a result, Colonel Machut was one of only a few reservists who retained command of his original battalion during the war.

The 7th Engineer Support Battalion, organic to 1st FSSG, was assigned the general engineering mission. Commanded by Lieutenant Colonel Scott H. Poindexter, the battalion's broad taskings included breaching operations at the border between Kuwait and Iraq, construction of combat service support areas and enemy prisoner of war holding facilities, and continuous route maintenance. The 7th ESB's habitual garrison relationship with 1st Marine Division and ample joint training and planning in California enhanced the battalion's ability to provide both direct and general engineering support to ground combat forces.

The 8th Engineer Support Battalion (8th ESB), based out of Camp Lejeune, North Carolina, and organic to 2d FSSG, was assigned the expeditionary bridging mission. Commanded by Lieutenant Colonel Niel E. Nelson, it was the only remaining battalion in the Marine Corps with bridging assets, and as such, was the obvious choice for this mission. In garrison, 8th ESB was structured like a typical multifunctional engineering battalion, and prior to deploying, Colonel Nelson had to rebuild his table of organization and table of equipment to that of a battalion-sized bridging force. This included adding two

A convoy of vehicles from 6th Motor Transport Battalion begin their move north into Iraq 21 March 2003.
Courtesy of 6th MT BN

reserve bridge companies from 6th ESB and recruiting bridging experts throughout the Marine Corps.[36]

Medical Support

Task organized to meet the medical support requirements during OIF, Health Services Battalion* also fell under CSSG-15. Its mission was to provide MEF units with level-two healthcare, which was the first level of medical care to include surgical support. Several surgical companies, organized from personnel in 1st, 2d, and 4th FSSG, were co-located with the FSSG support areas, where they provided a more permanent capability. In addition to the surgical companies, the battalion deployed 12 shock trauma platoons (STPs) and 6 forward resuscitative surgical systems (FRSSs).[37] Commander Gregory M. Huet (USN), commanding officer of 1st Medical Battalion, had spent several tours with Marine units and knew that the deployment of STPs and FRSSs was significant for the medical support field. Along with the traditional surgical support companies, these STPs and FRSSs, which were lighter and more mobile, were positioned across the battlefield, providing a critical level-two surgical medical capability.[38]

The STPs, whose functions were previously performed by collecting and clearing companies, were an outgrowth of the medical battalion. Their mission was stabilization, triage, and holding of patients. In terms of capability, they fit between a battalion aid station and a surgical company. Often called a "super-BAS," (battalion aid station) the STPs consisted of approximately 25 individuals, to include two emergency physicians, one critical care nurse, one physician's assistant, one independent duty corpsman, several additional corpsmen, enlisted Marine electricians, drivers, and security. The typical STP possessed everything that a modern-day emergency room would have, less a surgeon. While their mission dictated that they set up in less than one hour, most of the time they were able to accomplish this in less than 40 minutes, immediately treating patients upon arrival. At each repair and replenishment point, they worked closely with the landing support Marines because many of their casualties arrived by helicopter.[39]

A Forward Resuscitative Surgical System (FRSS), which could be moved by two High Mobility Multi-purpose Wheeled Vehicles (HMMWVs or humvees) or sling-loaded by CH-53, was small, self-contained, and mobile. The teams consisted of eight individuals: one general surgeon, one orthopedic surgeon, a critical care nurse, an anesthesiologist, and four hospital corpsmen (two of whom were operating room technicians).[40] They worked out of two shelters, each weighing about 6,000 pounds; possessed oxygen generation, laboratory, and ultrasound capabilities; and carried their own blood supplies. Characterized by minimal cubic weight and footage, the FRSS was a self-contained operating room designed to forward displace to treat those casualties who were not stable enough to survive a flight to a rearward surgical company. As it was not designed to handle all surgical patients, it was estimated that less than 10 percent of the surgical patients requiring an emergency evacuation would actually be treated by the FRSS. Its main purpose was to stabilize patients enough to evacuate them to the rear, and most treated by the FRSS required a second surgery once evacuated. With the supplies included in an FRSS, the eight individuals could perform approximately 18 surgeries in a 48-hour period. Both flexible and mobile, the forward surgical systems could be established within an hour of hitting the ground. However, without its own communications or security capability, it would have to be employed with a shock trauma platoon and another combat service support element. A necessary part of the FRSS concept was the en route care capability (someone to travel with the patient during a medical evacuation), however, the table of organization did not support this.[41]

The concept of combining and deploying STPs and FRSSs was pioneered by Navy Captain Harold R. Bohman and Lieutenant Commander Tracy R. Bilski. Borne on the need to be able to keep up with the rapid pace and flexibility of combat operations, the combined capabilities of an STP and FRSS was equal to that of a level-two medical care facility. After its initial conception in 1997, the STP/FRSS system experienced limited use during Exercise Bright Star in Egypt and again during Operation Enduring Freedom in Afghanistan. During Operation Iraqi Freedom, the STPs and FRSSs experienced their first full implementation and became one of the most significant accomplishments for I MEF.

716th Military Police Battalion

Largely due to the extensive command and control capabilities within its military police organizations, the U.S. Army was tasked by I MEF to provide military police support. The U.S. Army's 716th Military Police Battalion, one of the most decorated military police units in its service, has a rich history. An active duty battalion from Fort Campbell, Kentucky, it had always maintained a close relationship with the Army's 101st Airborne Division. For this operation,

---

* There was no number designation given to Health Services Battalion, because this was the only such organization that existed throughout the Marine Corps.

BGen Edward G. Usher poses with LTC Kim Orlando, USA, (left and right center), commanding officer of the 716th Military Police Battalion, USA, and his commanders. The battalion was attached to 1st FSSG during OIF-I.

however, the battalion was assigned to provide I MEF with security support of convoys, enemy prisoners of war, and established support areas. Upon assignment to I MEF, Lieutenant Colonel Kim S. Orlando and his staff began to develop a relationship with the 1st FSSG and started to integrate all of the unit's personnel, skills, and assets into the FSSG's organization.[42] He described several meetings that took place during January and February of 2003. "We did a series of coordination visits to Camp Pendleton; we got to know the command group, started to work with them in terms of how to best use Army military police and what we could bring to the table. That was really, in terms of spelling success, the most important step."[43] General Usher recognized that the Army brought capabilities that the Marine Corps either did not have or did not have in sufficient numbers. He also recognized the importance of properly integrating the Army battalion into 1st FSSG's operations.

You just position them and engineer them for success instead of looking at them as a bucket of resources that you can realign elsewhere to fit an operational scenario that might not be advantageous for them to operate in. So I just simply let the 716th execute its mission with guidance and some direction, and it seemed to work very well . . . . what they want to do, like everybody else, including the Marines, is to be given a mission, given an area of focus, and be given authority to make decisions to match up with each individual's responsibilities.[44]

In total, the battalion had more than 1,200 military police personnel supporting 1st FSSG, organized into seven companies. Originally, only the headquarters and one military police company from Colonel Orlando's battalion deployed into theater. Eventually, other military police companies arrived in theater to augment the 716th. These included several regular Army and Army reserve companies, as well as two Marine reserve companies: Company A deployed from Lexington, Kentucky, and Company C came from Dayton, Ohio.*

Its mission was to provide security throughout the 1st FSSG's area of responsibility, to include the routes of movement for supplies and equipment. The battalion also handled enemy prisoners of war, processing more than 1,400 captives for I MEF. Its mission in Iraqi towns included both acting as the police force and maintaining order so that local civil-

---

* Company B, from Pittsburgh, PA, was attached to CSSB-10.

Photo by MSgt Edward D. Kniery, USMC

Marines monitor local civilians as they pass through a checkpoint near Logistics Support Area Viper.

ians could rebuild their infrastructure and reestablish a stable existence. Their presence alone helped prevent combat looting. One of the challenges the MPs faced was the constant evolution of rules of engagement. As difficult as it was during combat operations to distinguish between the "good guys" and the "bad guys," it became even more difficult during stabilization operations. Colonel Orlando considered one of his primary responsibilities to work with company and platoon commanders ensuring that they always emphasized situational awareness and prudent application of force. With multiple force levels, his battalion had to be prepared to transition from the use of extreme lethal weaponry, such as AT4s (shoulder launched, anti-armor weapons), to nonlethal riot and crowd control weapons, such as pepper spray.⁴⁵

Ultimately, integration of the U.S. Army's 716th Military Police Battalion into 1st FSSG's organization and operations was a success. Colonel Orlando*

praised the relationship and cooperation between his battalion and the 1st FSSG:

> Our integration with the group has been nothing short of spectacular. They have been just wonderful professionals to work with . . . what laid the groundwork for that is our coordination and liaison visits that took place in the months preceding the deployment. That, in addition to the fact that they're just a fine bunch of professionals that want to give you the shirt off their backs, and they have . . . that has been a complete success story. Never once has anybody ever said anything about any differences between the Army or Marine way.⁴⁶

Headquarters and 4th FSSG Forward West

With the reorganization of 1st FSSG well underway, General Usher had to think about the composition of his own staff. Maintaining the typical staff sections and functions, the greatest change was in regard to personnel and increasing the staff size to support the FSSG's critical mission during OIF. A major part of this included the integration of 4th FSSG Forward West.

In December of 2001, Colonel James P. Sheahan,

---

* Tragically, LTC Orlando was killed on 16Oct03, while attempting to negotiate with a group of armed men near a mosque in Karbala. The 716th Military Battalion had been turned over by 1st FSSG to 1st Marine Division, and at the time, LTC Orlando was the highest-ranking Army officer killed by hostile fire in Iraq. (Associated Press, "Army LTC Kim S. Orlando," www.militarycity.com/valor/256881.html)

CSSB-19

While 1st FSSG was planning and reorganizing in anticipation of Operation Iraqi Freedom, Marine Expeditionary Unit (MEU) Service Support Group 11 (MSSG-11) was preparing for a scheduled six-month deployment as part of the 11th MEU. However, like the east coast MEU, the deployment cycle of western Pacific Marines was interrupted and elements were reassigned in accordance with I MEF's war plans. The 11th MEU and its ground combat element were redesignated as Task Force Yankee, the air combat element was absorbed into 3d MAW, and MSSG-11, which had been conducting port operations for the Amphibious Task Force West at 32d Naval Station in San Diego, California, redesignated as Combat Service Support Battalion 19 (CSSB-19). Commanded by Lieutenant Colonel David M. Kluegel, the battalion's assigned tasks involved enemy prisoner of war handling and processing in coordination with Task Force Yankee. Combat Service Support Company 191 (CSSC-191), commanded by Captain Christopher R. Lucas, was established and provided limited service to Task Force Yankee elements by constructing the I MEF prisoner holding area. Soon after the war's commencement, I MEF decided not to open this facility, and CSSB-19's focus of effort shifted to convoy and area security. For the duration of the war, CSSB-19 augmented existing force protection elements and traveled with more than a dozen convoys throughout southern and central Iraq.[47]

a reservist out of Saint Louis, Missouri, was serving as the executive officer of 4th FSSG Forward West when he was brought back on active duty. In January, Colonel Sheahan and 19 of his Marines from 4th FSSG Forward West were assigned to augment the headquarters staff of the 1st FSSG, which had already begun planning for possible contingency operations in both the Middle East and Korea. The FSSG's operations section had a tremendous need for augmentation, and the majority of the detachment immediately assumed key billets in this area. Colonel Sheahan, who later served as the 1st FSSG's liaison officer to the I MEF, became the deputy assistant chief of staff, operations, 1st FSSG. Then, in February 2002, I MEF began detailed planning for Operations Plan 1003V, and subsequent MEF exercises, called Desert Spear, were held in May and October. Colonel Sheahan's focus at this point was the daunting task of identifying which reserve units would be mobilized in the event of a contingency. As the key units were identified, their commanders were gradually brought into the planning. By the exercise that October, commanders of several reserve battalions, including 6th ESB, 6th MTBn, and 4th LSB, were participating.[48]

Colonel Darrell L. Moore, the commander of 4th FSSG Forward West and Colonel Sheahan's boss, had not been activated initially. However, in January 2003, General Usher spoke to General John W. Bergman, commanding general, 4th FSSG, and requested Colonel Moore's assignment as his Chief of Staff, 1st FSSG. Colonel Moore, an attorney from Pryor, Oklahoma, was subsequently activated on 20 February and flown directly to Kuwait, arriving on the evening of the next day.[49]

General Usher believed that augmenting the 1st FSSG with reservists was the only way they could go to war in support of a full MEF. "The integration of the reserves is an enduring requirement for our FSSGs. Over the years the active force structure has been lost in the FSSGs. It's really felt when we go to the battlefield as a MEF, and the only way to overcome that is through smart integration of our reserve force capability."[50]

Before he was assigned as the chief of staff, 1st FSSG, Col Darrell L. Moore was the deputy commander, 4th FSSG. While in the reserves, he spent tours as a company and battalion commander, as well as the G-3 Plans Officer, 4th FSSG Forward West.

Courtesy of 1st FSSG

One Reservist's Story

During the weeks following 9/11, Lance Corporal Joseph J. Klan, a New York City police officer, went to Ground Zero on his own time to help with the ongoing recovery and cleanup efforts. During those dark moments facing death and destruction, a chance meeting occurred with a fellow Marine. Klan felt that meeting and working with the gunnery sergeant—who happened to be a recruiter—was a bit of fate, as he had already been thinking about getting back into the Marine Corps. After his service in the first Gulf War, he felt that events would eventually lead him back to the Middle East, as there was a certain level of unfinished business. He later learned that two police officers that he knew had been killed in the 9/11 attack. These men were also Marine reservists, and Klan made it his personal mission to honor them by rejoining the Marine Corps. One of the two fallen Marines was retired Sergeant Major Michael Curtin, who had been the sergeant major of Klan's former unit, the 6th Communications Battalion. It took a year and a half of badgering the recruiter before he was able to rejoin. Finally, after contacting the career management team in Quantico, Virginia, and accepting a reduction from his previous rank, he was able to rejoin the Corps as a lance corporal. He was reassigned to 6th Communications Battalion, which had already been activated in late January 2003. It deployed to the Middle East before Klan had officially joined, but he flew over on 14 March with its rear party. He was 39 years old at the time.[52]

There were eventually over 4,000 4th FSSG reservists mobilized to support 1st FSSG, whose total table of organization was approximately 11,000; reservists accounted for roughly 36 percent of the personnel in 1st FSSG. One of the major factors that contributed to the overall success of reservist integration was that several key personnel had been involved in the planning process and subsequently had the opportunity to spend several months preparing for their specific missions. The entire process was a collaborative one, with 4th FSSG deeply involved with the planning.[51]

Establishing the Marine Logistics Command

Although the concept of a Marine Logistics Command (MLC) was established during the first Gulf War, when 1st and 2d FSSGs provided general and direct support logistics to I MEF, Brigadier General Michael R. Lehnert, commanding general of 2d Force Service Support Group (2d FSSG), had limited doctrine to work from when forming the Marine Logistics Command.[53] As General Usher explained, "the MLC concept has been whittled away at over the years . . . this is the first time we've employed an MLC in the true sense."[54] General Lehnert possessed a widely diverse Marine Corps background, including tours as both a maintenance and engineer officer, assignments within all four FSSGs, and several joint tours, to include both Operation Just Cause and Operation Sea Signal in Guantanamo Bay, Cuba. As a result, he was well equipped with the flexibility and creativity required to build such a critical, yet ambiguous organization. In developing the MLC, he drew from a Center for Naval Analyses study on the Marine Logistics Command and focused on the mission at hand. General Lehnert did not want the shape and size of the FSSG to drive the mission, but rather

Prior to assuming command of 2d FSSG, then BGen Michael R. Lehnert, an engineering officer, served as head of the joint task force charged with the custody of Taliban and al-Qaeda detainees at Guantanamo Bay, Cuba.

USMC Photo

for the mission requirements to drive the design of the MLC. He wanted a flat organization with minimal hierarchy: an organization that fulfilled its functional requirements without any nonessential components.⁵⁵

> We looked at the various logistics nodes of what was going to be expected of us and who we thought we were going to be doing business with, particularly within the Theater Support Command, and we did essentially a troop to-task redesign of the 2d FSSG . . . I didn't want a lot of hierarchy in it, and I wanted it focused on the functions that we were expected to provide and those tasks that we were expected to do. So if you believe in the concept of form following function, we took nothing with us for which we did not have a specific and identified mission and task.⁵⁶

The MLC's main function during OIF was operational level logistics. While 1st FSSG was the retail-level logistics organization, 2d FSSG or MLC was the wholesale-level logistics organization.* In large part, MLC interfaced between the 1st FSSG and the U.S. Army's 377th Theater Support Command,** the senior logistics command within the Coalition Forces Land Component Command. In specific terms, the MLC was responsible for brokering the gross sustainment requirements, such as ammunition, fuel, and water to the supporting theater agencies and pushing that sustainment out to the tactical logistics support areas across the battlefield. In an article that appeared in the August 2003 issue of the *Marine Corps Gazette*, co-authors General Lehnert and Colonel John E. Wissler, commanding officer of 2d Transportation Support Battalion, stated:

> The MLC manages the resources necessary to sustain the operational tempo of the modern campaign and extend Marine Forces' operational reach to distances more in keeping with the tenets of expeditionary maneuver warfare and advanced seabasing. Coming of age in the sands of Kuwait and Iraq, the MLC allows the warfighter to focus on the near battle.⁵⁷

While the majority of its tasks centered around receiving, storing, fixing, and moving logistics in general support of I MEF, the MLC's direct reporting relationship to Marine Forces Central Command (MarCent) gave them an even broader logistics mission during OIF. Specific tasks included establishing and operating required infrastructure, terminals, and facilities to provide general support to MarCent; coordinating arrival, assembly, and other force closure operations; coordinating with existing theater support systems; integrating host nation support; inter-service, common item, and cross-service support; and developing Marine Forces logistics requirements.

Transforming the 2d FSSG

Even before the planning of OIF began, 2d FSSG had already been undergoing transformation. For one, it had implemented parts of the integrated logistics capability (ILC) concept. The main points of this centered around supply consolidation, the re-alignment of maintenance processes—including bumper-to-bumper maintenance support—overall process improvements, and the development of integrated information technology. In short, ILC was an attempt at modernizing and improving the doctrine, organization, equipment, and technology of Marine Corps logistics.⁵⁸

The 2d FSSG had also executed CSS migration, which focused on the consolidation of its units around skill groups. As a result, the battalions within 2d FSSG were structured strictly along functional alignments: all maintenance personnel were in 2d Maintenance Battalion, all supply personnel were in 2d Supply Battalion, all engineers were in 8th Engineer Support Battalion. In many ways, this organization made 2d FSSG's transition to the Marine Logistics Command easier. As each battalion restructured to meet its deployed logistics requirements, they only had to look to one battalion for a specific functional resource, and the augmentees received offered much more depth in their training and skill levels.

One difficulty that 2d FSSG encountered was a shortage of planning staff and resources. Even as it transitioned into the MLC, the service group had to maintain its garrison role in support of II Marine Expeditionary Force. An illustration of this planning shortfall emerged in late January 2003, when the group had equipment staged on a train heading out

---

* Ironically, Gen Lehnert had often described I MEF as the wholesale MEF, due to the fact that II MEF, which he referred to as the retail MEF, often had many contingencies and small-scale response forces on their plate. Now, as commander of the MLC, he was the wholesale logistics provider and 1st FSSG was the retail logistics provider.

** During combat and sustainment operations, the 377th Theater Support Command forces numbered 43,000 and included a Transportation Command, Medical Command, Personnel Command, Finance Command, Movement Control Agency, Material Management Center, two Military Police Brigades, four Area Support Groups, a Transportation Group, a Petroleum Group, and an Ammunition Group. These forces provided combat service and combat service support, as well as life support operations in Kuwait and Southern Iraq.

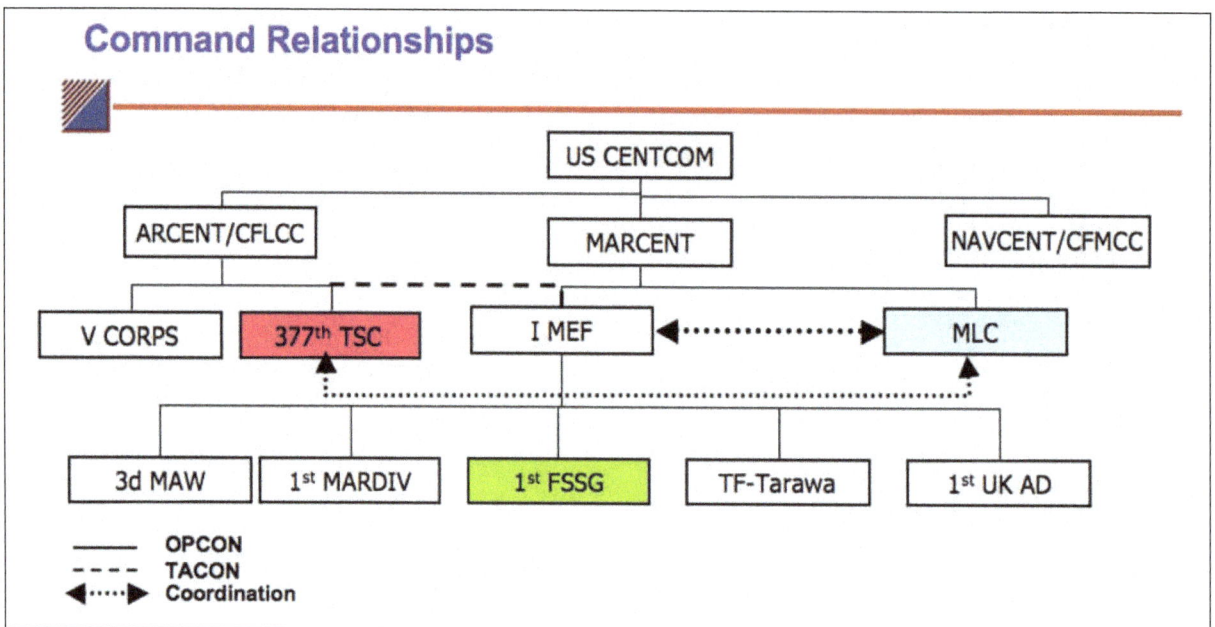

The U.S. Army's 377th Theater Support Command (TSC), the Marine Logistics Command (MLC), and the 1st Force Service Support Group (FSSG) represented three levels of logistics support during OIF.

to Twentynine Palms, California, to support a combined arms exercise. At the last minute, this movement was cancelled and the equipment was off-loaded to support the MLC missions instead.[59]

In garrison, 2d FSSG consisted of eight functional battalions: Headquarters and Service Battalion, 2d Supply Battalion, 2d Maintenance Battalion, 8th Engineer Battalion, 2d Medical Battalion, 2d Dental Battalion, 2d Transportation Support Battalion, and 2d Military Police Battalion. By table of organization, the FSSG typically carried between 8,000 to 10,000 Marines and sailors. By December 2002, 2d FSSG was reorganized and slimmed down to a lean, functionally aligned organization, totaling 4,500 personnel and officially assigned the MLC mission. The new operational structure consisted of an FSSG forward, and headquarters and service, transportation support, maintenance, supply, and military police battalions; as well as detachments from the engineer support, medical, and dental battalions.

Headquarters and Service Battalion, commanded by Lieutenant Colonel Craig C. Crenshaw, supported the command and control structure of the MLC. The three main units within H&S battalion were the services, communications, and food services companies. Deploying approximately one-quarter of its personnel, services company's operational tasks included the provision of a post exchange facility, postal, disbursing, and legal services in support of all Marine Forces Central Command (MarCent). The communications company, 2d FSSG's only organic communications capability, deployed its entire "footprint," to include $70 million of communications assets. Once in theater, the company integrated into the communications architecture, largely supported by augmentees from 8th Communications Battalion.* When the food services company arrived, it was apparent that most such services would be contracted out; therefore, the majority of the company was retrained and assigned to serve in a guard and security capacity.[60]

The 2d Transportation Support Battalion (2d TSB), commanded by Colonel John E. Wissler, had the broad, albeit critical mission of planning and executing battlefield distribution operations, providing both local- and line-haul distribution capabilities for MarCent theater stocks. In essence, 2d TSB was responsible for pushing sustainment items forward to the 1st FSSG's units, who were providing tactical combat service support to 1st Marine Division. In the initial planning, 2d TSB's distribution piece was limited in scope, based on assumptions that the MLC would be providing support at the operational level. Planners realized, however, even in the early stages, that there had to be a connection between MLC's operational and 1st FSSG's tactical level logistics, and MLC might have to fill this gap. As 1st FSSG moved further up

---

* The communications architecture that MLC setup during OIF is further discussed in Chapter 2.

Photo by LCpl Victor A. Barrera, USMC

An honor graduate of the United States Naval Academy and a distinguished graduate from the Marine Corps Command and Staff College, then-Col John E. Wissler was commanding officer, 2d TSB. He also served on the Commandant's Amphibious Plans Study Group in support of Operation Desert Storm.

the battlefield, setting up support areas to provide tactical support to ground units, MLC still had to deliver its support to their back door.[61] The important question was where on the battlefield this hand-off between operational and tactical level logistics would take place. In the weeks to follow, Colonel Wissler's battalion would be augmented with maintenance, supply, military police, engineer, communications, and intelligence capabilities. 2d TSB would push its own limits to provide the crucial link in the distribution of sustainment throughout the battlefield.

The 2d Maintenance Battalion, commanded by Lieutenant Colonel Brent P. Goddard, was the largest and most diverse battalion to deploy within the Marine Logistics Command. With approximately 1,975 Marines and sailors, the battalion covered a wide range of functional areas, to include motor transport, ordnance, electronics and communications, engineer and utilities, and general support maintenance. Leaving a sizeable rear element, 900 Marines remained at Camp Lejeune, North Carolina, to provide continuous support to remain-behind units and equipment, while seven companies deployed in support of Operation Iraqi Freedom. Disbursed throughout Kuwait and Iraq, the battalion's mission was to execute recovery, evacuation, and repair capabilities for Marine forces in theater, as well as internally focused maintenance support to MLC.

The 2d Supply Battalion, commanded by Colonel William F. Johnson, deployed five units in support of OIF: headquarters, supply, support, medical logistics, and ammunition companies. Operating at the wholesale level, the supply battalion managed a general account and intermediate supply support activity in theater and was responsible for maintaining theater stocks, to include all classes of supply.

The 2d Military Police Battalion, commanded by Lieutenant Colonel Christopher B. Martin, was a relatively new garrison battalion under 2d FSSG. During the past decade, there had been various attempts to reorganize the military police community within the Marine Corps. The latest attempt began in 1999, when the Force Structure Planning Group recommended that military police personnel be consolidated into single battalions. Within II Marine Expeditionary Force (II MEF), it was determined that this functionally organized battalion of three companies would fall under the FSSG. During the initial phase of Operation Iraqi Freedom, military police companies from 2d FSSG provided support during the Maritime Prepositioning Force offload and eventually, augmented by a reserve rifle company from 1st Battalion, 24th Marines, provided convoy and camp security. In addition to being the first time a military police battalion deployed intact, this was also the first time military working dogs were deployed to a tactical environment since the Vietnam War. The dogs possessed the ability to detect explosives and were primarily used for entry control points. Additional tasks assigned to 2d Military Police Battalion included enemy prisoner of war management, area and main supply route security, and traffic control at ports and terminals.[62]

While the majority of 8th Engineer Support Battalion was assigned to 1st FSSG as the "bridge battalion," Detachment Alpha was assigned to support MLC. Commanded by Navy Lieutenant Timothy A. Wallace, a Seabee exchange officer with the 8th ESB, the detachment's missions consisted of general construction of basic infrastructure and installation of power, water, and other utilities. Lieutenant Wallace was in a unique position as one of the first Seabee officers to command a Marine Corps engineer detachment. Adding to his challenges, he was also required to oversee the operations of bulk fuel and explosive ordnance disposal: two missions not traditionally performed by a standard Seabee unit.

Most of 2d Medical Battalion was split up during

Marines of 2d FSSG Military Police Battalion conduct canine training at Camp Fox, Kuwait.

OIF. Early on, Company A had been disbanded and divided among Companies B and C. By the end of January, having received personnel from the medical augmentation program,* those companies, as well as five shock trauma platoons from H&S Company, 2d Medical Battalion, deployed. They were immediately transferred to the Health Services Battalion, 1st FSSG, and integrated to support I MEF. The remaining personnel were combined into a single detachment, led by the battalion's commanding officer, Navy Commander Benjamin G. M. Feril, and deployed throughout January and February to set up an aid station at MLC's support area. They also provided overflow support to I MEF and medical regulating for MarCent.

2d Dental Battalion was also reorganized. During the deployment of the Marine Logistics Command, the battalion commanding officer, Navy Captain Stephen J. Connelly, was assigned as 2d FSSG's chief of staff and acted in this capacity at Camp Lejeune, North Carolina. Meanwhile, Captain Stephen M. Pachuta (USN), executive officer of Dental Battalion, deployed forward as the officer-in-charge of Dental Battalion Forward. Of the three expeditionary dental platoons, each of which had six dental officers and nine dental technicians, Bravo and Charlie platoons were assigned to augment the two surgical companies that were transferred to 1st FSSG's Health Services Battalion. The third, Alpha platoon, deployed in support of MLC and shared facilities at Camp Fox with the medical detachment.[63]

With operational flexibility and innovation, 2d FSSG transformed itself into the Marine Logistics Command. Although the concept was not new, there was limited doctrine, which made the task of reorganization and transformation a major challenge. However, this was just one of a series of challenges that General Lehnert and his operational level logistics command would face and overcome during Operation Iraqi Freedom.

> ### Remain Behind Staff
> While 1st and 2d FSSGs were deployed in support of Operation Iraqi Freedom, their remain-behind staffs were augmented with Marines from 4th FSSG to continue performing their mission in garrison. This included the management of a large quantity of remain-behind equipment, as well as continued training and the area commander responsibility. Marines from both 4th Supply Battalion and 4th Maintenance Battalion were activated to support the continental U.S. requirements during Operation Iraqi Freedom].[64]

---
* In the rear, the medical battalion is only approximately 65 percent staffed and is augmented through the medical augmentation program in times of war.

Chapter 2

Arrival in Theater

By the fall of 2002, 1st Force Service Support Group's (FSSG) transition to its wartime organization and 2d FSSG's transformation to the Marine Logistics Command were well underway. The main task at hand was getting Marine forces and all their equipment into theater and ready to fight.

The Offload

While in garrison, the 2d FSSG maintained a forward element, consisting of approximately 30 permanent personnel. Led by Colonel Stephen W. Otto, the 2d FSSG Forward mirrored a brigade service support group (BSSG) command and control structure. Yet when task organized for OIF, it was a flexible organization of more than 1,500 Marines and sailors.* During the fall of 2002, Colonel Otto and his staff planned for the spectrum of missions they might face, but it was difficult at best to pinpoint exactly how many Marines were needed to deploy at any given time.

In late November, the FSSG Forward received its first mission: to offload one ship bearing aviation ordnance materials, and be prepared to offload a second ship. Because this mission assignment was not a part of the request for forces associated with Operations Plan 1003V, Colonel Otto had to rapidly deploy an initial force to execute the ammunition offload, while maintaining the capability to handle other missions that would come their way. His planning proved to be on target; even as an eight-person advanced party was en route to Kuwait to prepare for the ammunition offload, Colonel Otto received another mission for his Marines: to offload two Maritime Prepositioning Ship Squadrons (MPSRONs).* The initial plan had called for 1st FSSG to conduct the first offload and 2d FSSG to handle the second; however, after lengthy discussions, it was decided that 2d FSSG would conduct both Maritime Prepositioning Force offloads, freeing up 1st FSSG to move forward and establish sustainment bases in support of the MEF.

Prior to the offload, General Lehnert and a small staff visited Camp Arifjan, Kuwait, to liaise with the 377th Theater Support Command. Intuitively, the FSSG's commanding general established a formal relationship between his Marines and the Army's theater logistics providers, ultimately deploying a command liaison element to Camp Arifjan to conduct continuous coordination with the Army throughout the war.[1]

As one of the first Marine Corps units to arrive in Kuwait, the 2d FSSG Forward's advanced party, led by Major Arthur J. Pasagian, the unit's executive officer, spent several days liaising with host nation contractors, the Kuwaiti government, U.S. Embassy officials, and other service organizations. Predeployment planning had the Army's theater support command providing basic infrastructure, transportation support, stevedore support at the port, cargo movement at the airfield, and general life support. To the FSSG's dismay, the Army had not yet received its own force enablers in theater, and short-fused

Vehicles are offloaded from one of eleven Maritime Prepositioned Force ships in Kuwait.

Photo by CNA

---
* Throughout Operation Iraqi Freedom, the table of organization of the FSSG Forward continued to fluctuate to meet the changing missions, at one point reaching almost 1,900 Marines and sailors, task organized from their parent battalions within 2d FSSG

The USNS PFC James Anderson Jr. *(T-AK-3002) docks at the Kuwaiti Naval Base, awaiting offload. The MPF ship was named in honor of the first African American Marine recipient of the Medal of Honor, which was awarded posthumously to PFC Anderson during the Vietnam War.*

arrangements had to be made with local contractors and third country nationals in Kuwait.[2]

On 27 December, the main body of the 2d FSSG Forward arrived in theater. Re-designated as Combat Service Support Detachment Kuwait Naval Base, these 450 Marines worked tirelessly to offload five ships carrying aviation ordnance. A total of 13,198 pallets of ordnance material was offloaded and distributed to various munitions storage areas by way of 153 convoys. This enormous responsibility became an even greater challenge when the Marines realized that locally contracted drivers and vehicles were not allowed on Kuwaiti bases. To overcome this obstacle, the Marines quickly began to train their own drivers to operate commercial vehicles on base. At the same time, 2d FSSG Forward created a beach operations group to support the reception, staging, onward movement, and integration (RSO&I) of the 15th and 24th Marine Expeditionary Units, as well as both Amphibious Task Forces West and East with initial sustainment and operational support. During the beach operations, they processed 7,717 personnel, 1,500 vehicles, and 6,182 pieces of cargo through the Kuwait Naval Base.

On 5 January, additional augmentees from 2d FSSG arrived in Kuwait, transforming the FSSG Forward into the Landing Force Support Party. Marines from Bravo Company, 2d Transportation Support Battalion provided the nucleus of the transportation support detachment, supporting the reception, staging, onward movement, and integration operations in Kuwait. The shore party's mission, to offload two MPSRONs consisting of 11 ships, presented 2d FSSG with an interesting command and control situation. Essentially, they were now answering to two separate commands: first as an operational force for MarCent, supporting the ordnance offload, and second as a tactical enabling force for I MEF, supporting the RSO&I of equipment to assembly areas throughout Kuwait.

To offload the MPSRONs, 2d FSSG established and maintained a seaport of debarkation at the Kuwaiti Port of Ash Shuaybah, where they offloaded, staged, and conducted throughput of 8,452 containers, 8,617 wheeled vehicles, 964 tracked vehicles, 5,112 trailers, 2,714 lifts of general cargo, 64 aircraft, and 18,000 personnel. The original goal, to complete the offload in 21 days, required that one ship be completed every 72 hours. Although few individuals believed that this was possible, given the shortfalls in vehicle drivers and equipment operators, both squadrons were unloaded in 17.5 days. This offload, one squadron in support of I MEF and a second in support of 2d Marine Expeditionary Brigade, was the largest Maritime Prepositioning Force offload since the first Gulf War and believed to be the most expedient in Marine Corps history, finishing four days ahead of schedule.[3]

While the offloads of the ammunition ships, as well as the Maritime Prepositioning Force Squadron ships, were underway, another element of 2d FSSG Forward was dispatched to the Kuwait City International Air-

Marine Order of Battle

By 0800 on 17 March 2003, the order of battle for I MEF, and the individual components strength and missions, were depicted in briefing charts at MarCent.

I MEF Command Element–4,638

1st Marine Division–20,606 Secure the southern oil fields; conduct a passage of lines through Task Force Tarawa, and attack toward Baghdad.

3d Marine Aircraft Wing–14,381 Shape I MEF's battle space; screen the ground combat element from attacks; support CFACC.

1st Force Service Support Group–10,504 Provide direct combat service support to I MEF; interface with the Marine Logistics Command, a theater-level command under operational control of MarCent.

I MEF Engineer Group–3,121 Maintain roads and bridges along the I MEF lines of communication; this unit was a composite of U.S. Navy construction battalions and Marine engineers.

Task Force Tarawa (2d Marine Expeditionary Brigade)–5,091 Secure An-Nasiriyah and crossings across the Euphrates River; secure lines of communication.

15th MEU–1,739 Attach to 1 (UK) Armored Division for Opening Gambit; attach to Task Force Tarawa.

1 (UK) Armored Division–21,045 Attack north from Kuwait; conduct relief in place in oil fields with 1st Marine Division; secure Basrah and vicinity.

I MEF Total–81,125

Other Marine Forces in Theater:
MarCent Command Element (Bahrain)–385
Marine Logistics Command (Kuwait)–4,525
CJTF/Consequence Management (Kuwait)–742
MarCent Total–86,777*

---

* This is the rendition of the MarCent morning report, 17Mar03, captured by the field historian attached to MarCent, LtCol Jeffery Acosta, and sent to the author by e-mail. The total does not show the Marines committed to CJTF Horn of Africa.

---

port. Their mission was to establish an aerial port of debarkation to receive and process all Marine Corps personnel and cargo arriving on inbound flights. Working around the clock, these Marines were able to handle 3,000 to 4,000 incoming Marines each day. Receiving minimal support from the Army, 2d FSSG Forward once again looked to commercial contractors for 20 buses to transport personnel and equipment to their assembly areas throughout the region. From the Kuwait Naval Base, the Port of Ash Shuaybah and the airport, 2d FSSG Forward facilitated the flow of Marine forces. Marines arrived in theater one day and were ready for war the next.[4]

Establishing a Base of Operations in Kuwait

During January and February of 2003, Marines arrived in Kuwait by the thousands. Following a series of requests for forces* and subsequent deployment orders, units arrived by both sea and air. Two 17-ship amphibious task forces brought 2d Marine Expeditionary Brigade (2d MEB) and Regimental Combat Team 1 (RCT-1), while the remainder of I MEF flew by a combination of military and civilian contracted aircraft. Eventually, more than 80,000 Marines and their equipment deployed into theater in support of Operation Iraqi Freedom.

When they arrived, the Marines dispersed to one of many camps built throughout the vast desert between Kuwait's capital city and its border with Iraq. The preponderance of I MEF headquarters was located at Camp Commando, a section of a Kuwaiti commando training facility that Marines and civilian contractors had transformed into a fortress of buildings, tents, and guard towers. 1st Marine Division and Task Force Tarawa were located at Camp Matilda and Camp Ryan respectively, large camps that had been erected in the Kuwaiti desert with hundreds of giant canvas tents and parking lots filled with equipment. 3d Marine Air Wing established its base of operations at two existing Kuwait Air Force bases located in al-Jaber and Ali al-Salem. Although still considered to be a field environment, where Marines lived and worked in tents, these two bases had been supplemented with such amenities as air-conditioned mess halls

---

* The Pentagon's decision to use deployment orders instead of the more sequential time-phased force deployment data (TPFFD) process to move forces into theater was not a popular one among many planners in the field.

Originally a barren patch of desert in northern Kuwait, Camp Coyote rapidly became a massive logistics hub for 1st Force Service Support Group.

with ice cream machines, showers, and post exchange facilities.

Camp Wake Island

1st FSSG had begun planning for campsites in Kuwait almost one and a half years prior to the war; actual execution of this plan, however, did not begin until November 2002. Before the first ship arrived at the port, Marines from the 1st FSSG established a 42-square mile arrival and assembly operations element in the Kuwaiti desert. Just a few days after their arrival in the first week of November, Major William L. Babcock Jr., assistant logistics officer for the 1st FSSG, and his Marines turned what was once an empty tract of desert into a receiving point for all 1st FSSG equipment. Camp Wake Island, as the area was named, served as the rallying point for all 1st FSSG personnel to link up with equipment and supplies from military aircraft and vessels. Major Babcock described their arrival to the area:

> We walked in looking at a flat area with an undeveloped road network. What we've done is completely shaped the terrain and the arrival and assembly area to accept Marine Corps assets quickly. It's the same concept that has been repeated and successful for the Marine Corps. The way we employ forces provides the Marine Corps the ability to assemble combat power quickly into a combined air-ground task force.[5]

Camp Coyote

While Camp Wake Island served as 1st FSSG's rallying point for personnel and equipment arriving in theater, Tactical Assembly Area (TAA) Coyote became its staging area while making the final preparations for war. On 3 January 2003, General Usher flew all of his commanders to Kuwait, to conduct a site survey of TAA Coyote. For five days, the commanders traveled extensively through the area, to include a trip up to the Iraqi border, and then returned to the United States to prepare their battalions for deployment. Construction began on 10 January, after a lengthy process of acquiring Kuwaiti approval. The La Nouvelle Company won the contract to build the camp and largely used locals for the actual construction. All supplies had to be flown into Kuwait from other countries; even the gravel being used for dust control was imported from the United Arab Emirates. There were challenges with weather, supplies, and shortened timelines, made all the more difficult because of the Muslim holidays local contractors celebrated. All in all, though, the camps were well equipped. For food services the Marines contracted ESS Support Services, a food subcontractor of Halliburton, to provide, construct, and manage large field kitchens and chow halls. While the original plan had the food services company supporting up to 30,000 troops, they ended up accommodating upwards of 60,000 with seven kitchens.

Complete with an expeditionary airfield,* TAA Coyote encompassed 58 square miles and was divided into 20 individual camps, each housing more

---

* In February of 2003, an expeditionary airfield was constructed within TAA Coyote. Marine Corps Air Station, Joe Foss was named in honor of Maj Joseph J. Foss, World War II Marine pilot and Medal of Honor recipient. At age 87, he had just died on 1 January of that year.

TAA Coyote	
Camp Iwo Jima	1st FSSG Headquarters
Camp Betio	7th Engineer Support Battalion
Camp Okinawa	Combat Service Support Battalion 18
Camp Tarawa	Combat Service Support Group 15 Combat Service Support Battalion 12
Camp Guadalcanal	Health Services Battalion
Camp Peleliu	8th Engineer Support Battalion
Camp Bougainville	Combat Service Support Group 11 Combat Service Support Battalion 10
Camp Solomon Islands	6th Engineer Support Battalion
Camp Guam	Transportation Support Group

than 500 personnel. The camps were designed with dispersion in mind, yet allowed for secure movement between them. All 20 were completed in 33 days, and 59 miles of security berm were constructed in 12 days.[6] All but two of the camps were named for Marine battles from the famous island hopping campaign of World War II; it was thought that each individual camp, housing one of several FSSG units, was like "an island or a self-contained and sufficient entity in the vast desert sand."[7]

By February 2003, the 1st FSSG Headquarters established itself at Camp Iwo Jima, Tactical Assembly Area Coyote. Although the smallest in geographical size, Camp Iwo Jima was the first of 11 built on Coyote and considered to be the "model home" for the remaining 1st FSSG camps to be built in area. Complete with hot shower trailers, portable commodes, and billeting tents with wood floors and electricity, the camp offered many amenities to the Marines that they did not expect to find in the Kuwaiti desert. Major David V. Raimo,* Camp Iwo Jima commandant, stated that "from the junior troops up to senior officers, a lot of them said [that] this is the best field living [they've] ever experienced."[8]

Marines from Combat Service Support Group 11 (CSSG-11) arrived at Camp Bougainville, 1st FSSG's northernmost camp in Kuwait, during late January and early February. The Marines were largely impressed with what they found. As one described, "instead of a vast wasteland, there was a berm-surrounded area that had Bedouin tents with lights and wooden decks, shower trailers, and a chow tent that served two hot meals daily. These were a welcome surprise to the Marines and sailors so recently removed from the conveniences of the United States and expecting to live in two-man tents."[9]

In mid-February, the 1st FSSG staff was directed to establish a forward command post. Captain Kevin P. Coughlin, a staff judge advocate who had initially been assigned as a prosecutor for the Legal Support Services Section, was pulled from his job working in operational law and rules of engagement to be the camp commandant. Together with Gunnery Sergeant Wesley M. Wentz, the company gunnery sergeant, Captain Coughlin successfully developed tables of organization and equipment that would support the requirements for a forward headquarters camp. They established Camp Midway just a few hundred meters away from the main FSSG camp. This was a practice run for the 1st FSSG Forward, testing their ability to conduct independent operations while split from the main element and to remain self-sufficient for an ex-

---
* Maj Raimo, like many officers in 1st FSSG, had arrived in Kuwait under the auspices of Exercise Internal Look, a CentCom exercise based on the current version of the plan for the invasion of Iraq.

The FSSG Forward headquarters is assembled at Camp Coyote February 2003.

tended period of time. This satellite camp, which became the blueprint for future FSSG Forward constructs, housed the operations center that directed all of 1st FSSG's combat service support on the battlefield.[10]

Camp Fox

While 1st FSSG established Tactical Assembly Area Coyote, the Marine Logistics Command was busy developing its own logistics support area. Colonel William A. Meier, a 27-year combat engineer veteran, was given the task of building Logistics Support Area (LSA) Fox. Having previously served as General Lehnert's chief of staff in Guantanamo Bay, Cuba, Colonel Meier was transferred from his current assignment at Marine Corps Base, Camp Lejeune, North Carolina, to serve as the deputy operations officer for 2d FSSG. After arriving in Kuwait during January 2003, he was assigned as the "area" or "camp commander"* of what became a sprawling logistics support area. Two-hundred-fifty Marines from the FSSG Forward were reassigned as a quartering party to assist in the buildup of LSA Fox, a 50-square-mile area in the vast Kuwaiti desert.

While a more northern location was originally designated as the site for LSA Fox—also known as Camp Fox—this area was home to a large number of Bedouins. To avoid any added conflicts or complications in the construction of the camp, the FSSG opted to move and find a new site. A vast stretch of empty desert to the south was eventually selected as an alternative. The engineer detachment from 8th Engineer Support Battalion (8th ESB) worked on the basic infrastructure of the camp, including utilities, water, power, and fuel. Additionally, the detachment's small explosive ordnance disposal team worked to uncover and remove a large quantity of ordnance discovered during the construction of Camp Fox. The size and breadth of the camp required the engineers to work long, often 18-hour days for the first six weeks. During the initial construction phases, 2d Military Police Battalion provided command and control to integrate security elements from the Marine, Navy, and British units. This combined security force implemented a comprehensive, multi-layered anti-terrorism/force protection plan.[13]

The camp's new location was extremely remote, and the lack of trafficable roads and a usable airfield* presented an enormous challenge. Ultimately, an entire road network had to be laid down. For Colonel Meier, this proved to be one of the most challenging aspects of developing Camp Fox. Materials available through local contractors, a combination of a clay-like substance called "getch" and a low-grade gravel, did not hold up well when wet, and severe rainstorms made the roads unusable for days at a time. Another challenge that Colonel Meier and his Marines

---

* Because the decision to build the camp came prior to the official "stand-up" of the Marine Logistics Command, the camp commander managed all internal aspects of the camp, to include several million-dollar contracts, which would normally have been the responsibility of the G-4. After the MLC was officially in place, these internal functions remained under the camp commander's responsibilities, therefore overshadowing the need for a G-4 on the MLC staff. With the exception of military police, all internal logistical requirements continued to be managed by the camp commander.

* Although there was no formal airfield at LSA Fox, two helicopter landing zones were constructed.

Classes of Supply

Class I	Subsistence (food), gratuitous (free) health and comfort items
Class II	Clothing, individual equipment, tentage, organizational tool sets and kits, hand tools, unclassified maps, administrative and housekeeping supplies and equipment
Class III	Petroleum, Oil and Lubricants (POL) (package and bulk): Petroleum, fuels, lubricants, hydraulic and insulating oils, preservatives, liquids and gases, bulk chemical products, coolants, deicer and antifreeze compounds, components, and additives of petroleum and chemical products, and coal
Class IV	Construction materials, including installed equipment and all fortification and barrier materials
Class V	Ammunition of all types, bombs, explosives, mines, fuzes, detonators, pyrotechnics, missiles, rockets, propellants, and associated items
Class VI	Personal demand items (such as health and hygiene products, soaps and toothpaste, writing material, snack food, beverages, cigarettes, batteries, alcohol, and cameras—nonmilitary sales items)
Class VII	Major end items such as launchers, tanks, mobile machine shops, and vehicles
Class VIII	Medical material (equipment and consummables) including repair parts peculiar to medical equipment
Class IX	Repair parts and components to include kits, assemblies, and subassemblies (repairable or non-repairable) required for maintenance support of all equipment
Class X	Material to support nonmilitary programs such as agriculture and economic development (not included in Classes I through IX)

faced was working with the Kuwaitis and foreign contractors, who generally did not work at the same pace or maintain the same work habits as Marines.[14]

Within Camp Fox, there were seven self-contained subordinate camps, a large ammunition supply point encompassing 18 square miles, a perimeter berm with guard towers and Arabic warning signs, a post exchange, a post office, and medical facility. Complete with warehouses, maintenance pads, hardstand billeting areas, a road network, and a command and control network, it became the base of operations for the Marine Logistics Command and its subordinate units. Additionally, the camp was home to two tenant units: the British Army's 6th Supply Regiment and Seabees from the Navy Mobile Construction Battalion 4 and the I MEF Engineer Group.

Headquarters and Service Battalion, 2d FSSG focused its efforts on establishing a variety of services, such as mail, exchange facilities, disbursing, administration, and communications. The battalion established a joint military mail terminal at Subhan, Kuwait, as well as subordinate post offices at the Kuwait City International Airport, the Kuwait Naval Base, and Camp Fox. Although the food services company was originally prepared to feed Marines within MLC, they were transformed into a provisional rifle company and used for internal camp security after their food service mission was contracted out to local civilian companies.

The Buildup of Sustainment Capability

Once in theater, MLC focused their efforts on developing its sustainment capabilities. Nobody could predict how long operations would continue, and ultimately, it was MLC's responsibility to provide logistics support for the duration of the war. It had only been a few months earlier when the decision was made to deploy 2d Supply Battalion as part of the Marine Logistics Command. Led by Colonel William F. Johnson, a 28-year veteran of Marine Corps supply, this battalion was tasked to provide operational supply support to I MEF and 1st FSSG, to include all classes of supply. However, by the time Colonel Johnson was finally able to deploy his Marines into theater and begin to build the battalion's stocks of supplies, he already faced one obstacle: a large backlog of orders for repair parts that I MEF units had been accumulating during the past few months. With priority placed on ammunition, rations, and medical supplies, emerging requirements for repair parts became a secondary concern. The challenge presented by this early backlog of requests was amplified by a major system challenge: 1st and 2d FSSGs were operating within two incompatible supply systems, which prohibited the ability to maintain visibility across the battlespace. Another challenge that Colonel Johnson faced was that as 2d Supply Battalion built its supply stocks in support of Operation Iraqi Freedom, it remained responsible for providing consumable repair parts support to all II MEF, 22d and 24th Marine Expeditionary Units, Combined Armed Exercises, Unitas, Joint Task Force-Horn of Africa, Rolling Thunder, and Operation Enduring Freedom.

Support Company, 2d Supply Battalion, was responsible for managing the MLC's container operations terminal lot. Having recently transferred the equipment record keeping of more than $200 million worth of 2d FSSG assets to the battalion level, Support Company, 2d Supply Battalion, was now able to focus its time and effort on building and maintaining this lot, which housed high usage items, to include over $1.5 million of office and administrative supplies, construction equipment, personal hygiene items, and large equipment.

In addition to building sustainment stocks in support of the war effort, Colonel Johnson took the opportunity to address problems encountered during Desert Storm. Coordinating with the British 14th Geographic Squadron, 2d Supply Battalion established a field map depot to facilitate the issue of paper and

The Supply System

Historically, during combat operations, logisticians deal with challenges such as poor visibility of supply requisitions and subsequent status updates. This was certainly no different during Operation Iraqi Freedom. In a testimony given to the House Armed Services Committee, Brigadier General Usher commented on this deficiency:

Our greatest shortfall during OIF was the lack of in-transit visibility information to incorporate into our command and control effort. The FSSG had large, extended convoys moving hundreds of miles in unsecured terrain supporting Marine forces spread across thousands of square miles in demanding weather conditions. The lack of asset visibility on unit stocks and in-transit visibility on ordered items made it difficult to identify actual shortages, to locate needed items within stocks for reallocation, and to direct and track the movement of ordered items to requesting units. This lack of visibility resulted in delays, shortages, and at times an inability to expedite critical parts.[15]

With the long distances the MEF was traveling and the number of units spread out across the battlefield, visibility of supply requisitions was poor. Additionally, because 1st and 2d FSSG were using different versions of the Asset Tracking Logistics and Supply System (ATLASS), there were problems with the supply system from the start. Technical workarounds provided temporary solutions, but the big disconnect and frustration was in the lack of visibility. Ultimately, it did not hamper the execution of the mission; however, the mission accomplished was often done so through "brute force logistics," which General Usher described as "simply a way of applying what had to be done . . . not pretty . . . not elegant . . . and not sophisticated. Sheer adrenaline pushed to move sustainment and to provide other elements of combat service support as quickly as possible across an increasing line of communication."[16]

Demonstrating the kind of initiative and ingenuity that allowed the 1st FSSG to step so far outside its doctrinal box, Major Brandon D. McGowan, CSSB-18 supply company commander in 1st FSSG, helped alleviate the problem of poor visibility by marrying the ATLASS system with satellite phone technology to provide supply units hundreds of miles apart on the battlefield the ability to send and receive supply requisitions. Working closely with systems command and 2d FSSG, he also aligned the separate systems being used by the two FSSGs to facilitate data flow between them.[17]

Courtesy of 2d FSSG
Gen Michael R. Lehnert greets a locally contracted driver at Camp Fox.

digital maps to all Marine forces in theater. This facility warehoused over two million maps and imagery products, and during Operation Iraqi Freedom, it issued more than 330,000 maps to I MEF and Coalition forces.

MLC's Growing Distribution Mission

The original distribution plan for moving supplies throughout the theater had MLC vehicles concentrated on transportation from the ports of entry to Logistics Support Area Fox and Tactical Assembly Area Coyote. The preponderance of the long-haul requirement of moving supplies forward into Iraq had initially been allocated to U.S. Army theater assets. Although the Army provided limited resources, such as heavy tank haulers and fuel trucks, the theater assets did not materialize in the expected numbers, because the Army's 377th Theater Support Command could not support both V Corps and I MEF. It was also determined that 1st FSSG did not possess the vehicles to reach back to TAA Coyote from their forward support areas in Iraq. Additionally, the original flow of forces into theater focused on the push for combat troops; deployment enablers, to include truck drivers, were limited. General Lehnert, Commander of MLC recognized the shortfall early on:

As soon as we got into country, it became very obvious that the distribution assets that had been promised by the theater support command were not available at that time and were not likely to be available for some time. So what we had to do was use our expeditionary contracting capability to contract for almost 300 tractor-trailers driven by third country nationals.[18]

When 2d FSSG had begun operating in Kuwait they had contracted with local vendors to help support the offload of equipment from the ports to LSA Fox. When this contract was due to expire they had renewed it, but shifted the fleet of vehicles and drivers to new transportation missions within Kuwait. As the plan unfolded, and it became more obvious that 2d Transportation Support Battalion would move forward into Iraq, stretching the logistical lines even further up the battlefield, another missing link in the distribution chain became clear. As a result, the Marine Logistics Command established another contract for third country national drivers, vehicles, and maintenance support to cover the distance between TAA Coyote and forward bases in Iraq. General Lehnert described:

If you're a student of history, you'll know that that was done during Desert Storm, and this wasn't particularly an original concept. What was original in this particular case is not only were they initially contracted to move the over 5,000 containers that came off the MPS shipping—because once again, we could not get that support from the Theater Support Command in at least the speed and the quantities that we desired—but after that mission was over with the TCNs, the third country nationals in the contracted vehicles actually were integrated into our battlefield distribution plan and went all the way north and actually up to about 250 to 300 miles into Iraq.[20]

To manage and support contracts with over 230 third country national drivers from 11 nations and their large fleet of commercial vehicles, General Lehnert established the MLC Support Detachment 1 (MSD-1). This 545–Marine and sailor unit, commanded by Major Tyson B. Geisendorff, was staged at Camp Tarawa, TAA Coyote, where it could move supply convoys north to points in Iraq. MSD-1 also fulfilled a number of other functions to include providing military police, medical, communications, utility engineers, bulk fuel, maintenance, supply, and ammunition.

Request for Forces

In early 2003, when forces began arriving into theater, it was not by the time-phased force deployment data (TPFDD) process, but rather through the request for forces (RFF)/deployment orders. The more traditional TPFDD process formed the basis for all deployments in support of Operations Plan 1003V and was based on force planning, support planning, and transportation planning; it addressed both force requirements and prioritized transportation movement. On the other hand, the RFF/deployment orders process required Central Command to request packages of forces, each of which had to be approved by the Secretary of Defense. General Lehnert commented on the impact of this decision on the Marine Corps' ability to provide logistics support to its own forces:

> When the force came here, the decision was made at the highest levels to move the forces: the RFF as opposed to TPFDD, and the net impact of that was that in many cases the deployment enablers were not moved in the right sequence. So you had combat forces that showed up expecting sustainment, expecting the maintenance, the transportation and the food to be in place when the deployment enablers were still moving . . . We worked through that, but having the RFF process rather than a TPFDD was not a plus, and it certainly made the level of difficulty much harder than it needed to be.[19]

Another challenge posed by the decision to use deployment orders was that units could not be alerted until the deployment order was signed. This was especially difficult for the large number of reservists who supported 1st FSSG during Operation Iraqi Freedom. Final decisions often came very late and left units scrambling to deploy.

General Lehnert recognized that hiring third country national (TCN) drivers from Kuwait and asking them to drive into Iraq posed new challenges and potential for mission abandonment. He quickly implemented a program of team building among the foreign drivers to address the human dimension and allay any fears they had regarding their mission. He understood the criticality of the third country national truck force and focused on their well-being and self-confidence. To start, the drivers were provided with shelter, food, and fuel for their trucks. Additionally, they were given Geneva Convention photo identification cards, gas masks, and an armed Marine as an assistant driver. This helped to boost their confidence. General Lehnert also believed that the foreign drivers would excel at their mission more if given additional incentives. Besides visiting the camp, sharing meals and taking photographs with the drivers, he implemented a simple reward system where Marine Corps emblem decals would be affixed to the vehicles to reflect a driver's successful mission into Iraq. A seemingly trivial program paid dividends in the end, as the drivers were motivated and demonstrated great resolve in supporting the MLC team.[21]

Setting up a Communications Architecture

By table of organization, each FSSG possessed its own communications company. 2d FSSG's communications company supported connectivity between MLC's multiple sites, to include the beach operations group at Kuwait Naval Base, the seaport of debarkation at the Port of Ash Shuaybah, the aerial port of debarkation at Kuwait City International Airport, the Arifjan Army Base, and Camp Fox. Although this worked during the build-up of forces, it was obvious to Lieutenant Colonel Kenneth S. Helfrich, 2d FSSG's communications officer, that for Operation Iraqi Freedom this would not suffice. For example, the communications company did not possess satellite capability, which was an absolute necessity for long-range and distributed operations.

As a result of this shortfall, the Marine Logistics Command relied heavily on assets from 8th Communications Battalion, II MEF,* commanded by Lieutenant Colonel Roarke L. Anderson. Almost immediately upon receiving its mission to conduct the ammunition offload, 2d FSSG received the support of an additional communications company from 8th Communications Battalion, which did possess the satellite capability. Although the battalion had not been considered in the initial planning for Operation Iraqi Freedom, various missions developed over the course of several months, including a requirement to provide basic communications support to 2d Marine Expeditionary Brigade (Task Force Tarawa). During subsequent planning conferences, the communica-

---

* 8th Communications Battalion had at one time been a part of the FSSG, but was now a standalone battalion within the II MEF Headquarters Group.

tions requirements for both Marine Forces Central Command (MarCent) and MLC were identified, and as a result, Support Company was assigned to MarCent's command element, and Bravo and Charlie Companies were assigned in direct support of MLC. This presented a complicated command structure, as the battalion's headquarters element was attached to MarCent, which was located in Bahrain, but the majority of the battalion was co-located with, and tactically controlled by, MLC at Camp Fox in Kuwait.[22]

In addition to the support provided by 8th Communications Battalion, the MLC received assistance from both the U.S. Army and Air Force to address the emerging communications requirements. In the interim, however, while the communications architecture was being built, cellular phones were a critical, but temporary and expensive, solution.

During the next several weeks, the focus of 2d FSSG shifted from the offload of the ammunition and MPF ships to the construction of Logistics Support Area Fox and the establishment of the MLC. To make this happen, 2d FSSG required additional aid from 8th Communications Battalion. Arriving in theater during the second week of February, advanced planners for the battalion began to tackle the complex problems of setting up a communications network. Essentially, two companies had to create a communications network to link multiple locations in the southern area of operations, which encompassed Kuwait's ports, its airport, and MLC's expansive Camp Fox. Problems included interference caused by power lines and city structures. Adding to this, the complicated command relationships meant that the battalion headquarters could not task its own companies.

It was immediately identified that MLC required a more substantial communications architecture than it had originally anticipated and the communications planners established a centralized Operation Systems Control Center (OSCC). Major Julie L. Nethercot, the communications battalion operations officer and director of the OSCC described their operations:

> We pulled open a couple of doctrinal pubs, and we found what would best fit this situation. Usually when the battalion would deploy, I, as the [S-3], would run the systems control. In this instance, we have not only 8th Comm Bn, but we have 2d FSSG communications company, and Marine Wing Communications Squadron 48: three very unique groups, units, missions . . . so what we did is we stood up what's called an Operations Systems Control Center, which takes all three units and gives communications control to one entity, the OSCC . . . and by putting that in place, that gave MarCent one unit that they talked to, one organization that they tasked.[23]

While the concept of the OSCC was well conceived, its implementation was not. The original plan had the OSCC co-located with the MLC's Combat Service Support Operations Center and positioned at the center of "the hub and spoke" setup, with communications lines stretching out to battalions. Although this plan would have optimized the communications capabilities support, when units began to arrive in Kuwait and set up at Camp Fox, the arrangement was more linear, prohibiting execution of the original plan.[24] Despite these limitations and a number of other challenges, including new gear, environmental obstacles, and command and control complications, the OSCC was able to process a daily average of 12,000 phone calls.[25]

Preparing for Battle

In the weeks leading up to the start of Operation Iraqi Freedom, both 1st and 2d FSSG shifted their focus from "getting into country" to "preparing for battle." Rehearsing realistic scenarios and identifying unknown factors helped prepare the Marines for what was to come. Training was emphasized at all levels, from senior staff officers down to the individual Marines. At the upper levels this materialized as rehearsal of concept (ROC) drills.

Recognizing the complexities associated with the logistics and combat service support missions, General Lehnert orchestrated a ROC drill on 23 February 2003. The purpose was to test supportability concepts, introduce trafficability and distance limitations and probable enemy responses, and to challenge preconceived unit employment plans. This drill, attended by general and senior officers from the Marine Logistics Command, the 377th Theater Support Command, I Marine Expeditionary Force, 1st Marine Division, 3d Marine Aircraft Wing, and 1st Force Service Support Group, forced units to address potential problems and alternate solutions, while establishing a common baseline for theater, operational, and tactical level logistics forces.

On 5 March, the 1st FSSG hosted its own drill at Camp Midway. Lasting five hours, this exercise allowed members of the group staff and other major commands, such as the Marine Logistics Command and 3d Marine Air Wing, an opportunity to identify discrepancies in their plan and coordinate support

BGen Edward G. Usher III listens during a rehearsal of concept drill at Camp Midway, TAA Coyote, Kuwait.

requirements and deconfliction of movement and mission. Lieutenant Colonel Adrian W. Burke, 1st FSSG future operations officer and a veteran combat service support commander from the first Gulf War, orchestrated the rehearsal. Representatives from each battalion and group briefed their schemes of maneuver for multiple phases of the war, providing the attendees with an opportunity to view the entire picture of combat service support across the battlefield.[26]

Combat Service Support Group 11

At the unit level, training focused on both job proficiency and general battle skills. Because they were in direct support of 1st Marine Division, it was highly likely that Marines in Combat Service Support Group 11 would find themselves in combat situations. CSSG-11 had conducted close cooperative planning efforts with 1st Marine Division through constant exercises and rehearsal of concept drills. These events, occurring both stateside and in Kuwait, had begun in the summer of 2002 and continued up to the day prior to crossing the line of departure into Iraq. Additionally, the commanding officer, Colonel John J. Pomfret, conducted a Marine Corps combat readiness evaluation system test to ensure that his Marines were well prepared in both their combat skills and military occupational specialty skills. Combat skills included firing, maneuver, movement, chemical decontamination, and security. Further, the colonel and his subordinate commanders continuously conveyed to each Marine the importance of realistic preparations for war. The uniform of the day for Marines at Camp Bougainville included helmet, flak jacket, and gas mask carried at one's side. Because of the potential for biological and chemical attacks, mission oriented protective posture (MOPP) suits were required to be accessible within 60 seconds. This uniform standard, which mirrored that of 1st Marine Division, was above and beyond that of other units within 1st FSSG. Reaction drills for both enemy conventional and chemical attacks were also conducted on a regular basis.

Training was emphasized during the weeks leading up to the war, and all units within CSSG-11 participated. For example, within the group's five shock trauma platoons were many medical augmentation personnel who were not accustomed to being in the field. Prior to the war, their training in Kuwait focused on being able to set up quickly both day and night. High standards were set, and the Marines and sailors in CSSG-11 met all of them.[27]

Meanwhile, as the group's Marines were preparing

for potential combat operations, they began providing combat service support to division units. One tool that provided Colonel Pomfret and his staff with the ability to better track incoming requests and outgoing support was the logistics tasking order. Created by Major James C. Caley, executive officer of CSSG-11, this tool was loosely based on the aviation community's air tasking order and was designed to take rapid requests, consolidate requirements, and produce an order that would lead to mission accomplishment.[28]

In Combat Service Support Battalion 10 (CSSB-10), Colonel Weinkle had great concerns for his Marines' safety. Although his battalion normally followed closely behind 1st Marine Division, setting up repair and replenishment points in anticipation of ground combat advances required that the combat service support convoys move in between and in front of division units, which increased the potential for friendly fire incidents.[29] One thing that helped to minimize this danger was that CSSG-11 had already begun providing direct support to 1st Marine Division in Kuwait, and procedures were already in place. Even as they prepared their own equipment and personnel for operations in Iraq, CSSG-11 and CSSB-10 had the mission of providing 22,000 Marines and sailors in 1st Marine Division with their water, food, and fuel, as well as preparing their ammunition loads for combat. This early implementation of support helped strengthen the bonds that had already been established through months of integrated planning.

Combat Service Support Battalion 22

While elements of I MEF arrived from the West Coast, forces from II MEF began arriving from the

Marines from CSSG-11 train in search and seizure techniques.
Courtesy of CSSB-10

Photo by LtCol Melissa D. Mihocko, USMCR

Chemical Protection

The higher the MOPP—Mission Oriented Protective Posture—level, the greater the threat of chemical attack. There are four levels MOPP, which require the wearing of different protective items of clothing. Level I consists of wearing a protective suit (trousers and jacket) and carrying the suit's boots, gloves, mask, and hood. Level II includes wearing the boots, while carrying the gloves and mask with hood. Level III adds the wearing of the mask with hood. Level IV requires the entire outfit, including the gloves, to be worn.

East Coast. On 16 February, one of the eastern units, Combat Service Support Battalion 22 (CSSB-22), arrived at the Kuwait Naval Base and immediately began offloading their personnel and equipment from the USS *Saipan* (LHA 2). They then headed to Camp Ryan, the new desert home for Task Force Tarawa. Operational tempo was extremely high, as the Marines in CSSB-22 not only prepared for upcoming combat operations, which included last minute planning and reshuffling of support capabilities, but also spent long days providing combat service support to both Task Force Tarawa and Regimental Combat Team 2 (RCT-2), which consisted of three infantry battalions, an artillery battalion, and companies attached from the combat engineer, light

Courtesy of CSSB-10

During the weeks prior to the start of the war, MajGen James N. Mattis, commanding general of 1st Marine Division, made several visits to Camp Bougainville to emphasize the critical relationship between the division Marines and those of CSSG-11 and CSSB-10.

armored reconnaissance, assault amphibian, tank, and reconnaissance battalions.[30]

One of the most significant efforts for CSSB-22 in the weeks leading up to war was the reorganization and establishment of mobile resupply teams in direct support of combat operations. In essence, these teams, which augmented the battalion logistics trains with one day of food, water, fuel, and ammunition resupply, served the same purpose for RCT-2 as the combat service support companies in CSSG-11 did for the regimental combat teams of 1st Marine Division. Similar to CSSG-11, the battalion had to balance both their responsibility to provide combat service support to Task Force Tarawa and RCT-2 with their need to train for upcoming operations. During the weeks following their arrival, the Marines of CSSB-22 continued the training they had been conducting on ship, but also added many live-fire weapon shoots on Udairi Range, Kuwait, while training daily for immediate action drills and convoy procedures.

Another significant CSSB-22 element was its shock trauma platoon. While preparing for combat operations, Lieutenant Colonel Thomas N. Goben, commander of CSSB-22, recognized the importance of his medical unit. "Our shock trauma unit has the capability to reinforce any Task Force Tarawa combat unit. During the fight, their mission is to stabilize any casualty for follow on medical care."[31] Unfortunately, in the days to come, the platoon's capabilities would indeed be tested.

General Support Arrives in Country

In early February 2003, Combat Service Support Group 15's (CSSG-15) main body arrived in Kuwait. Throughout the month, the Marines conducted reception, staging, onward movement, and integration operations, moving both equipment and personnel to their designated locations. They also began to focus training on combat operations center procedures, reporting processes and actions, force protection, and nuclear, biological, and chemical (NBC) detection and personal defensive measures. War seemed imminent during February and March. The Marines observed a number of senior leaders, to include the Commandant, General Michael W. Hagee; the Marine Forces Central Command, Lieutenant General Earl B. Hailston; and the I MEF Commanding General, Lieutenant General James T. Conway, who visited at that time to deliver motivational "go to war" speeches.[32]

Falling beneath the CSSG-15 headquarters, Combat Service Support Battalion 12 (CSSB-12), Combat Service Support Battalion 18 (CSSB-18), and Health Services Battalion* also began to arrive in country during February. When they reached their respective camps at Tactical Assembly Area Coyote, CSSB-12 and CSSB-18 each established a base of operations, focusing heavily on training in areas such as combat service support operations center procedures; nuclear, biological, and chemical alerts; force protection drills; media handling; mortuary affairs; explosive ordnance disposal; rules of engagement; and civil affairs. During this period, CSSB-12, however, had the additional responsibility of providing combat service support to I MEF, which had already arrived in Kuwait. This support included food, water, fuel, ammunition, repair parts, medical supplies, and maintenance capabilities. Additionally, CSSB-12 provided full-service capabilities to include disbursing, postal, legal, and a post exchange selling sundries, hygiene products, and junk food. Two Boeing 747s with $2 million worth of Army and Air Force Exchange Services material were brought in to supply the post exchange. Services were stationary at CSSB-12's camp, but a small mobile services unit was pushed out to support the Marines at other camps.[33] Meanwhile, CSSB-18 remained "in the box," to be prepared for a short notice order to move into Iraq. Similarly, Health Services Battalion had one of its companies establish a fully operational surgical capability, while the two other companies awaited orders to move north into Iraq.

---
* During Operation Iraqi Freedom, CSSG-15 also received many augments to their organization, including the U.S. Army 7th Biological Integrated Detection System Platoon, 7th Chemical Company, 83d Chemical Battalion; A Company, 63d Signal Battalion; the 1st Platoon, 51st Chemical Company, 83d Chemical Battalion; and the U.S. Air Force Aeromedical Evacuation Liaison Team and Mobile Air Staging Facility Team, 320th Expeditionary Aeromedical Evacuation Squadron. (Combat Service Support Group 15 ComdC, 1Jan03–30Jun03.)

6th Engineer Support Battalion

Lieutenant Colonel Roger R. Machut, the commanding officer of 6th Engineer Support Battalion (6th ESB), arrived in Kuwait on 8 February and assembled his battalion at Camp Solomon Islands, Tactical Assembly Area Coyote. Although he had completed several tours with 6th ESB during his career, this was the first time the entire battalion had been mobilized. To support its massive mission to generate, transport, and provide both fuel and water to I MEF forces, the battalion received numerous augments from other units, including a utilities platoon and bulk fuel company from 7th Engineer Support Battalion (7th ESB). Among them, Bulk Fuel Company, 7th ESB, commanded by Captain Jennifer A. Esch, had previously been involved in the planning of the tactical fuel system, and logically transferred over to 6th ESB as Delta Company. The complement of 6th ESB eventually totaled more than 1,600 Marines and sailors, a large battalion by Marine Corps standards.

Having been assigned the mission to construct and maintain a tactical fuel system, the battalion immediately began conducting extensive training on the procedures surrounding the implementation of the hose-reel system. This included route reconnaissance and land clearing, digging the required V-ditch, laying the hose, and establishing booster stations. This training was critical as few of the Marines possessed practical experience acquired while working in a deployed environment. Anticipating the inevitable movement of forces into Iraq, Colonel Machut was confident that his Marines would be able to accomplish the mission and establish the hose-reel system in the required four days; his concern was focused more on the enemy. While they would not be laying hose in populated areas where intense fighting was expected, any random insurgent wielding a knife could easily sabotage the success of the entire tactical fuel system.[34]

While most Marines in 6th ESB trained in the Kuwaiti desert, others continued to receive gear from MPF ships, as the battalion had initially arrived with only 19 percent of its standard equipment. It received more than 6,000 short tons of cargo over the next few weeks, which included over 1,000 large pieces of equipment, from five ships arriving at the Port of Ash-Shuaybah.

On 17 February, Colonel Machut's Marines reached Breach Point West, where the battalion's command, security, and construction elements had been prepositioned. Just five miles from the border

Photo by MSgt Edward D. Kniery, USMC

Corpsmen of Alpha Surgical Company, Health Services Battalion set up Forward Resuscitative Surgical System #5 for incoming casualties.

between Kuwait and Iraq, these Marines were among the forward-most positioned units of I MEF. In early March, when the arrival of some U.S. Army bulk fuel units was delayed, Colonel Machut received a request from the Coalition Forces Land Component Commander to provide a bulk fuel company to operate the Army's tactical petroleum terminal at Breach Point West. This last-minute tasking yielded the largest field fuel farm ever operated by Marines and it became the primary source of fuel for both I MEF and the Army's 3d Infantry Division.[35]

7th Engineer Support Battalion

By 5 February, the 7th Engineer Support Battalion had arrived in Kuwait. Located at Camp Betio, Tactical Assembly Area Coyote, their designated engineering mission consisted of construction, mobility and countermobility, and survivability. As a result, the Marines had an endless number of engineering projects to pursue as the 1st FSSG's new home at TAA Coyote was being developed. Commanded by Lieutenant Colonel Scott H. Poindexter, the Marines constructed 14-foot berms, 10-foot-by-15-foot anti-tank ditches, trenches and bunkers, and portable com-

modes for the array of camps supporting the Marine Expeditionary Force. Concurrently, elements of 7th ESB conducted various training exercises to prepare for what would become their primary tasks during the war: combat service support area construction, main supply route maintenance, breaching, and follow-on breaching.

Bravo and Charlie Companies, which were responsible for the initial breaching and obstacle reduction along the Kuwait-Iraq border, trained continuously for this critical task. To simulate the actions that were required at the commencement of combat operations, the Marines constructed a replica of the enemy's Kuwait-Iraq border obstacle belt. Such innovations provided more realistic training than had been received prior to this deployment. Other areas of training included chemical and biological decontamination drills, convoy operations, small arms and crew served weapons employment, nighttime equipment operation, first aid, patrolling, and perimeter defense. Captain Susan Bird had Charlie company conduct combined training with 11th Marines and 3d Light Armored Reconnaissance Battalion, further solidifying integration with their supported combat units. These mounted rehearsals and training in tactical convoy operations would pay dividends in the near future.[36]

8th Engineer Support Battalion

Like many other battalions, 8th Engineer Support Battalion had the daunting task of reorganizing late in the game and retraining its Marines to work together as a team. Additionally, because the battalion fell under of 2d FSSG, which was designated as the Marine Logistics Command for Operation Iraqi Freedom, Lieutenant Colonel Niel E. Nelson, the battalion commander, also faced unique manpower challenges. Many of his personnel and equipment, especially in the area of transportation and maintenance, had already been attached to other battalions within 2d FSSG. Additionally, because 2d FSSG had been assigned the operational logistics role in the Marine Logistics Command (MLC), he had forfeited resources to meet the MLC's requirement for an organic engineering capability. Colonel Nelson looked to 1st FSSG's commanding general, Brigadier General Usher, to help fill the gaps in his battalion's manning structure and received augmentation from 1st Transportation Battalion, 1st Supply Battalion, 6th ESB, 7th ESB, 6th Motor Transport Battalion, 1st and 2d Combat Engineer Battalions, and Headquarters and Service Battalion, 1st FSSG. Lieutenant Colonel Nelson described the reorganization process:

> This loss of core competencies from within the battalion is analogous to an infantry battalion consolidating its mortars and crews at the regiment or division level and then getting back a pick up team of mortar men who did not have the culture and training of the infantry battalion. The Marines and sailors that were placed under the command of 8th ESB were highly motivated, but required extensive training in order to be independent bridge builders under wartime conditions.[37]

An additional challenge faced by 8th ESB was the lack of transportation assets. Arguing the need for two mobile-loaded bridge companies to support movement of both 1st Marine Division and Task Force Tarawa, Colonel Nelson was faced with the fact that his battalion simply did not possess the as-

Marines of 8th Engineer Support Battalion build Lake Coyote in Kuwait to train in building bridges across rivers.

Courtesy of 8th ESB

sets required to transport the necessary equipment. Ultimately, the burden was lessened by the use of commercially procured trailers to move ten bridge erection boats and the adaptation of a new loading method for the MK48/14 logistics vehicles system/container transporter rear body unit. By rotating the bridge pallets 90 degrees, the Marines were able to load twice the equipment on a single vehicle. This type of resourcefulness was a testament to the battalion's motto, Whatever It Takes.[38]

The bridging mission was unique and required master skills down to the squad level. With an unknown number of potential crossings and the added loss of both equipment and personnel to man each of the crossings emplaced, the battalion trained and prepared by building and removing three full-scale 70-ton capacity medium-girder bridges every 48 hours for more than four weeks. The companies also conducted numerous day and night convoys around Camp Coyote to practice loading, unloading, and transporting the combat loads, as well as to prepare immediate action plans. During the month of February, 8th ESB Marines conducted training in the middle of the Kuwaiti desert. As many of the battalion's boats came from all parts of the United States and off the Marine Corps maritime preposition shipping, it was important to water test each one to ensure its reliability and functionality. As a result, their training centered on simulated water crossings, a unique challenge to overcome in a desert environment. The Marines exercised ingenuity by successfully creating both a dry-gap pit and large pond, called Lake Coyote, to test both their bridging skills and equipment. Extensive training in the art of bridge building culminated in a battalion competition, which Charlie Company won. The company, commanded by Captain Christopher M. Haar, later helped construct a medium-girder bridge across the Diyala River, allowing 1st Marine Division to cross the river and continue their final assault into Baghdad.[39]

Transportation Support Group

No training was more critical to the Marines of Transportation Support Group (TSG) and 6th Motor Transport Battalion (6th MTBn) than that of convoy control procedures. To identify and work through uncertainties that they would inevitably face during combat operations, Colonel David G. Reist and Lieutenant Colonel Patrick J. Hermesmann had the newly formed Convoy Control Company escort actual sustainment convoys being run in support of I MEF. Together, drivers from the TSG and 6th MTBn began transporting equipment from the port to the arrival assembly operations group, and then to their new home at Camp Guam and Camp Saipan in Tactical Assembly Area Coyote.

As the operational tempo increased, it became obvious that even combined, TSG and 6th MTBn lacked the equipment necessary to support I MEF. Although they contracted for host nation support vehicles, most were different from the tactical vehicles the Marines normally operated. An eight-day licensing program was subsequently established and Marine drivers from both 6th MTBn and TSG, as well as all officers and staff noncommissioned officers, were trained to operate large tractor trailers, lowboys, buses, and fuel and water tankers.[40]

Another TSG unit that provided a critical capability was the Landing Support Company. To complement the successes of the Marine forces on the

A helicopter support team member guides a CH-53 Super Stallion to land near the ammunition supply point, LSA Viper.

Photo by MSgt Edward D. Kniery, USMC

Photo by LtCol Melissa D. Mihocko, USMCR

1st FSSG deputy commander, Col John Sweeney (second from left) speaks to Marines at Breachpoint West prior to the commencement of the war.

battlefield, the Landing Support Company would provide air support to transport sustainment items to forward units. Major Matthew S. Cook, landing support company commander, understood the potential for his 282 Marines to enhance ground combat effectiveness and focused their attention on training helicopter teams, arrival/departure airfield control groups, and shipping and receiving platoons. In buttressing Combat Service Support Battalion 10, many of the company's Marines were assigned traffic control duties in their repair and replenishment points. Others provided critical service to the mobile medical units by coordinating and controlling landing zones for lifesaving evacuations. Additionally, Combat Service Support Battalions 12 and 18 used shipping and receiving platoons to track the movement of battlefield sustainment.

As the commencement of combat operations loomed, vessels carrying critical equipment continued to arrive at the port in Kuwait. Two ships arriving on 14 and 18 March provided TSG with 93 percent of its table of equipment, most of which was cargo trucks.[41] Until the start of hostilities, the TSG Marines continued to load these trucks in support of units preparing for war. Of note, 91 of them were loaded with bridging equipment for 8th ESB, in anticipation of assault bridging requirements, and 68 carried critical hose-reel equipment in support of 6th ESB's tactical fuel system mission.

Breach Point West

On 18 March, Colonel John L. Sweeney Jr., deputy commander of 1st FSSG, and the group's Sergeant Major Manuel J. Sanchez, travelled to Breach Point West to visit each group element staged at the frontline. Poised just a few miles south of the Kuwait/Iraq border, several of these units had been staged in this remote location for days. If and when the war began, they would be among the first 1st FSSG Marines to cross the line of departure. Colonel Sweeney and Sergeant Major Sanchez delivered words of praise and encouragement to the Marines, as they stood informally in groups beneath camouflage netting. The colonel also provided much-appreciated updates on current events and the impending conflict. The Marines were motivated; they had been "away from the flagpole" and enjoying a bit of independence and solitude, all the while preparing themselves and their equipment for the moment they would cross the border into Iraq. Colonel Sweeney knew this would be the last command visit to the frontlines before the start of Operation Iraqi Freedom, and he took the opportunity to give the Marines some of his own advice on the days to come.[42]

Chapter 3

Opening Days of the War (17–22 March 2003)

On 17 March 2003, President George W. Bush issued a 48-hour ultimatum for Saddam Hussein and his sons to leave Iraq. For most Marines, the significance of this broadcast was that G-day—the start of the ground war—was now imminent. In one long-awaited speech, a timeline for war emerged. Following the announcement, the forces in I MEF began to move to their dispersal areas.

For Operation Iraqi Freedom, Lieutenant General James T. Conway, Commanding General, I Marine Expeditionary Force, concisely laid out the Marines' mission in his Operations Plan 1003V:

> The purpose of this operation is to remove the Iraqi regime. We will support the CFLCC (Coalition forces land component commander) by rapidly defeating Iraqi forces in the MEF AO (area of operation) in order to protect the Main Effort's (V Corps') eastern flank throughout the operation, and by isolating Baghdad from the east. Additionally, the early seizure of the key oil infrastructure will be central to preventing environmental disaster in the region while facilitating a smooth transition to a new Iraqi government.[1]

The 1st Marine Division's first task at hand was to move north into Iraq and secure key oil infrastructures. During the Persian Gulf War of 1991, Iraqi forces retreating from Kuwait set fire to Kuwaiti oil wells. Many of these fires burned out of control for months, primarily because it was too dangerous to dispatch firefighting crews to areas surrounding the oil wells that had not been cleared of mines and unexploded ordnance. The result was widespread pollution of Kuwait's soil and air. In the current operation, it was feared that the roughly 500 oil wells located in Iraq's southern Rumaylah oil fields would be targets of destruction or sabotage by the Iraqi forces, and the goal was to secure them immediately, preventing any destruction and mitigating environmental disaster. Beyond this initial task, 1st Marine Division would focus on defeating Iraqi forces in their area of operations and clearing main supply routes to allow follow-on forces and logistical support to flow north of the Euphrates River to al-Kut and eventually Baghdad.

Photo by LtCol Melissa D. Mihocko, USMCR

Marines in the 1st FSSG Combat Operations Center watch a live broadcast of President George W. Bush as he delivers the ultimatum to Saddam Hussein to leave Iraq or face war.

Movement to the Dispersal Areas

On 18 March, 1st Marine Division received the order to move to its dispersal areas in preparation for attack. In close coordination, all three combat service support companies from Combat Service Support Group 11 (CSSG-11) followed their respective regimental combat teams as they moved to their own dispersal areas. Combat Service Support Battalion 10 (CSSB-10), the unit within CSSG-11 that aided the combat service support companies also began to move. To evenly support all three companies, Lieutenant Colonel Robert K. Weinkle Jr., split his battalion into three functional elements. Two were named "Repair and Replenishment Point 3 Opening Package"* or "East Opening Package" and "Repair and Replenishment Point 4 Opening Package" or "West Opening Package," and were designed to follow in trace of Regimental Combat Teams 5 (RCT-5) and 7 (RCT-7) and their direct support combat service support companies. The third element, which did not

---

* In the pre-deployment phase, the commanding officer of CSSG-11, Col J. J. Pomfret, frequently utilized the term "Opening Package" to refer to the advance capability set. The term became the standard of usage after CSSB-10 crossed the line of departure into Iraq.

have a designation of "opening package," was specifically designed and configured to support the preparatory and ensuing fires of the 11th Marines. Combat Service Support Company 111 was followed in trace by the CSSG-11 tactical command post.

The initial movement of the combat service support companies to their dispersal areas and CSSB-10 to Repair and Replenishment Points 1 and 2 was the first real test of convoy movement, command and control, and communications. One CSSB-10 convoy had a vehicle footprint of more than seven miles. This lengthy stretch of vehicles was common throughout the rest of the war. Although the designated repair and replenishment points were just 30 miles north of Camp Bougainville and still on the Kuwait side of the border, the Marines were anxious to move to their new locations. First Sergeant Gonzalo A. "Butch" Vasquez of Transportation Support Company described the atmosphere as they moved north. "The Marines were apprehensive about what they were about to encounter, but more than ready to get out of Bougainville. They didn't know what they were asking for, but ready to get out of the situation they were currently in."[2] Located near the RCT-5 and RCT-7 dispersal areas, just south of the Kuwait/Iraq border, Repair and Replenishment Points 1 and 2 were designed to provide division units with a final resupply prior to crossing the line of departure. For the most part, the regimental combat teams used these points as an opportunity to top off on fuel prior to moving north toward the enemy.[3]

While elements of CSSG-11 stayed in close coordination with 1st Marine Division's units, other elements of the 1st FSSG were assembled at Breach Point West, preparing for movement across the border. Just a few miles from the border between Kuwait and Iraq, Breach Point West served as a staging area for vehicles, equipment, and personnel from the most forward elements of 6th, 7th, and 8th Engineer Support Battalions, Combat Service Support Battalion 12 (CSSB-12), Combat Service Support Battalion 18 (CSSB-18), Transportation Support Group, and the 1st FSSG Forward. Here they waited and prepared for the inevitable command to cross into Iraq.

On the evening of 19 March, 11th Marines unleashed a bombardment of artillery on Safwan Hill, an Iraqi observation post overlooking the Kuwaiti border. Just a few miles north of the border, this position sat on a raised point, 551 feet in elevation, offering the Iraqis an unobstructed view of advancing Coalition forces. Additionally, it was suspected of having sophisticated surveillance equipment oriented toward the main highway, which runs north from Kuwait to al-Basrah and on to Baghdad. Destruction of the observation post was imperative before Coalition troops could begin crossing into Iraq. The attack, supported by both U.S. Marine and Navy aircraft, continued through the night, ultimately destroying the post beyond recognition.[4]

While elements of 1st FSSG along the border prepared for the move north into Iraq, elements of the Marine Logistics Command (MLC) also began to shift.

A convoy of Medium Tactical Vehicle Replacement seven-ton trucks from Transportation Support Group moves into Support Area Chesty, 1st FSSG Forward Headquarters, IMEF, Iraq.

Photo by MSgt Edward D. Kniery, USMC

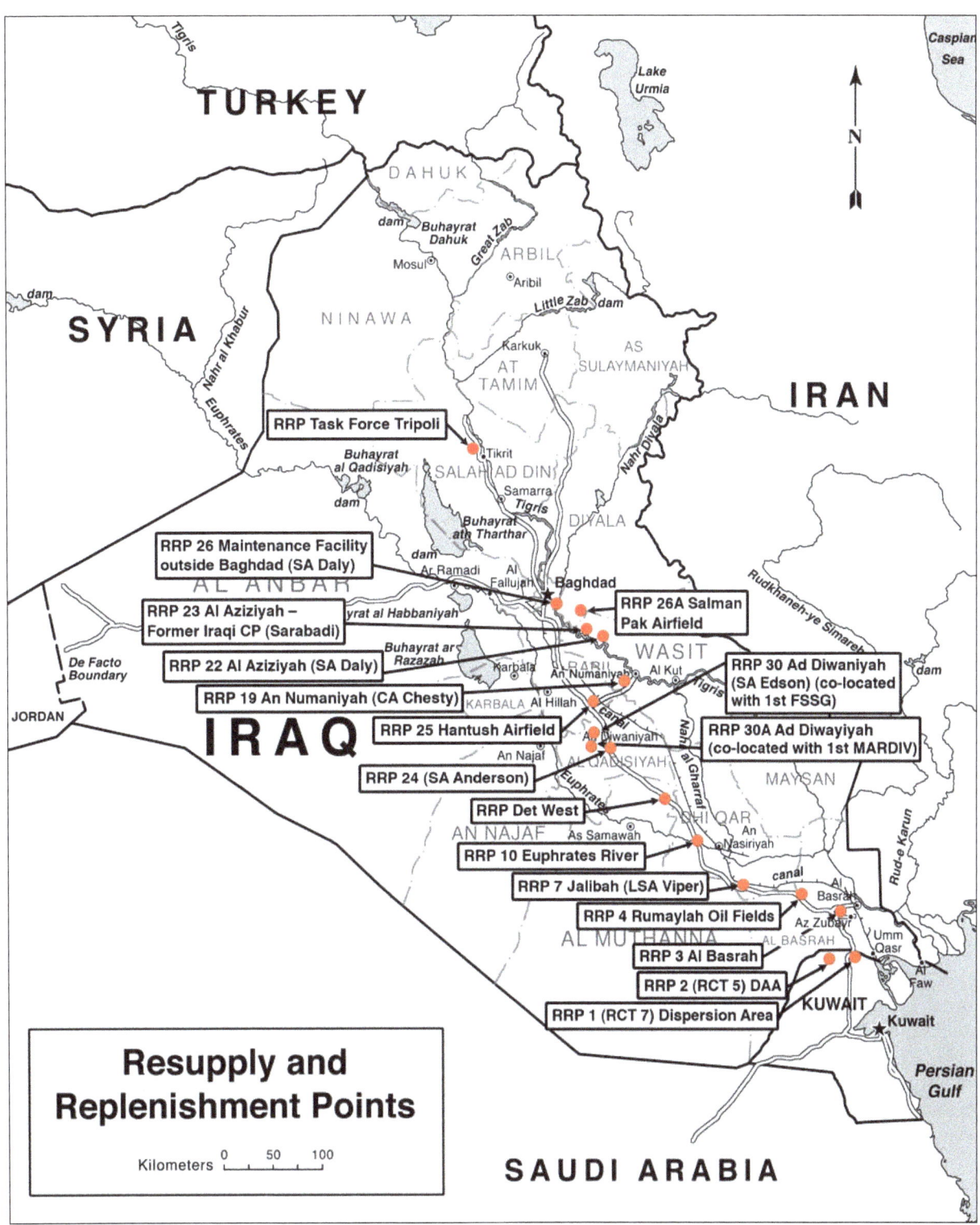

Resupply and Replenishment Points

2d Transportation Support Battalion (2d TSB) or Task Force Pegasus, commanded by Colonel John E. Wissler, moved from Logistics Support Area (LSA) Fox to Camp Solomon Islands, Tactical Assembly Area (TAA) Coyote. This move, which occurred over the course of three days, better positioned their assets to augment 1st FSSG's transportation capabilities and provide responsive battlefield distribution. Throughout the three days, continuous Iraqi missile attacks on Kuwait forced the drivers to be on constant alert

A U.S. and British helicopter support team waits to hook up fuel bladders to a British CH-47 Chinook at Camp Fox.

for any attack and often required them to drive while dressed in the highest mission-oriented protective posture level.

Meanwhile, the Marine Logistics Command Support Detachment 1 (MSD-1), which had been developed to manage and support the contracted commercial vehicles and drivers at TAA Coyote, had also begun conducting convoys. During the previous week, Major Tyson B. Geisendorff and his detachment had worked tirelessly to build up a combat service support operations center and a billeting camp for the third country national drivers.

Back at LSA Fox, the MLC amassed stocks of combat service support supplies in anticipation of a requirement to help maintain the velocity of I MEF's combat units. Meals ready-to-eat (MREs), engineering equipment, and repair parts were among the supplies that the MLC pushed forward to Combat Service Support Battalions 12 and 18, which would be providing general combat service support to all ground forces on the battlefield. Similarly, they pushed supplies to Combat Service Support Company 151 (CSSC-151), the MEF's direct support element, as well as Combat Service Support Companies 133 (CSSC-133) and 134 (CSSC-134), the direct support elements of 3d Marine Air Wing. Colonel Wissler's Beach and Terminal Operations Company, led by Major Robert A. Kaminski, took over responsibility for the transportation battalion's convoy operations originating out of LSA Fox. With this came the mission to manage all host nation transportation assets, including 121 commercial tractor trailers and third country national drivers. Helicopter support teams were also used for deliveries by air and had been conducting multiple helicopter support missions during the past few weeks to build their proficiency.

On 20 March, the United States began launching air attacks at strategic targets in Baghdad. What some Marines had expected to be a heavy-hitting air campaign to shape the battlefield, similar to the 43-day air war of Desert Storm turned out to be a precise and almost restrained approach in the use of Coalition air forces.

A Reminder

On 20 March, at approximately 1030, an enemy HY-2 Seersucker missile flew directly overhead at TAA Coyote. Several 1st FSSG Marines watched as the missile slowly flew overhead at an unbelievably low altitude. More than one Marine reported later that they had initially thought it to be a low flying cargo jet. The missile continued on and impacted just outside the perimeter of Camp Commando, the I MEF headquarters in Kuwait. Fortunately, there were no casualties. Although the explosion caused a loud boom and shook the camp's extensive infrastructure, it did not cause much damage. The shock value of the missile itself and the fact that it had literally come in under the radar had the greatest impact. As if to symbolize the Iraqis' determination to fight the Coalition's inevitable offensive, this missile was a reminder that even those Marines who would remain in Kuwait were on the verge of war; one with a technologically inferior, yet unpredictable and desperate enemy. More than anything, the event caused chaos and disbelief that the Iraqis could get that close to hitting a major Coalition headquarters.[5]

Photo by LCpl Dick Kocketi, USMC

Firefighters work to plug a burning oil well in the Rumaylah Oil Fields, Iraq, on 27 March 2003.

Later that same evening, the ground attack began with 1st Marine Division's Regimental Combat Team 5 moving across the border into Iraq to secure the Rumaylah gas and oil separation plants. Intelligence reports had indicated that Iraqi sabotage of their own oil resources was likely, and when reconnaissance photos began to show several wellheads on fire in the Rumaylah oil fields, the United States responded with a preemptive attack that occurred 10 hours earlier than the initial plan specified.[6] In February 2004, Lieutenant General Conway, I MEF commander, spoke in an interview with PBS *Frontline* about the intelligence he and his Marines had prior to the start of the war.

> We knew that there were seven or eight key nodes in the southern oil fields that we needed to preserve in order to establish the reconstitution of oil production in the wake of the war. So when we saw that Saddam was starting to destroy some of those oil heads, I think that's principally what prompted our higher headquarters to tell us to attack.[7]

About six hours after the first battalion in RCT-5 entered Iraq, Combat Service Support Company 115 (CSSC-115) crossed the line of departure at the Route Dallas breach site and traveled north to their first objective near the intersection of Routes Dallas and Tampa. Company commander Captain Suzan F. Thompson and her 240 Marines typically traveled with the regimental combat team's fuel trains; however, she often sent small convoys of supplies forward to support individual battalions within the regiment. As RCT-5 maneuvered to its objective at the southern gas oil separation platforms of the Rumaylah oil fields, CSSC-115 followed closely behind, ready to provide combat service support at a moment's notice. They moved with the regiment at all times except when the infantry forces were heading directly into a combat mission.[8]

Just behind Captain Thompson's company, Combat Service Support Battalion 10's Repair and Replenishment Point Opening Package 4, led by the battalion's military police company commander, Major Edward P. Wojnaroski Jr., left its position at Repair and Replenishment Point 2 and crossed the border into Iraq. En route to its next location, Major Wojnaroski's convoy maneuvered through blazing oil fires. Moving through enemy territory, the Marines saw for the first time a number of dead Iraqi soldiers strewn along the roadside, the unfortunate casualties of 5th Marines' deadly firepower. Upon arrival at Repair and Replenishment Point 4, the Marines established a hasty security perimeter, with oil fires

Women at War

Captain Suzan F. Thompson was one of many female Marines simply doing their job as they filled billets traditionally assigned to men. However, an overarching policy put in place by General Usher, which may have gone unnoticed by many, was very significant to women in the Marine Corps. During the months of pre-war planning at Camp Pendleton, California, the general felt it was important to outline a definitive policy regarding women in the 1st FSSG. It stated that, aside from those areas specifically identified by Department of Defense policy, the FSSG would employ all of its Marines (including women) to the fullest extent possible. Ultimately, the direct combat service support elements within CSSG-11, that would be integrated with 1st Marine Division and its regimental combat teams, would be provided with the most qualified Marines, regardless of gender. Women would be very close to, or even at times right on, the frontline. With the aid of 1st FSSG's Staff Judge Advocate, Lieutenant Colonel Vaughn A. Ary, General Usher researched the existing policies to ensure that his employment of women, especially in the direct support elements, was legal. While there may have been some apprehension from division in the beginning, especially at the battalion and regimental level, no issues ever surfaced regarding women in the FSSG.[9]

marking both the northern and southern ends of the area. One element of the major's unit, a military police company, constructed a 2,000-man prisoner collection point during the night and set up a control center to support prisoner operations. No prisoners would be processed at this location; however, a surplus of enemy weaponry, including AK-47s, rocket-propelled grenades, and mortars were found within 200 yards of the repair and replenishment point, and it was determined that a number of the enemy had recently occupied the same area.[10]

Meanwhile, two companies from 7th Engineer Support Battalion (7th ESB), augmented by 2d Transportation Support Battalion's Support Company, had moved forward to the Iraqi border to conduct breaching operations for 1st Marine Division and Task Force Tarawa. Their mission involved removing berms, tank ditches, and electrical fences, marking the lanes, and providing security and mobility through the breach. On 20 March, Company B, led by Captain Andrew R. Winthrop, breached the Kuwait and Iraq obstacle belt at Breach Point West, opening four lanes for Task Force Tarawa to cross. Company C, commanded by Captain Susan Bird, breached the Green Breach Zone or Breach Point North, allowing 3d Light Armored Reconnaissance Battalion and 11th Marines to pass through. Once all forces had pushed through Breach Point North, Charlie Company closed the breach and moved back to Breach Point West, where they joined the rest of 7th Engineer Support Battalion. Bravo Company remained at Breach Point West for the next four days, maintaining the open lanes to allow other units, including 7th ESB to pass through.[11]

Crossing the Breach

While Combat Service Support Group 11's direct combat service support elements entered Iraq trailing their supported regimental combat teams, the general support elements had a different objective to meet: setting up Logistics Support Area Viper, the Marine expeditionary force's first logistical support area in Iraq. On 20 March, Combat Service Support Battalion 18's advanced party and a smaller quartering party crossed the line of departure and moved north towards Jalibah, a town along the eastern flank of the Task Force Tarawa and 1st Marine Division advances. The role of these elements was to arrive at the objective ahead of the battalion, clear the area of mines and unexploded ordnance, set up initial communications capabilities, and coordinate pre-arranged camp areas for all supported units.

While CSSB-18 managed the overall buildup of the logistics support area, there were several other tenant organizations occupying the vast desert of nearby Jalibah. I MEF set up their forward base, 3d Marine Air Wing established an airfield, and several units from 1st FSSG built camps within LSA Viper. At the start of the war, General Usher knew that he needed to move a command element from the 1st FSSG headquarters forward to establish command and control. In the evening on the first day of the war, he had his chief of staff, Colonel Darrell L. Moore, lead an advanced party across the border toward Jalibah. Their convoy experience through the breach was similar to that of most units trying to make their way into Iraq. Breach lanes were crowded, especially the few that were hard surfaced and allowed for commercial vehicle passage. All units were jockeying for position and movement through the breach, and the convoy was stretched out across distances too great to maintain a consistent speed and direction. As con-

Photo by MSgt Edward D. Kniery, USMC
A fleet of seven-ton trucks from 6th Motor Transport Battalion are staged at LSA Viper.

voy commander Captain Kevin P. Coughlin described, speeds that seemed feasible to the lead vehicles left the trailing end of the convoy literally in the dust. Visibility was poor, communications mechanisms were scarce, and vehicles broke down. Several times during the night, the convoy split up and regrouped, covering only 60 miles during 13 to 14 hours of travel.[12] The security threat during this initial movement through Iraqi desert was unknown, but most drivers and passengers were too busy dealing with the challenges of the convoy movement itself to even worry.

On 21 March, the remaining forces of 1st Marine Division began their attack into Iraq. Regimental Combat Team 7 attacked west of al-Basrah to secure Safwan and the Az Zubayr Pumping Station, while Regimental Combat Team 1 (RCT-1) attacked to the east.[13] Combat Service Support Company 117 (CSSC-117) crossed the line of departure and followed RCT-7 up Highway 1. That evening, Combat Service Support Battalion 10's Repair and Replenishment Point 3 Opening Package, led by Lieutenant Colonel Weinkle, departed their initial repair and replenishment point and followed closely behind CSSC-117. Crossing the border just before midnight, Colonel Weinkle's Marines saw firsthand the path of destruction left by 1st Marine Division en route to their objective near al-Basrah. The Marines drove in complete blackout conditions, with only the light from fire trenches and burning oil wells ignited by the retreating Iraqis, to guide their way. As they crossed the line of departure, the colonel observed the eerie atmosphere and noted that his Marines now found themselves alone. This would be indicative of their experiences throughout the war, as their logistics vehicles often drove into areas that had only been recently cleared by the division's lead elements.[14]

Movement during this convoy was difficult. Blackout light conditions and the speed required to keep up with 1st Marine Division's momentum were two major factors in a serious vehicle accident that occurred just 40 miles north the border. A troop-carrying seven-ton truck rammed the rear end of a communications vehicle, which in turn collided with a high-back humvee. As one Marine in the battalion described, "one minute we were racing north, and the next I was running toward our wounded Marines trying to provide what medical support I could."[15] Once the injured Marines were stabilized by the shock trauma platoon, the convoy continued on toward its objective. A second accident occurred in a later serial of the convoy, as they crossed the border. Because of the narrow highway and border gate, the convoy slowed. Despite this, several vehicles that had not been traveling with the proper distance between them crashed into the vehicles to their front. Injuries to personnel were minor, but the convoy suffered damage to several vehicles, and Marines were reminded that even without direct enemy contact, they faced many dangers.

At approximately 0300, the convoy halted once again for Colonel Weinkle to lead a small reconnaissance party forward on Route Tampa (Highway 80). Having received a warning from CSSC-117 that they were entering an area that had not been secured by RCT-7, the team, comprised of Colonel Weinkle, Captain Forrest C. Poole III (battalion operations officer), Captain Jamie Jones (transportation company commander), and First Lieutenant Leith R. Habayeb (military police platoon commander), cautiously dismounted their humvees and walked the terrain in the dark. While seeking a suitable repair and replenishment point ingress/egress route, they surprised a small Iraqi Army contingent that hastily departed, abandoning their command post and three ZU-23 antiaircraft positions. Later, an Iraqi sheep herding family was found wandering the area, and through translators, told the Marines they had been held hostage by the Iraqi contingent that used them as a human shield to avoid helicopter strafing. After receiving humanitarian rations and cigarettes from the Marines, the family gladly provided useful intelligence on weapons caches and the absence of mines in the area.

The battalion arrived at Repair and Replenishment Point 3 early the next morning. Located just south of Highway 80, the site was geographically well suited for their mission of providing combat service support. With ample space, each section had its own area to set up. The Marines in CSSB-10 worked tirelessly to emplace their combat service support capabilities, but found that the requirements for support were fairly minimal. Meanwhile, CSSG-11's tactical command post, led by Colonel Pomfret, trailed RCT-1 and Combat Service Support Company 111 (CSSC-111) as they crossed the Iraqi border early in the morning on 21 March. Their objective was to establish Repair and Replenishment Point 7, in the vicinity of Jalibah.

To the west of 1st Marine Division, Task Force Tarawa followed closely behind the U.S. Army's 3d Infantry Division. The task force's role was to secure the bridge crossings in an-Nasiriyah to allow movement through to Highways 1 and 7. Accompanying Task Force Tarawa, 8th Engineer Support Battalion (8th ESB) was assigned to provide direct support bridging to the ground combat forces. Just days earlier, the engineer battalion had been under the administrative control of 2d FSSG, the operational control of 1st FSSG, and assigned in direct support of 1st Marine Division; a complex command and control situation in any circumstance. The difficulties would not lessen. Just 72 hours prior to the commencement of fighting, 8th ESB was reassigned to the operational control of Task Force Tarawa. Facing these last minute organizational changes was only part of the engineers' challenges. Because of the battalion's specific bridging mission, there was always a level of uncertainty as to when and where they would be required to execute a mission. For every crossing that the ground forces approached, the battalion would have to design a complete plan as if the existing bridgehead had been destroyed. Lieutenant Colonel Niel E. Nelson, commanding officer of 8th ESB, was designated as the force crossing engineer and located his battalion with Task Force Tarawa, in preparation for movement across the line of departure on G-day and potential bridging missions across the Euphrates River in the vicinity of an-Nasiriyah. He described the roadblocks associated with his battalion's unique and changing assignments. "It is difficult to describe the chaos that took place in this crossroads of maneuver, but with the 3d Infantry Division, Task Force Tarawa, and the 1st Marine Division's simultaneous usage of Route Tampa, all with a different mission, the small unit command and control became paramount to the success of the battalion."[16]

Getting Fuel to the Fight

As units were still crossing through the breach and slowly making their way to their objectives, Lieutenant Colonel Roger R. Machut and his Marines in 6th Engineer Support Battalion (6th ESB) began to

USMC Photo

Shown here as a colonel, LtCol Robert R. Machut worked in his civilian career as a civil engineer before being activated to command 6th Engineer Support Battalion during OIF-I.

build the hose-reel system that would enable the flow of fuel from Kuwait to forward bases in Iraq. These Marines had been staged at Breach Point West for several days, preparing their equipment and planning the execution of the 60-mile tactical fuel system. The line would run from a six million-gallon U.S. Army bulk fuel farm at Breach Point West to a location deep inside Iraq, where Marines would establish their own bulk fuel farm. "It's a way of transporting fuel without motorized support," commented Chief Warrant Officer–4 Thomas M. Cierley, a bulk fueler who had served in Vietnam over three decades earlier. Back then, they were using slower pumps, smaller fuel bladders, and relying on trucks for transport. "We're getting bigger, better, and more efficient." A significant part of this improvement came with the implementation of the hose reel, which would alleviate much of the need for trucks in transporting fuel to forward based units.[17]

The Marine Corps' hose reel, better suited for implementation in a hostile environment than the U.S. Army's more permanent Inland Petroleum Distribution System, consisted of three steps. First, Marines conducted a reconnaissance of the route to find and dispose of any unexploded ordnance. Second, a team of Marines operating heavy equipment, such as graders and excavators, followed the route to grade

Photo by LtCol Melissa D. Mihocko, USMCR

A Marine from 6th ESB indicates the beginning of the hose-reel system at Breachpoint West.

the surface and dig a V-ditch. Third, another team of Marines pulled the six-inch diameter rubber hose off of large, truck-loaded spools and carefully laid it down into the V-ditch, actually walking on the hose to ensure its emplacement. Two teams worked simultaneously on this task. One started at Breach Point West and the other at the halfway point between that point and Jalibah, the fuel system's destination. Colonel Machut designated this midpoint as the "Golden Spike," a reference to the historic Promontory Point, Utah, where the eastern and western portions of the transcontinental railroad were linked in 1869.[18] By the next day, 15½ miles of hose reel had been laid. Meanwhile, 6th ESB's Bulk Fuel Company Alpha moved across the line of departure up to Logistics Support Area Viper, where they established a 1.2 million-gallon fuel farm.[19]

Logistics Support Area Viper

When Combat Service Support Battalion 18 (CSSB-18) arrived at Jalibah, it immediately initiated the establishment of Logistics Support Area Viper. With Alpha Company, 7th Engineer Support Battalion in direct support to provide engineering capabilities, the battalion began the daunting task of clearing the vast area. The engineers, led by Captain Jose M. Lopez, worked to clear unexploded ordnance and mines, built an ammunition supply point, constructed guard towers, and created security berms.[20] At this time, CSSB-18 expected to have four days to setup, while Combat Service Support Battalion 12 (CSSB-12) continued to provide support to I MEF from Tactical Assembly Area Coyote. On the day of its arrival, however, CSSB-18 immediately began receiving requests from customers such as 1st Marine Division, Task Force Tarawa, and units within 3d Marine Air Wing. The challenges of moving over 70 miles from points in Kuwait to Jalibah had been great. Fuel had been quickly depleted, and equipment had broken down, causing a surge in the requirement for repair parts.

Arriving on the morning of 21 March, Colonel Moore's advanced party waited throughout the day to get clearance from explosive ordnance disposal personnel to set up their camp at LSA Viper. Unfortunately, because several units were trying to establish camps simultaneously, these highly trained and skilled Marines were in short supply. The area was absolutely barren, but the ground was visibly littered with unexploded ordnance. Using a global positioning system (GPS) receiver, he and Captain Coughlin selected a grid square for the 1st FSSG Forward to setup. Unable to obtain a team of explosive ordnance disposal personnel, Colonel Moore decided to have the Marines walk the ground looking for unexploded ordnance. If anything suspicious was found, they marked the ground with a flag and moved forward. Although this was a somewhat risky approach, time constraints and operational necessity dictated that the Marines could not sit and wait. It was imperative that

Photo by MSgt Edward D. Kniery, USMC

Marines from CSSB-18 sandbag a bunker at LSA Viper.

the 1st FSSG Forward establish itself and initiate communications with General Usher back at Camp Coyote. After marking the area and retrieving the rest of the convoy, they finally obtained the explosive ordnance disposal personnel, who were able to more expeditiously clear the site by investigating the marked ground. Numerous pieces of ordnance were found, and due to a lack of heavy-lift equipment, the Marines had to manually remove some of it. In at least one incident, they chained an unexploded warhead to the back of a humvee and dragged it to a deserted spot two miles away. By the end of the first evening, they occupied the area and began setting up the camp. At the end of the second day, the camp was up and running, and the forward element was able to communicate with the 1st FSSG at Tactical Assembly Area Coyote. Although there may have been some security threats in their area of operations, the Marines were minimally concerned about them because they were so busy. However, despite their focus on providing combat service support, they set up a perimeter security and dug fighting holes around the camp.

One of the largest support areas built in enemy territory, LSA Viper was constructed within the first four days of the war, during a severe sandstorm, and simultaneously with combat operations occurring in southeast Iraq. Lieutenant Colonel Thomas N. Collins, commander of CSSB-18, was the designated base cluster commander, responsible for the area/terrain management and force protection and security coordination with both I MEF and the 3d Infantry Division units. Ultimately, LSA Viper encompassed a 3d Marine Air Wing forward operating base, the I MEF command element, an expeditionary medical facility, and the majority of 1st FSSG units. It was the major logistics hub for I MEF operations up to the Tigris River. From a temporary combat service support operations center, Colonel Collins and his Marines provided critical and timely ammunition and medical support to Task Force Tarawa during intense combat operations in an-Nasiriyah. Simultaneously, his Marines established an equipment collection and salvage point, conducting recovery operations to retrieve invaluable 1st Marine Division equipment, such as M1A1 Abrams tanks and light armored vehicles that had become inoperable during combat operations. Bulk fuel, bulk water, medical, and supply support rounded out the capabilities that CSSB-18 put in place to support I MEF through a period of intense fighting, extreme weather, and fast-paced movement.[21]

Another critical capability that Colonel Collins possessed at LSA Viper was maintenance. The mission of 1st FSSG's maintenance companies was to provide third- and fourth-echelon maintenance to units on the battlefield, as well as first- and second-echelon maintenance, as needed. For the maintenance companies of both CSSB-18 and CSSB-12, their primary customer was Combat Service Support Battalion 10, however, they supported any and all units who requested help. Each company was divided into several functional areas including motor transport, engineer, communications and electronics, and ordnance maintenance.[22]

CSSB-18's maintenance company did not waste any time moving its Marines and equipment up to LSA Viper; they knew their expertise would be greatly needed in the harsh desert environment. Movement up to Viper, though, was extremely difficult due to the general conditions of the roads. When they arrived there, they found the area to be quiet and unpopulated and proceeded to set up. Because some of their contracted civilian vehicles got stuck, numerous pieces of their equipment were left behind, limiting their maintenance capabilities. Marines had to piece together the limited tools and resources they had to repair as many vehicles and other equip-

Photo by MSgt Edward D. Kniery, USMC
A Marine with CSSB-18's Maintenance Company works on a disabled LVTP-7 at LSA Viper.

ment as possible. The mechanics borrowed shipping containers from supply to live in because they did not have tents. Unfortunately, the influx of broken equipment was almost immediate. Less than a day after the start of the ground war, several assault amphibian vehicles were turned in for maintenance due, at least in part, to the fact that the vehicles had recently come off ships, where they had been sitting unused for a long time. The sheer age of some equipment was one of the root causes of some maintenance problems, but Captain Mark F. Birk, the company's executive officer, also noted that the infiltration of fine desert sand was causing problems with nearly all equipment. The company's goal was to repair equipment and return it to the owning unit within seven days, however, with a shortage of tools, this was not always feasible. If they were not able to fix a piece of equipment within seven days, the Marines evacuated it to higher echelon maintenance at Marine Logistics Command. One challenge with this process, however, was the lack of transportation. Because they did not have an organic transportation capability, they were competing with every other unit for transportation support.[23]

On 21 March, elements of the transportation support group (TSG) crossed the border into Iraq. They had been staged at Breach Point West for the past three days and were now on the move to LSA Viper. Portions of both TSG and 6th Motor Transport Battalion were heading up to the large support area near Jalibah, so they could quickly establish a forward operations capability. From there, TSG would be in a better position to conduct distribution operations in support of combat forces fighting in and around the city of an-Nasiriyah, which held a key crossing on the Euphrates River. Additionally, a small element consisting of Marines from the landing support company crossed the breach on 21 March and moved to Viper, where they established a landing zone, an arrival/departure airfield control group, and a helicopter support team capability. This critical capability assisted in the opening of the airfield at Jalibah and allowed for continued integration of Marine air and ground assets. From this point on, supplies and personnel could be directly transported by air to points within Iraq.

The next day, Alpha Company, 2d Transportation Support Battalion, also moved to LSA Viper. Hauling over 1,000 short tons of ground ammunition, this 121-vehicle convoy, Task Force Pegasus' largest con-

Photo by LtCol Melissa D. Mihocko, USMCR

Marines board a CH-53 near their base camp in Kuwait for transportation to Iraq.

voy of the war, established a command and control center for the task force.[24] The company's presence at LSA Viper allowed for quick convoy turnaround. Concurrently, the battalion's support company established a trans-load point at Tactical Assembly Area Coyote, enabling the rapid transfer of cargo and equipment between host nation trucks and tactical vehicles within the task force.

Early in the morning that same day, Colonel Pomfret, commanding officer of Combat Service Support Group 11, and his Marines conducted a site reconnaissance and established Repair and Replenishment Point 7 (RRP-7). This was located north of Jalibah and in the vicinity of LSA Viper, and it was here that elements of CSSG-11's tactical command post came under direct small-arms fire from a squad-sized enemy unit while conducting reverse osmosis water purification unit reconnaissance operations. The Marines returned fire and forced the enemy to withdraw, but a 75-meter wide canal* denied the Marines the ability to pursue the enemy. A report was immediately submitted to Regimental Combat Team 1, and shortly after, two UH-1N helicopters arrived on scene to conduct an aerial reconnaissance, observing personnel in civilian clothes. Later in the afternoon, both CSSG-11 Forward and CSSG-11 Main elements linked up with the tactical command post at RRP-7. The following day, after spending roughly 24 hours at Repair and Replenishment Points 3 and 4, both elements of CSSB-10 moved north to link up with CSSG-11's tactical command post. Upon arriving the evening of 23 March, they joined CSSG-11 and faced their first crisis: 1st Marine Division was experiencing major fuel shortages. The division's momentum at this point needed to be maintained, and the CSSG-11/CSSB-10 staff worked tirelessly to provide the 160,000 gallons of fuel needed. While they were able to acquire small amounts of fuel from LSA Viper, it was a large convoy from the Transportation Support Group traveling from Kuwait that arrived early the next morning and delivered the much-needed fuel "just in time." The 1st Marine Division had dubbed the first 96 hours of the war the "Opening Gambit," and all resupply during this period followed a precise execution matrix. This critical delivery of fuel was the last preplanned resupply for 1st Marine Division, as they approached the Euphrates River. Also, while at RRP 7, CSSG-11 began receiving their first prisoners from various combat units. In response to this, CSSB-10 established a prisoner collection and holding facility under a bridge. In total, they processed 232 Iraqis (88 enlisted and 144 officers). Less than 24 hours after their initial arrival and setup of RRP 7, CSSG-11/CSSB-10 prepared to depart for their next location.[25]

Civil Affairs

During the planning for Operation Iraqi Freedom, there was no doubt that the Marines would come in contact with civilians. Among many potential prob-

---

* This canal (southeast of the Euphrates River in the vicinity of an-Nasiriyah) was the same location where two Marines in 6th Engineer Support Battalion drowned, trying to swim across and secure the far side of what they ended up using as a reverse osmosis water purification unit site. This incident is described in more detail in Chapter 4.

A convoy of civilian fuel trucks contracted by Transportation Support Group moves north in Iraq.
Photo by MSgt Edward D. Kniery, USMC

lems, this could hinder the mobility of commanders as they tried to advance rapidly across the battlefield. To aide commanders in their responsibility to deal with civilians, civil affairs teams were integrated into each command. These teams, mainly assigned at the battalion level, came from one of the two existing Marine Corps civil affairs groups, and advised commanders on issues relating to civilians. They served as eyes and ears on the ground to forewarn commanders about prospective civilian problems or issues. They ultimately developed a civil-military operations center

Civil affairs Marines hand out radios to local civilians to promote good will and open communications.
Photo by MSgt Edward D. Kniery, USMC

Khuder al Emeri

Civil affairs Marines worked directly with members of a program called the Free Iraqi Forces. This program enlisted several Iraqi opposition volunteers to assist U.S. and Coalition forces in civil-military operations during Operation Iraqi Freedom. Among the Free Iraqi Forces attached to 1st FSSG was a man named Khuder al Emeri. Following Operation Desert Storm in 1991, he had led his Shiite town of Qalat Sikar in an uprising against Saddam Hussein. The rebellion was crushed, and he soon had a 50,000 Iraqi dinar bounty on his head. With nowhere to hide from the Ba'ath party's vengeance, he sought refuge in the United States with relatives in Seattle, leaving his wife and sons behind with a promise that someday he would return. Twelve years later during OIF, Al Emeri was finally able to return to his hometown with Marine forces and reunite with his family.

to coordinate interaction with the local population.

Lieutenant Colonel Valerie E. Thomas, a detachment commander from the West Coast 3d Civil Affairs Group, was responsible for eight four-man teams, assigned specifically to 1st FSSG. In addition to advising commanders, the teams acted as the focal point for local civilian interaction.

As reservists, civil affairs Marines were well suited for their mission; their training had prepared them to interact with civilians, and they came across as less threatening to the locals than average Marines. Bringing a multitude of specialties and civilian career experience to their mission including Environmental Protection Agency specialists, law enforcement officers, businessmen, and cultural anthropologists, their goal was often to win the hearts and minds of the local population. Two of the primary missions they conducted were large-scale humanitarian projects and handling displaced civilians. On a smaller scale, they were involved in numerous goodwill projects with local communities, hospitals, and the general population. They sought opportunities to demonstrate to civilians that U.S. Marines were there to help them. In return, the civil affairs teams received useful information from the local populace, which they turned over to the intelligence section. In the end, the real value of civil affairs was that it gave the commander one less thing to worry about.[26]

Chapter 4

Battling for An-Nasiriyah and Beyond (23–26 March 2003)

A Day to Remember

As 1st Marine Division advanced north to secure Iraq's vulnerable Rumaylah oil fields, Task Force Tarawa was fast on the move toward an-Nasiriyah. Traveling through open desert because the U.S. Army's 3d Infantry Division's convoys filled the roads, the task force, led by Brigadier General Richard F. Natonski, was tasked with securing the city's bridge crossings on the Euphrates River and Saddam Canal. This would allow 1st Marine Division's Regimental Combat Team 1 passage to move north on Highway 7 towards al-Kut. A second bridge lay further west in a more rural area outside the city limits of an-Nasiriyah. Under the control of the 3d Infantry Division, this crossing would provide Regimental Combat Teams 5 and 7 access to Highway 1, leading northwest to ad-Diwaniyah.

Combat Service Support Battalion 22 (CSSB-22), Task Force Tarawa's combat service support element, had crossed into Iraq late in the day on 21 March. During two days of movement, the main element of CSSB-22, led by Lieutenant Colonel Thomas N. Goben, followed in trace of Regimental Combat Team 2 (RCT-2), periodically sending smaller mobile elements to travel in direct support of the individual infantry battalions. By 23 March, they had arrived at a location near Jalibah Airfield, where they co-located with RCT-2's administrative and logistics operations area.[1]

It was largely believed that the people of an-Nasiriyah would support the Coalition's presence, due to the large Shia* population. Not anticipated, however, were the high numbers of *Fedayeen*, regular Iraqi soldiers, and an assortment of Ba'ath loyalists already dispersed among the thousands of fearful Iraqi civilians. In the early morning hours of 23 March, elements of RCT-2 departed Jalibah to enter the city and take control of the key bridge crossings. From the start, there were signs that the plan would not go smoothly. Even as they approached the outskirts of an-Nasiriyah, lead elements of the 1st Battalion, 2d Marines, came under attack by Iraqis. To make matters worse, the same day Task Force Tarawa entered an-Nasiriyah, an Army convoy from the 507th Maintenance Company had gotten lost and erroneously traveled into the heart of city, alerting the Fedayeen fighters of the Americans' approach. This fatal mistake set off a series of tragic events, including several enemy ambushes and a suspected A-10 Warthog friendly fire incident that resulted in 18 Marines from Company C, 1st Battalion, 2d Marines, killed in action—the single worst day of casualties for Coalition forces during the war.*

By the end of the day on the 23rd, CSSB-22's shock trauma platoon had sprung into action, receiving and treating 14 casualties from 1st Battalion, 2d Marines. They also treated five wounded soldiers from the 507th Maintenance Company who were rescued from an-Nasiriyah by a team of Marines. This was a difficult test for Lieutenant Colonel Goben's Marines and sailors, as it was their first encounter with casualties during the war. The battalion commander described the events of that night:

> It was some of the most horrific sights I had ever seen . . . the AAVs that were attacked, just blown up completely and burned to the ground. I later saw the remnants of the hulls. . . . that was a very long day; that was a very trying day for everybody. . . . if anything is going to be remembered [about CSSB-22] it's the efforts of every one of my Marines who assisted in that whole process . . . dragging litters in and off of helicopters and moving around for the medical folks . . . . I can't say enough about how well the medical folks performed . . . it was just absolutely phenomenal . . . everybody was going here, there, and everywhere, talking to the Marines, comforting them. It's a day I will never forget.[2]

Days later, the bodies of the Marines killed during the battle at an-Nasiriyah became the first group of

---

* The Shia constitute more than 50 percent of the Iraqi population and suffered extensive discrimination and brutality during the regime of Saddam Hussein and the Ba'ath Party.

* Although none of the casualties were officially ascribed to the A-10s, as investigated by Central Command, many Marines in Charlie, 1/2 suspected that rounds from the airplanes hit some of the Marines.

Photo by LtCol Melissa D. Mihocko, USMCR

Marines killed in An-Nasiriyah were brought to the mortuary affairs tent at Camp Iwo Jima, TAA Coyote, for processing.

combat remains the mortuary affairs detachment received back at Camp Iwo Jima, Tactical Assembly Area Coyote. Transported by air from Jalibah Airfield to Joe Foss Airfield, they arrived late at night. Working through the night and making several sprints to the Scud bunkers as a result of frequent incoming missile alerts, Lieutenant Colonel John M. Cassady Jr., officer-in-charge of the mortuary affairs team and his deputy, Chief Warrant Officer–4 Cheryl G. Ites, a reserve Marine and mortician in her civilian career, focused on identifying the individuals and processing the required paperwork. Marines trained in mortuary affairs had not yet arrived in theater; as a result, a group of volunteers worked side-by-side with Colonel Cassady and relied on his expertise and experience to guide them through an otherwise overwhelming procedure. CWO-4 Ites described the challenges in having Marines work such a difficult job. "For many of them, this was the first remains they had ever seen . . . and it wasn't 'grandpa at the funeral home' type remains. These are someone who's roughly their age group; they see themselves in that same situation, so it's a little more stressful for them; harder for them to deal with."[3] Carefully and reverently, they opened each body bag to view the remains inside. As one body bag was opened, a Marine with no obvious wounds on his front lay peacefully with an American flag crumpled in his hands. The sight was more emotional than any amount of blood or open wounds. One could imagine his comrades hastily stuffing the flag in their friend's hands as his body was being carried away. His fatal injury, a large exit wound in his back, was later found when mortuary affairs Marines carefully turned the body over.[4]

Positive identification was the most critical part of the process, as the inevitable confusion during combat casualty evacuation often prevented a unit from distinguishing individuals killed in combat from those who lay injured in a field medical facility. Unit commanders often relied on the timeliness of the mortuary affairs processing to aid in unit accountability and accurate casualty rates. Beyond this, however, mortuary affairs, supported by more than 200 years of tradition among Marines, ensured that those who paid the ultimate price in combat would be rapidly and respectfully returned to their loved ones.[5]

1st Marine Division's Advance North

As Task Force Tarawa fought through the streets of an-Nasiriyah to secure the key bridge crossings on the Euphrates River and Saddam Canal, which would open the passageway for Regimental Combat Team 1 (RCT-1), the rest of 1st Marine Division continued to execute its plan, which called for 3d Light Armored Reconnaissance (3d LAR) Battalion to lead an attack up Highway 1. West of an-Nasiriyah, Regimental Combat Teams 5 (RCT-5) and 7 (RCT-7) moved through the countryside, challenged mostly by traffic jams and poor weather.

Mortuary Affairs

Lieutenant Colonel John M. Cassady Jr., officer-in-charge of mortuary affairs in Operation Iraqi Freedom, became involved in the formerly named "graves registration" in 1989 while assigned as head of the combat service support doctrine at Marine Corps' Warfighting Center. He was the leading mortuary affairs officer during Operations Desert Shield and Desert Storm, and throughout his career, did much to both document and advance mortuary affairs operations. The Marine Corps' foremost expert in this field, Colonel Cassady came out of retirement to head up the mortuary affairs mission in Iraq. This was to "establish mortuary affairs collection points which receive, process, and expeditiously evacuate I MEF remains to the theater mortuary evacuation point; and be prepared to assist in the search, recovery, and tentative identification of I MEF remains and decontaminated remains as they are moved to the mortuary affairs collections points."

The original concept of operations included the employment of five 50-man platoons, all of which would be operationally controlled by Colonel Cassady. This was to maintain adaptability on the battlefield; in essence, to have the flexibility to move the platoons where the necessity existed. This was a lesson learned from Desert Storm. For this campaign, there would be one fixed collection point at Camp Iwo Jima, Tactical Assembly Area Coyote, in support of Surgical Company Alpha. The numbers at this point were expected to be lower, due to the high survival rate in the surgical companies. At this collection point, the remains would also be processed for shipment by way of the Joe Foss Airfield at Camp Coyote to the U.S. Army's theater mortuary and evacuation point. Three other collection points would be forward positioned in support of maneuver elements and mobile, so they could leapfrog across the battlefield to support mission requirements. This concept of operations characterized the "rapid response" approach unique to the Marine Corps' mortuary affairs program.

During the weeks preceding the start of the war, a U.S. Army UH-60 Black Hawk helicopter crashed in the Kuwaiti desert, resulting in the deaths of four soldiers. Although the Army handled the initial recovery of the remains, the Marine Corps mortuary affairs platoon was assigned the secondary recovery mission. This tragic event for the Army turned out to be useful training for the mortuary affairs Marines, as it would be the first operational experience for many of the Marines in the platoon. For five days, they conducted a site assessment, involving gridding and locating the debris field, and cataloguing and flagging items found on the site. Due to sandstorms, many pieces of the remains were already covered by sand, and the Marines, in their protective gear, conducted operations by hand and on their knees to recover any elements of human remains and personal effects. Every fragment of the helicopter was inspected and sand was sifted to a depth of six inches, in hopes of recovering remains not visible to the untrained eye.[6]

Mortuary affairs Marines sift through the wreckage of a downed U.S. Army Black Hawk helicopter.
Photo by LtCol John M. Cassady Jr., USMC

Their objective was the intersection between the Hantush Airstrip and Highway 27, from where RCT-5 would move in and seize the airstrip. Up until this point, all resupply missions into Iraq had been accomplished through ground transportation and were not without challenges. Securing control of the airstrip would enable the KC-130 Hercules aircraft to provide resupply and guarantee the uninterrupted momentum of 1st Marine Division toward their ultimate objective, Baghdad.[7]

On 23 March, 3d LAR Battalion moved cautiously up Highway 1, where they fully anticipated enemy contact. By nightfall, the battalion was engaged by a large element of Fedayeen fighters that was quickly defeated by the Marines' overwhelming firepower. By the next morning, RCT-5 completed a forward passage of lines with 3d LAR Battalion and continued north as the division's main effort. Meanwhile, Combat Service Support Company 115 (CSSC-115), which had been at Repair and Replenishment Point 7 retrieving supplies from Combat Service Support Battalion 10 (CSSB-10), moved to an area north of the Euphrates River, where they continued to jump between the regimental combat team's individual battalions to provide much needed resupply of fuel and maintenance contact team support. To maintain effective command and control, Combat Service Support Group 11 (CSSG-11) forward command post traveled with the 1st Marine Division forward command post, just behind RCT-5. They remained there all the way to Baghdad.

As CSSB-10 departed Repair and Replenishment Point 7 and continued north toward the Euphrates River, its movement was slow because of road congestion and broken-down vehicles, both enemy and friendly. Just south of the river, the battalion established Repair and Replenishment Point 10 near the intersection of Highways 1 and 8. CSSB-10 remained in this position only long enough to provide an overnight refueling point for division units as they waited to cross the Euphrates River bridge. During the next 16 hours, the battalion supported an endless stream of division units, meanwhile, living side-by-side with an Iraqi family and its yard of donkeys, dogs, and sheep. Second Lieutenant Sarah M. Stokes, a watch officer for CSSB-10, described the location of this repair and replenishment point, which was strategically important to the mission, yet unpopular among the Marines.[8]

> After spending two months in Kuwait, we were beginning to wonder whether the Fertile Crescent actually existed. As we neared the Euphrates, we quickly discovered all of this green stuff came with a price. The RRP was set on a mile-long triangular plot of rich, dark earth—an abandoned manure lot. The gnats were thrilled with our arrival. The crawling black specks soon covered our face and hands.[9]

Fortunately for the Marines in CSSB-10, they

Air Delivery

On 23 March, Air Delivery Platoon, 2d Transportation Support Battalion, conducted its first combat air delivery mission since the Vietnam War. Two drops, made from C-130s, were scheduled for the same time at two different locations. One site was on the far bank of the Euphrates River where Highway 8 crosses. The other was at a repair and replenishment point about 12 miles northwest of Viper. Each drop consisted of approximately 88 warehouse pallets or 3,780 cases of meals ready-to-eat, prepared and rigged with a parachute by air delivery Marines. About three hours before the aircraft were to take off, Major Matthew S. Cook, company commander of 1st Landing Support Company, called the Logistics Movement Control Center to notify them that the 1st Marine Division was not across the Euphrates yet and to divert that drop to a location near LSA Viper. He later learned that his request never made it to the pilots, and they made the drop at the original grid. Putting a positive spin on it with his Marines, he told them to view it as the first humanitarian drop of the war. The second drop went better, but had its own problems. The original grid that was provided had changed, and the location was further away from Logistics Support Area Viper than expected. Marines on the ground saw the helicopters and suspected that because the original drop zone at the repair and replenishment point was so crowded with gear and personnel, the pilots diverted a few miles away to avoid injury or damage to personnel on the ground. The supplies ended up in a marshy area nearby, and seven-ton trucks were sent to the location, where Marines loaded pallets of MREs by hand.[10]

packed up and headed for their next location less than 24 hours from the time they arrived at Repair and Replenishment Point 10. They crossed the Euphrates River, but another major obstacle that would hinder the movement of all forces on the ground and in the air stood in their path.

The Sandstorm

During the evening of 24 March, a severe sandstorm blew through southern Iraq, slowing the momentum the Marines had gained since crossing the line of departure. The harsh combination of severe winds, sand, and rain prompted General Usher to label it "the worst sandstorm in 20 years." Marines faced gusts of wind up to 50 knots, blowing clouds of fine sand, and visibility so limited that navigating, driving, and other essential functions become impossible. Major Michael J. Callanan, Combat Service Support Group 11 operations officer commented on the harsh conditions. "The sky went black and then red . . . visibility was zero. Vehicles continued to move north at [three miles per hour] and then ground to a halt. Compasses couldn't be seen, and GPS receivers were no longer able to track satellites for reference."[11]

Convoy movement, which had been slow to begin with, suffered the most from the storms smothering effects. Essentially, all movement came to a halt, as drivers, who donned gas masks to keep their eyes open in the blowing sand, could not see two feet in front of their vehicles. During a 24-hour period, Combat Service Support Battalion 10, struggling to maintain pace with the ground combat forces, moved a total of approximately 24 miles.[12] Major Edward P. Wojnaroski, one of CSSB-10's convoy commanders, commented on their efforts to move during the storm. "After crossing the Euphrates, . . . [we] stopped at points along the side of the road where a hellacious sandstorm ensued. The blinding effects of the storm were so severe that night vision goggles proved useless."[13] Many of Colonel Weinkle's Marines in CSSB-10 were from Twentynine Palms, California, where they were "used to riding out these conditions," but even he conceded that this sandstorm was unlike any they had experienced before, and that their convoys back in California were never this large.[14] The next day, when they were finally able to move again, the air was filled with a yellowish hue from the previous night's storm.

By this point, Task Force Tarawa had seized control of both bridge crossings in an-Nasiriyah, opening up access, albeit along the dangerous route dubbed "ambush alley," for Regimental Combat Team 1's movement toward al-Kut. Combat Service Support Battalion 22 moved from Jalibah to a location south of an-Nasiriyah, where they set up a defensive

Harsh conditions and zero visibility during a sandstorm debilitated the Marines' ability to continue movement forward.

USMC Photo

Photo by MSgt Edward D. Kniery, USMC

During a sandstorm, Marines from 6th ESB install the second portion of the hose reel system north of LSA Viper, Iraq.

perimeter. During the next 10 days, they continuously convoyed back-and-forth between their location and Logistics Support Area Viper, obtaining necessary support from Combat Service Support Battalion 18 to keep Regimental Combat Team 2 fully supplied. Each trip, which consisted of approximately 60 to 70 miles, took a convoy 13 to 15 hours. Additionally, CSSB-22 Marines augmented the regimental combat team in guarding more than 400 prisoners. On the night of 26 March, the battalion took part in a firefight where one cargo truck was damaged, but the battalion sustained no casualties. Unfortunately, other Marines in the task force were wounded, and once again, CSSB-22's shock trauma platoon came into action, treating 32 Marines.[15]

On 24 March, 6th Engineer Support Battalion (6th ESB) continued its task of laying the tactical fuel system down across barren desert, and as the debilitating sandstorm blew through the area, the challenges became even more daunting. The Marines laying the hose reel had to seek cover behind the truck deploying it, and the trucks could only inch along, guided by Marines walking directly in front of them. Basically, the Marines had to take a "touch and feel" approach to laying the hose reel, continuing on with the mission in 20-hour shifts despite the high winds, blinding sand, and minimal communications. Even with these added complications, the Marines were able to complete the tactical hose reel within three days, one day less than the original estimated completion time. On 25 March, the tactical fuel system was complete. Measuring 57 miles from Breach Point West to Jalibah Airfield, the pipeline included 17 booster stations located 3.5 miles apart. At the booster stations, two 600-gallons-per-minute pumps and two 20,000-gallon fuel bags helped ensure that the flow of fuel to LSA Viper, which began on 26 March, would be continuous.[16]

According to Colonel Machut, "no one thought it would work, but we made it work."[17] In reality, if the hose reel had failed, there would have been significant consequences on the entire war effort. Coalition forces were advancing at such a rapid rate that any lapse in the fuel supply would have caused a delay in operations. For the first three weeks of the war, while the Army was still installing their hard-line fuel system, the Marine Corps had "the only fuel in town."[18]

While the hose reel took care of fuel requirements, another group of 6th ESB Marines worked on the bulk water requirement. On 24 March, water operations began at LSA Viper with the utilities platoon from 6th ESB's Engineer Support Company establishing a water point 10 miles north of the battalion's combat operations center on the Saddam Canal. Engineer Company C, commanded by Major Michael P.

Photos by MSgt Edward D. Kniery, USMC

The bulk fuel point (above)—Replenishment Point 26—operated by CSSB-10 was located at Camp Daley, south of Baghdad. Water is pumped from the Euphrates River into 3,000-gallon water bladders at the LSA Viper water point (below). Marines in 6th ESB set up the water point to operate their reverse osmosis water purification units.

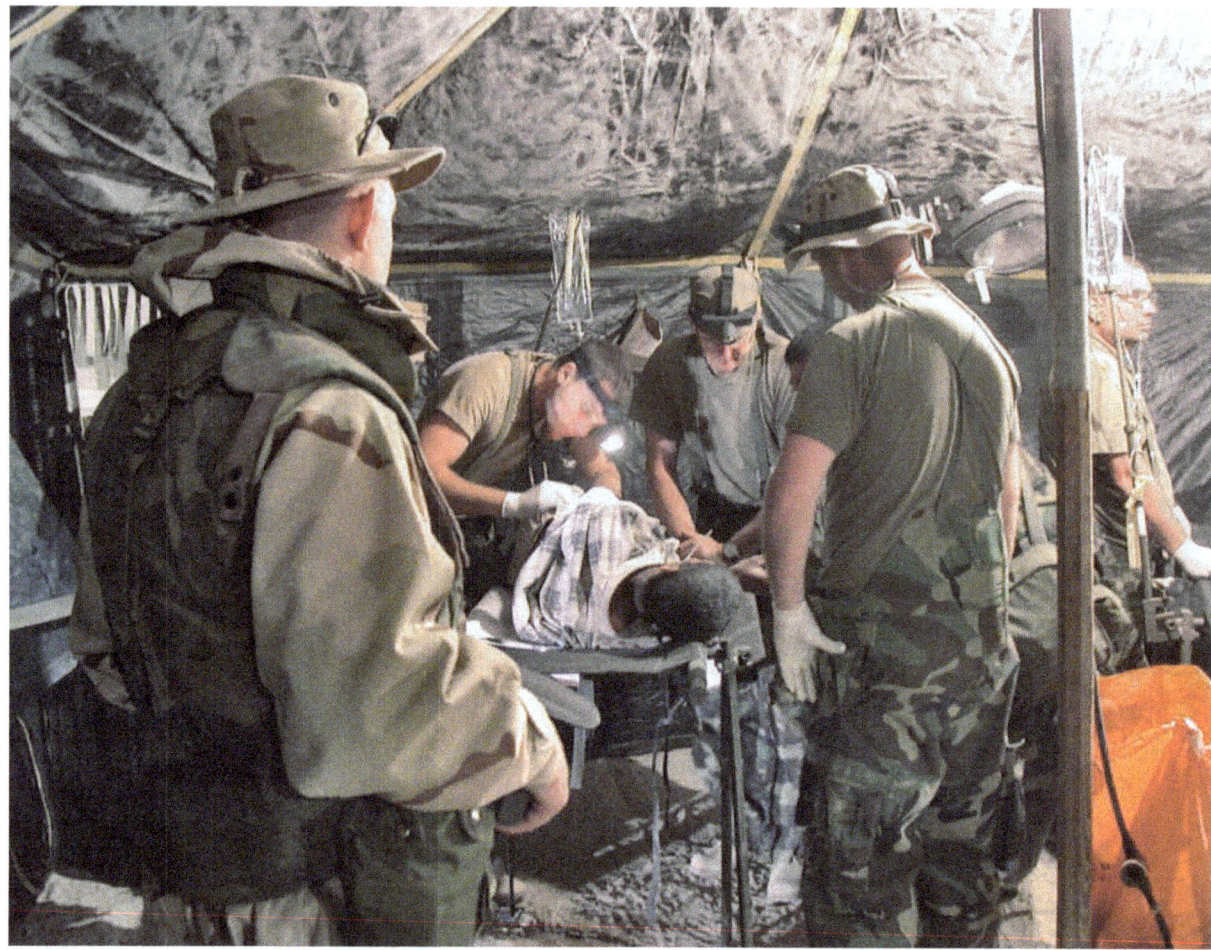

Photo by MSgt Edward D. Kniery, USMC

Corpsmen and doctors in Charlie Surgical Support Company provide medical aid to an Iraqi prisoner at LSA Viper.

McCarthy, provided security. It was on this day that tragedy first struck the reserve engineers. While swimming across the canal to provide security on the far bank, two Marines, Sergeant Bradley S. Korthaus and Corporal Evan T. James, drowned. Major McCarthy led a small team of Marines in an attempt to recover their bodies, but was unsuccessful. Later in the day, as the sandstorm blew through with full force, Navy Seabees were enlisted to help find the bodies. As weather conditions made it nearly impossible to see, the divers continued to search the canal for the two Marines, ultimately recovering them that evening.[19]

Since their activation in January and throughout the opening sequence of the war, 6th ESB had surpassed all expectations, and beat all scheduled deadlines. Perhaps the lowest point for an otherwise successful deployment, the tragic deaths of the two reservists reminded the engineers that in their critical mission, the enemy was not the only threat to their safety. Determined not to allow this tragic event to disrupt its support to the troops, Colonel Machut's battalion once again excelled—beating projected timelines and exceeding planned production of fresh water. Fourteen reverse osmosis water purification units at LSA Viper produced a one-day supply of 120,000 gallons of water, allowing 6th ESB to support the 1st Marine Division, Task Force Tarawa, 1st FSSG, and 3d MAW, as well as U.S. Army units passing through the area.[20]

Treating the Casualties

While shock trauma platoons and forward resuscitative surgical systems moved across the battlefield attached to their combat service support elements, another type of medical support arrived at LSA Viper within the first few days of the war to provide much needed surgical support. 1st FSSG's Surgical Support Company C flew in by helicopter on 24 March, just in time to feel the full effects of the sandstorm. Even

Photo by MSgt Edward D. Kniery, USMC

Litter bearers move a wounded Marine from an Army Black Hawk medevac helicopter to Charlie Surgical Support Company at LSA Viper.

in the blinding and debilitating weather, the surgical company experienced an extremely busy first three days. They treated close to 150 patients and conducted 25 to 30 operations, including complex abdominal and chest procedures. The majority of the patients treated by Company C were Iraqis. This was the same night that they had a large number of incoming patients, and the difficulty in treating patients was devastating for some of the troops. The breakdown of Marine and Iraqi patients was about 50/50, and while patient care was the first priority, Iraqi combatants, who were now U.S. prisoners had to be specifically identified during the process and guarded by Marines. This was a difficult task, as it was not always easy to distinguish the prisoners from Iraqi civilians. Navy Commander James P. Flint, a surgeon from Jacksonville, Florida, who had been mobilized as part of the medical augmentation program, commented on the challenge that a Marine faced in keeping his calm when a prisoner antagonized him by talking about "his shooting of two Americans." Aside from that incident, Commander Flint thought the prisoners had been fairly well behaved and had been giving valuable information to the intelligence interrogators. They saw several gunshot and shrapnel wounds, as well as injuries from vehicle accidents.[21] One night, they received several casualties from a landmine, requiring amputations. Included was a two-year-old child who did not survive.

The surgical company was limited in dealing with the post-treatment phase of patient care. They were equipped to provide a maximum of 48 hours care before moving the patient to another facility or discharging them. Most patients were medically evacuated to the next higher level of care at facilities such as the Army combat support hospital or the Navy Hospital Ship USNS *Comfort* (T-AH 20). The majority of the Iraqi captives were sent to the ship.[23]

Another significant capability of Surgical Company C resided in its combat stress platoon. Double the size of a normal combat stress platoon, which typically has one psychiatrist, two psychologists, and three psychiatric technicians, it treated cases of combat stress, which was considered to be a normal reaction to a combat environment. Commanded by Navy captain Glenn M. Goldberg, a clinical psychologist from Naval Hospital Jacksonville, Florida, the combat stress platoon's main goal was to provide its

A Muslim Burial

On 29 March, a two-year-old little Iraqi boy who had been brought to Surgical Company Charlie, died from wounds he obtained after stepping on a landmine. Without any identification or family members, he had been medically evacuated to Surgical Support Company C and underwent surgery to amputate both of his legs; sadly, he did not survive the trauma. After a cautious investigation of the proper Muslim burial procedures, the 1st FSSG civil affairs liaison officer, Lieutenant Colonel Valerie E. Thomas, arranged to have three Muslim gentlemen, Khuder Al Emeri, a Free Iraqi Force member; Ali Hassam, a Kuwaiti interpreter; and a third unidentified Muslim perform the burial in a prescribed location. The location was designated ahead of time, just outside of the Viper Logistics Support Area, to facilitate civilian visitation without incident. The grave was dug about six feet deep and oriented such that the child could be placed on his side, facing in the direction of Mecca. Next to the grave, a smaller shallow area was prepared. At the gravesite, Ali Hassam, who went by Sam, prepped the area by pouring water into the shallow area next to the grave. Meanwhile, Khuder stepped down into the grave to dig a side hole facing Mecca. When the child's body was removed from the ambulance on a stretcher, it was immediately placed on the ground. The first part of the burial ceremony took place, as the three Muslims knelt in front of the child's body, facing Mecca. Sam knelt in front of the other two and led them in Muslim prayers. When they were done, they unwrapped the child's body to ensure that there was no plastic inside the shroud and that his face was covered. Sam then picked up the child's body and handed it to Khuder, who was standing in the grave. The child's body was placed in the grave with his right shoulder down and his face towards Mecca. Wet sand formed into balls (about the size of oranges) were used to encase the child's body in the grave. Once the child's body was in place, Sam, Khuder, and the third

Photo by MSgt Edward D. Kniery, USMC

Ali Hassam, a volunteer translator, leads prayers during a burial service conducted for a two-year old boy killed when he stepped on a land mine. The boy was brought to the Charlie Surgical Support Company at LSA Viper, where he died of his wounds.

Muslim man began shoveling sand into the grave. After a short while, they asked for any Christians to help out by shoveling sand into the grave. When the grave was completely filled, the sand was kept flat and a line of rocks was laid at the head of the grave. This was left primarily to mark the grave site. At the conclusion of the burial, Sam sprinkled water over the grave.[22]

---

patients respite and relief from the danger, noise, and activity of combat and enable them to return to their units within 72 hours. Additional roles of the combat stress platoon included treatment and evacuation of patients with psychiatric disorders as well as counseling and supportive services to the Marines and sailors. While the platoon was still in Kuwait, they provided ample training to the surgical company on combat stress, and opened a wellness center. Once the war began, the combat stress platoon moved forward to LSA Viper with Surgical Company C. After just one week, the doctors noted that, surprisingly,

Photo by MSgt Edward D. Kniery, USMC

Members of Fleet Hospital 3 construct the first expeditionary medical facility in Iraq at LSA Viper.

they had only treated a handful of classic combat stress cases.* Navy Commander Patrick H. Bowers, a doctor with the combat stress platoon, discussed their initial caseload:

> We've only been here for one week, so it's still kind of early on to really know exactly what all we're going to be seeing and what our success rate will be getting people back to the front. So far, as far as classic combat stress type patients, we've seen relatively few . . . we've seen maybe half a dozen or so true combat stress type of patients and overall . . . it looks like our success rate with sending people back to their units is . . . a little bit less than 50 percent, which is lower than the numbers we were told we should expect. . . . We had [thought] we should be able to return up to 70 percent back to the front.[24]

Doctors noted that they had not received any undue pressure from the units to have their Marines returned to the frontlines. In contrast, one mentioned that in a particular case, the unit was very supportive of getting the Marine necessary medical support back in the rear area.[25]

Level-two medical care consisted of the FSSG's surgical companies, shock trauma platoons, and forward resuscitative surgical systems. However, another more robust capability was added when Fleet Hospital 3 arrived and constructed the Navy and Marine Corps' first expeditionary medical facility (EMF). On 25 March, elements of the EMF moved north to LSA Viper and began construction of the field hospital. The doctrinal timeline for setting up a facility of this size is ten days, but Navy Captain Peter F. O'Connor (USN), the EMF commanding officer, set an aggressive schedule to be up and running because of the impending battle and its expected number of casualties.[26] He commented that "the result is a significant increase in our ability to save lives. The sooner our forces receive the robust care available here at a fleet hospital, the better their chances."[27]

After working 24-hour days for five days straight,

---

* In a recent study conducted by the Walter Reed Army Institute of Research Land Combat Study Team, Marines from two battalions in I MEF were assessed for the condition of their mental health following operations between March and May 2003 during Operation Iraqi Freedom. While many gaps still exist in the understanding of the full psychosocial effect of combat, results generally showed that there was a higher occurrence of major depression, generalized anxiety, and post-traumatic stress disorder among individuals who served in Iraq during this period than those who had served in Afghanistan. There has been difficulty in comparing these results to other past wars, due to the lack of subjects studied so soon after their involvement in combat operations. Previous methods of such studies were often conducted years after the individuals' military service had ended. (Charles W. Hoge, MD; Carl A. Castro, PhD; Stephen C. Messer, PhD; Dennis McGurk, PhD; Dave I. Cotting, PhD; and Robert L. Koffman, MD; MPH, "Combat Duty in Iraq and Afghanistan, Mental Health Problems, and Barriers to Care," *New England Journal of Medicine*, 1Jul04.)

they opened the expeditionary medical facility on 1 April and immediately began receiving patients. The facility had a 20-bed intensive care unit, as well as 96 additional beds. It was configured with two operating rooms and four operating beds. During the course of the next seven days, they received 220 admissions and performed 119 surgeries. Similar to the surgical support companies, the expeditionary medical facility received both American and Iraqi patients whose injuries and need for medical care varied widely. It did not take long for the physicians and corpsmen to understand and accept the complexities of their unique role as medical care providers. One hospital corpsman described his initial thoughts when receiving simultaneous American and Iraqi patients.

> It took me a split second. I was assisting an injured Marine who was just outside our CasRec (casualty receiving) door. Just then, another gurney came around me with an Iraqi. For a split second, I thought it was wrong to let our guy wait. But then I looked closer and saw the Iraqi was in worse shape. Right then and there, it was crystal clear to me. We're here as healers. It made perfect sense to me from that point on.[28]

By the end of April, the expeditionary medical facility had received more than 500 patients, and performed 280 surgical procedures.

8th Engineer Support Battalion Reorganizing on the Move

At the start of the war, 8th Engineer Support Battalion (8th ESB) was in direct support of Task Force Tarawa. Once the western bridges were secured, however, it planned to detach and join the 1st Marine Division as they passed south of an-Nasiriyah. Task Force Tarawa was becoming engaged in the fight for the eastern bridges and was reluctant to release the bridge force. After some persuasion, 8th ESB was released and moved quickly to the western bridges over the Euphrates River, where it met up with two multi-role bridge companies (MRBCs) from the 3d Infantry Division.* While they were a welcome addition to the bridge battalion, the Army units were out of fuel and now the responsibility of 8th ESB. With some quick thinking, Major Timothy B. Seamon secured Marine CH-53 support and had fuel airlifted to the MRBCs. Once refueled, the battalion moved up Highway 1, emplacing four medium girder bridges over large gaps and supporting elements of the combat engineer battalions with bulldozers and bucket loaders to fill in more than 35 culverts and small gaps. This support ultimately led to the improvement of the logistics throughput required to sustain 1st Marine Division. The 8th ESB continued to support 1st Marine Division's attack up Highways 1 and 7, in the vicinity of the western Euphrates Bridge. With the two U.S. Army companies adding to their end strength of personnel and equipment, the engineers could now be divided and provide dual-axis support to 1st Marine Division. One element designated as Crossing Area Engineer 5 (CAE-5) was formed with Bridge Company C and the Army's 459th Multi-Role Bridge Company. They supported Regimental Combat Team 1 (RCT-1) as they traveled up Highway 7.[29]

Another element, designated as Crossing Area Engineer 1 (CAE-1)* was formed with Bridge Companies A and B, and supported Regimental Combat Teams 5 and 7 traveling up Highway 1. Colonel Nelson and his engineer command element were co-located with the 1st Marine Division forward command post also on the highway. The battalion's headquarters and engineer support companies, containing spare bridge parts, maintenance and service capabilities vital to the battalion, combined to form a third separate command under Major Joseph J. Klocek, the battalion executive officer and followed in trace of 1st Marine Division. Essentially three commands under one battalion—CAE-5, CAE-1, and the battalion main—provided Colonel Nelson, who had also been designated as the force crossing engineer, the maneuverability and flexibility needed to sup-

---

* The U.S. Army's 3ID requested the return of one of the MRBCs within days of its assignment to 8th ESB. This bridge company, the 574th MRBC had just employed its medium girder bridge on Hwy 1 and was moving north when the call came for their detachment. With the volume of combat and combat support vehicles moving forward in support of 1st Marine Division, the Army company, minus its medium girder bridge components, was ordered out of the line of march and subsequently had to wait several days prior to being able to travel south on Hwy 1 to rejoin the 3ID's westward movement.

* The crossing area engineer is a doctrinal concept that puts a river crossing command and control unit co-located with the supported regimental combat team headquarters. The idea behind this is the force crossing engineer (battalion commander and support staff) would be co-located with the Division forward headquarters and provide over-arching command and control of all of the bridge assets assigned to the FSSG/Division, allocating companies to crossing area engineers where and when they are needed. Each supported regimental combat team would have a crossing area engineer, who would provide command and control over the bridge build and then control the crossing area as the regiments passed through the river crossing area. They would also coordinate all resupply of bridge assets through the force crossing engineer. Crossing area engineers would report directly to the regimental combat team's operations officer or commanding officer, and to the force crossing engineer.

Courtesy of 8th ESB

Marines of 8th Engineer Support Battalion constructed medium girder bridges along Iraq's Route 1.

port 1st Marine Division's wide front and quick advance.*

As they followed RCT-1 along Highway 7 through

---

* A third crossing area engineer, CAE-7, had been part of the original plan to support each regimental combat team with a CAE, but never materialized for two reasons. There were not sufficient lift assets to mobile load additional bridging companies, and because RCT-7 and RCT-5 took the same axis of advance, they could be supported by one CAE, CAE-1. Maj Brian W. Ecarius, originally assigned to command CAE-7, worked as a liaison for the force crossing engineer.

an-Nasiriyah, CAE-5, commanded by Major Thomas M. Pratt, ran a gauntlet of indiscriminant small arms and rocket-propelled grenade fire. The extensive combat skills training that the Marines in 8th ESB had conducted prior to the war paid dividends for themselves and for their army counterparts. In an article written by Colonel Nelson and his executive officer, Major Joseph J. Klocek, the authors described the Marines' actions:

> The Army's 459th [Multi-Role Bridge Company], encountering its first enemy contact and

unfamiliar with the execution of immediate action drills, required direct supervision from the Marines of CAE-5 in order to conserve ammunition and continue its forward movement. To ensure the unit was ready for their next contact, CAE-5 Marines provided immediate action drill training and stressed the need for small unit leaders to take charge and effectively employ their organic weapons to neutralize the threat.[30]

This would prove useful several days later, as the 459th Multi-Role Bridge Company built an improved ribbon bridge across the Diyala River while under enemy fire.

Meanwhile, Colonel Nelson and CAE-1, commanded by Major Timothy B. Seamon, traveled with the 1st Marine Division main assault force up Highway 1, and during the sandstorm on 25 March, installed four medium girder bridges over box culverts along the highway to improve trafficability. Sections of this main supply route were under construction at the time of attack and existing bypasses proved extremely difficult for logistics vehicles to pass. Without 8th ESB's construction of the four medium girder bridges, Marine forces would have suffered a signif-

Marines of 7th Engineer Support Battalion repair the runway at a former Iraqi air base near Al Kut.
Photo by MSgt Edward D. Kniery, USMC

icant degradation of logistics throughput, ultimately affecting the division's speed and momentum.

Early in March, Lieutenant Colonel Nelson had commented that one of his greatest concerns was depleting his inventory of bridging supplies before being able to complete all required missions.[31] By 26 March, just six days into the war, the two companies in CAE-1 had already exhausted their entire inventory of medium girder bridges.[32]

Movement Following the Storm

All combat service support companies suffered the disabling effects of the sandstorm, but continued to provide resupply support to their regimental combat teams. Combat Service Support Company 111 (CSSC-111), following in trace of Regimental Combat Team 1, moved forward in the early morning of 25 March, and as it moved through an-Nasiriyah with light armored reconnaissance support, came under attack of sustained enemy machine gun fire. Returning fire, the company eventually crossed the Euphrates River and arrived at RCT-1's location. Later that evening, it also came under mortar and small-arms fire.

Combat Service Support Battalion 10 had now joined up with the Combat Service Support Group 11 Forward element and established a hasty repair and replenishment point along Highway 1 just north of the Tigris River near al-Mu'aytyah. Meanwhile, CSSG-11 main departed Repair and Replenishment Point 7 and followed closely behind. Plagued by the harsh conditions of the sandstorm and poor road conditions, many units traveling up Highway 1 were intermingled with one another. CSSG-11's main command post, co-located with 1st Marine Division's main, was strung out along Highway 1.

Once the sandstorm began to clear, CSSB-10, together as a single battalion again, moved to its next designated location, Repair and Replenishment Point 24 (RRP-24), which had previously been an Iraqi ambush site and only recently cleared by 3d Light Armored Reconnaissance Battalion. Along with CSSG-11's forward element and Combat Service Support Company 115, it arrived in the late afternoon of 26 March to the sight of over 20 dead Iraqi soldiers lining the roadway and their ambush positions. Still in convoy formation, the Marines immediately began taking mortar, machine gun, and small-arms fire from the surrounding area. Staff Sergeant Perry H. Shane, the ordnance maintenance chief for CSSB-10, riding atop an M88 Hercules tank recovery vehicle, spotted three enemy gunmen to his flank and neutralized them with his M240G medium machine gun. All remaining enemy instantly fled the area, but they would continually provide harassing fire throughout the battalion's next six days at RRP-24. This was the first experience of close combat for the CSSB-10 Marines.[33]

CSSG-11's main command post, following behind the 1st Marine Division main, meanwhile, was scattered along Highway 1 during the sandstorm, but by 26 March, had arrived at a position south of Repair and Replenishment Point 24, a location that became known as the "mud hole." Combat Service Support Company 117 (CSSC-117) halted along Highway 1, where they conducted resupply operations with Regimental Combat Team 7 (RCT-7). While at this position, the company came under enemy machine gun and small arms attack. The Marines repulsed the attack by forming a skirmish line and using the firepower of the nearby 1st Tank Battalion. Combat Service Support Company 111 followed closely behind RCT-1, which continued to fight its way through numerous Fedayeen and sniper attacks along Highway 7.

CSSG-11 and CSSB-10 continued to build logistical stockpiles at Repair and Replenishment Point 24. This position, which would eventually be named Support Area Anderson, provided the support Marines their first break from constant movement. They remained there for approximately six days, providing division units with a continuous supply of food, water, petroleum, oils and lubricants, ammunition, and medical supplies. At this point in the war, the requirement for repair parts had become a priority. Because critical parts were in short supply in theater, units began stripping disabled vehicles and equipment for necessary parts. CSSB-10 collected these "carcasses" and established its first "junkyard."

Dividing and Conquering the General Engineering Missions

While 6th and 8th Engineer Support Battalions had their specific missions of the hose reel and bridging, 7th Engineer Support Battalion had a more general engineering mission. As a result, the battalion was often split, conducting several different missions across the battlefield. Alpha Company, led by Captain Jose M. Lopez, continued to construct the massive Logistics Support Area Viper, while Charlie Company, led by Captain Susan Bird, was assigned a new mission. They would move north to Qalat Sikar and conduct rapid runway repairs and potentially construct Support Area Basilone. Captain Bird and her company staff planned this convoy movement with elements of Combat Service Support Battalion 12 and Marine Wing Support Squadron 373.

Meanwhile, a small contingent from Support Company, named Task Force Dirt Pig, conducted road repairs along Highway 1 to allow for better movement of ground forces. Bravo Company, 7th ESB provided security. Throughout the war, 7th ESB's missions were diverse and often segmented at the company level. Later in the war, in addition to their construction efforts, elements of 7th ESB were also tasked with providing security, conducting urban mobility and counter-mobility engineering.*[34]

---
* Due to a shortage of vehicles, 7th ESB experienced some difficulty in movement forward. As a result, the more mobile Seabee units under the MEF Engineer Group helped fill the gaps within general engineering missions across the battlefield.

Chapter 5

Northern Support Areas (27 March–3 April 2003)

Establishing Support Area Anderson

As ground forces moved north toward Baghdad, logistical lines were stretched. The distance between the direct support elements trailing 1st Marine Division and Logistical Support Area Viper (LSA), the forward-most logistical support area on the battlefield, was increasing by the day. The hundreds of miles equated to lengthy and time-consuming convoy operations, often stretching the already limited supply of trucks and threatening the precious momentum achieved by the maneuver forces. The result was that repair and replenishment points and subsequent support areas had to be repositioned to keep up with the maneuver forces. Combat Service Support Company 181 (CSSC-181), commanded by Captain Patryck J. Durham, became the supply node that would extend further north to support forces moving forward. A miniature version of Combat Service Support Battalion 18 (CSSB-18), which had opened up LSA Viper, CSSC-181 had been planned long before the battalion's arrival in theater. However, it was not until they were at Viper that Lieutenant Colonel Thomas N. Collins received the order from FSSG headquarters to stand up the company and have them displace to Combat Service Support Group 11's (CSSG-11) forward location near ad-Diwaniyah, Repair and Replenishment Point 24. The company did not have the same robust capability as the CSSB-18, but it would be able to provide more direct support to Combat Service Support Battalion 10 (CSSB-10) and 1st Marine Division.[1]

Although CSSC-181 had been formed prior to the start of the war, Captain Durham, an infantry officer by trade, crossed the line of departure with Combat Service Support Battalion 22 (CSSB-22), accompanied only by an explosive ordnance disposal detachment and a handful of communicators. Without a specific pre-assigned mission at the onset, his other detachments had rejoined their own companies while at Breach Point West and remained with them when they arrived at LSA Viper. Just days later and during the sandstorm, Captain Durham received word to reunite his company in preparation for movement to a forward position. He spent the next 24 hours coordinating and constructing the 100-vehicle convoy that he would lead up to CSSG-11's position. Within his company were detachments representing all of CSSB-18's companies including headquarters, engineering, supply, maintenance, and motor transport. He also had attachments that were in direct support of the company, including an engineer company from 7th Engineer Support Battalion (7th ESB), a shock trauma platoon, two forward resuscitative surgical systems, and a bulk fuel company. After departing on the morning of 26 March, they traveled for 24 hours across approximately 150 miles of desert, often having no communication with anyone outside the convoy. This lack of communications had become the norm for 1st FSSG operators. The only means of on-the-move communications was the limited supply of blue-force tracker systems.

On 27 March, CSSC-181 arrived at its destination and linked up with CSSG-11, which was especially thrilled to see that they carried with them a 75,000-gallon supply of fuel. Immediately, the company took over a section of the repair and replenishment point's defensive perimeter, where it received enemy small arms and mortar fire. Enemy probing actions continued throughout the night, but Captain Durham's Marines maintained their position. The next morning, their focus shifted to establishing communications and setting up a combat service support operations center. Simultaneously, Captain Durham and his Marines began providing support to CSSB-10 and other division units. During the next few days, the Marines of CSSC-181 integrated with CSSG-11's operations at Repair and Replenishment Point 24. From this location, later known as Support Area Anderson, the company also sent out maintenance contact teams to retrieve disabled equipment. In the immediate surrounding area, Captain Durham's Marines retrieved more than 200 vehicle hulls.[5]

Rumor of an Operational Pause

By 27 March, all three combat service support companies had resumed movement and followed in trace of their regimental combat teams. Regimental Combat Team 1 (RCT-1) had passed through a narrow and treacherous edge of an-Nasiriyah and was

Shortfalls in Communications

Many commanders within 1st and 2d FSSG, including the two commanding generals, often commented on the major communications shortfalls that severely challenged their mission and frequently put Marines at additional risk during Operation Iraqi Freedom. General Lehnert spoke plainly about the implication of this shortfall:

> I will say that the decision by the Marine Corps as an institution not to properly resource the FSSGs with the appropriate communications to be able to go 600 miles is an institutional failure and it is a situation that has me very concerned, because what it says institutionally is that the life of a grunt is worth a great deal more than the life of a truck driver.[2]

General Usher also recognized the problem early on:

> We always knew that we were going to be stretching our communications capability. We certainly did in a very real sense during the execution of the operation. We relied on a lot of ingenuity and individual effort, but institutionally we just did not have the communications architecture to be able to operate in such a broad environment as we found ourselves in Operation Iraqi Freedom.[3]

He added that because e-mail had become such a dominant means of communications in this day and age, any limitation in that area created real problems; command and control could essentially breakdown without e-mail capability. Even beyond the issues of safety and security, improvements in information processes and assets would need to be implemented to replace the "iron mountains" that General Lehnert described as hindering the FSSG's ability to keep up with modern warfare.

> We have iron mountains because operators don't trust us to get it right, and they don't trust us to get it right because there have been times when they have gone without food and they have gone without a repair part. With that said, ultimately we cannot afford to continue to move piles of stuff across the battlefield and still achieve the speed that modern warfare dictates. So what do you use to replace the iron mountains? You replace it with information.[4]

Despite the shortfalls experienced in the FSSGs, the Marine Corps had experienced many communications improvements since the first Gulf War. For instance, the blue force tracker system, which consisted of a laptop computer utilizing a global positioning system to automatically broadcast a vehicle's 10-digit grid coordinate every five minutes, as well as a limited e-mail capability, was reported to be possibly the most effective means of communicating with and locating logistics forces. Without the tracker, command and control of the transportation link of combat service support would have been nearly impossible. Unfortunately, where technology had advanced, supply could not keep up with demand; similar to other communications assets, the blue force tracker was in short supply.

---

now advancing toward the city of al-Kut. Regimental Combat Teams 5 (RCT-5) and 7 (RCT-7) had attacked up Highway 1, repeatedly engaging enemy elements, and were poised to seize the Hantush airstrip. As the sandstorm subsided, the Marines resumed their movement across the battlefield. At this point, the rumor of an operational pause began to filter its way down to the individual units and troops. Within a day, this rumor became a reality, and ground movement virtually halted for four days. No definitive reason or cause was revealed, leading to much speculation among the Marines. One of the more popular beliefs was that the suspension of movement was caused by the inability of U.S. Army logistics to keep pace with their supported ground troops. In reality, logistics support for both the Marine Corps and Army had already been stretched. Long, slow-moving convoys across miles of open desert were vulnerable to attack and rear areas were still swarming with pockets of enemy resistance.

Giving insight into the challenges that Marine logistics faced, Captain Suzan F. Thompson, commander of Combat Service Support Company 115 (CSSC-115), commented on the ongoing predicaments as her company struggled to maintain the fast pace of their regimental combat team while continuously obtaining their own resupply. "The regimental commander would brief his scheme of maneuver and his concept of [operations] and he would ask, 'Captain Thompson and Major Bryant (who was the Regimental S-4), are we going to outrun the logistics?' And we usually told him, 'Yes, sir, you are.' But we . . . executed the mission anyway."[6] The reality was that because all three regimental combat teams and their support companies were so spread out, the support battalions, which provided general support were not always positioned on the battlefield to best accommodate every maneuver element. To overcome this challenge, the combat service support companies, which struggled to keep up with their regimental combat teams and provide them with sustained resupply, often had to break off and form independent convoys back to the support battalion to maintain their own needs. They would then have to catch up to the regimental combat team, which was continuously on the move. In some ways, it was 1st Marine Division's successes that pushed the logistics near—but not quite to—the point of failure. The Marine logisticians were able to sustain the ground forces, however, largely due to their intrinsic ability to adapt to any situation, even as each day brought new challenges. Throughout the war, General Usher recognized that the logisticians' original plan had to be constantly re-evaluated for its ability to support the ground forces.

> The success of the operation has been more significant than planned and so therefore we've got the division a little further out ahead of us . . . it's caused us, in the planning cycle, to go back to our base plan and re-look at some of those planning assumptions and at the allocation of equipment and reposition and refocus.[7]

During the four-day operational pause, although there was minimal movement forward, 1st Marine Division continued to fight. All three regimental combat teams conducted aggressive security and ambush patrols to their flanks. They secured their zones and sought out any remnants of retreating enemy forces. RCT-5 suffered regular attacks by hit-and-run enemy elements firing mortars and artillery, and enemy ambushes, although not very effective, were frequent. The combat service support companies continued to conduct convoy movement to retrieve and deliver much needed supplies to their regimental combat teams. Combat Service Support Companies 115 and 117 (CSSC-117) remained spread out along Highway 1 and continued to pull logistical support from Repair and Replenishment Point 24, while Combat Service Support Company 111 (CSSC-111) moved to a location north of Qalat Sikar, establishing another repair and replenishment point. En route to this location, near ar-Rifa, they received heavy and sustained fire, and when they initially set up their repair and replenishment point, they faced a group of hostile civilians, causing them to once again move to a location south of the intersection between Highways 7 and 17. This new site, Repair and Replenishment Point 14, later became Support Area Basilone.

Turnover of Combat Service Support Battalion 12

On 27 March, Lieutenant Colonel Adrian W. Burke, future operations officer of 1st FSSG, assumed command of Combat Service Support Battalion 12 (CSSB-12)*, one of the two general support battalions under Combat Service Support Group 15. Lieutenant Colonel Burke, who had commanded a mobile combat service support detachment during Desert Shield/Desert Storm, took the assignment in stride, focusing on his new mission: to command the battalion and lead his Marines as they supported I MEF. With good reason, his efforts were concentrated on the unknown that his Marines would face in Iraq.[8]

The same day that Colonel Burke took command of CSSB-12, the battalion's advanced party, led by Major John E. Vincent, the unit's executive officer, and about 60 Marines, moved north to set up Support Area Basilone, near Qalat Sikar. With Charlie Company, 7th Engineer Support Battalion attached, they planned to link up with Combat Service Support Company 111, which had set up near Qalat Sikar, and expand their capabilities to include a forward resuscitative surgical system, a shock trauma platoon, an aeromedical evacuation liaison team, and a mobile aeromedical staging facility. As they moved north of an-Nasiriyah, elements of Marine Wing Support Squadron 371 (MWSS-371) joined their already lengthy convoy, bringing the total number of vehicles to more than 200 and the number of Marines to over 700. MWSS-371 was tasked with repairing and rebuilding the runway at the Qalat Sikar Airfield, to create the possibility of resupply operations by air.

In the vicinity of Ash Shatrah, the convoy began receiving small arms, machine gun, mortar, and rocket-propelled grenade fire. Although they had light armored vehicle support from the 15th Marine Expeditionary Unit dispersed throughout, the risk of damage to the convoy was too great, and they decided to turn around, move south to a point just outside of an-Nasiriyah, and await air support. In the evening, they made another attempt to move north,

---

* LtCol Burke replaced LtCol Kathleen M. Murney.

Courtesy of LtCol Adrian W. Burke, USMC

LtCol Adrian W. Burke, commanding officer of CSSB-12, conducts a berm reconnaissance in Iraq. Prior to assuming command of the battalion, LtCol Burke served as the 1st FSSG future operations officer and was instrumental in the reorganization of the group for OIF.

but again, the enemy was waiting for them. This time, Major Vincent's convoy was moving in blackout conditions, and the Marines did not have night vision goggles; however, they had the added security of four AH-1 Cobra gunships as escorts. Major Vincent described the sight:

> I was the lead vehicle. Right off to my side, about 75-100 yards, one of the Cobras shot a van . . . and this thing blew up and lit up the whole sky. . . . the Cobras were firing the rockets and the sparks from the rockets were falling across the hood of the vehicle. . . . when this thing blew up, you could feel the heat. We could hear the bullets dinging off the LAVs. . . . it was probably more exciting than anything . . . just because we knew we had air support and those guys would take care of us.[9]

Major Vincent's Marines made it through the ambush without any casualties. Further back in the convoy, however, MWSS-371 suffered casualties of both personnel and vehicles. Gunnery Sergeant Melba L. Garza, the squadron operations chief, commented on the fog of war they experienced during the attack on their convoy:

> We could hear on the radio, 'one humvee down, one LVS [logistics vehicle system] broken' and in the kill zone, we can't do anything but abandon the vehicle. There's nothing we can do mechanical-wise to go ahead and try to get them up. We actually didn't have the casualty count till we were in the RCT section . . . when we stopped at the RCT-1 site, we actually found out that one of our seven-tons had rolled over, we had one leg casualty . . . and we lost a Marine. That was the most gut-wrenching moment.[10]

Sergeant Fernando Padilla-Ramirez was the Marine whose status was initially classified as missing in action. He was later classified as killed in action when members of the 24th Marine Expeditionary Unit recovered his body nine days later.[11]

Around 0100 in the morning, the convoy finally arrived at 1st Marine Regiment's position near Qalat Sikar. Once the Marines arrived, they established Support Area Basilone with the hope of utilizing the nearby Qalat Sikar Airfield for resupply by air. This location would primarily support I MEF forces moving toward al-Kut.[12]

Two days later, Lieutenant Colonel Burke and his command element from CSSB-12 arrived at Support Area (SA) Anderson. They assumed tactical com-

> ## Loved Ones in Combat
>
> Among the many stresses that a Marine might go through during combat operations is the loss of a comrade or friend. There were several Marines participating in OIF, though, that had the additional stress of worrying about their loved ones: siblings, spouses, and even children. Major Vincent was one of many Marines who had a close relative deployed to Iraq at the same time. His brother was a helicopter pilot with the 101st Airborne Division, and the night Major Vincent went into Iraq, he heard that an Apache from his brother's battalion had been shot down. For five days he kept in the back of his mind the possibility that his brother had been hurt or killed; fortunately, he was later informed that his brother was safe.[13]
>
> Captain Patryck J. Durham, commander of CSSC-181 remembers that when his wife, a helicopter pilot with 15th MEU, initially left Camp Pendleton in the fall, he had a pretty good idea that he would also be heading out to the desert. Among his most memorable moments from the war were the three chance meetings when he was able to see his wife; on the flip side, some of the most stressful moments occurred when he would hear about a helicopter crash, but not know the identity of the pilot.[14]

mand of Captain Durham's company and responsibility for the support area once CSSG-11 departed. In addition to providing general combat service support, SA Anderson housed several medical units, which received and treated numerous casualties from the front lines of the battlefield. Additionally, while maintaining both the massive hose-reel system and water supply point at Logistics Support Area Viper, 6th ESB once again stretched its capabilities even further up the battlefield by sending a bulk fuel company to SA Anderson. Here, they were in direct support of CSSB-12 and were tasked to establish a 300,000-gallon fuel farm. While en route to their destination, the convoy came under enemy attack just north of an-Nasiriyah, but it was able to continue without casualties.

1st FSSG Headquarters Moves to Logistics Support Area Viper

Traditionally, at the FSSG headquarters level, the "main" and the "forward" were terms that largely reflected the structures required to echelon an organization's command and control forward. However, during Operation Iraqi Freedom, 1st FSSG implemented a different utility of the main and forward elements. The forward element of the FSSG, where General Usher remained throughout the war, was structured to support the combat operations center, which managed the daily operations of the combat service support forces moving across the battlefield. In the forward element, portions of all staff sections were consolidated into the combat operations center to shape the future operations, or next 72 hours, of combat service support. This structure significantly reduced the decision-making time and allowed General Usher to make the critical decisions when necessary. A major challenge that surfaced with this structure was the culture change for the staff sections. General Usher noted that:

> Some sections, like the G-3 and G-4, are used to having immediate issues that have to be resolved. Other staff sections, by the very nature of the business they do, are more deliberate. And so doing things quickly is a cultural shift, and that is not a negative connotation because some of the things you just have to do some research before you can make a decision.[15]

The FSSG main consisted of the staff that provided the sustained support, such as the administration (G-1) and the comptroller. Colonel John L. Sweeney Jr., the group's deputy commander,* remained with its main element at Tactical Assembly Area (TAA) Coyote, Kuwait. These functions were important to the day-to-day operations of the FSSG, however, were not critical to the immediate decisions being made on the battlefield.

On 28 March, General Usher and his forward headquarters element left Camp Iwo Jima, TAA Coyote, and moved forward to Logistics Support Area Viper. With elements of 1st Marine Division pushing farther up the battlefield toward Baghdad, the lines of communication were stretched to nearly 400 miles. Additionally, with 1st FSSG's direct support units set up hundreds of miles into Iraq and Combat Service Support Battalion 18 positioned at LSA Viper to provide general support to I MEF, it was imperative that the general and his staff have better visibility and control over what occurred on the battlefield. This new location would provide both. It was also at this

---
* In garrison, Colonel Sweeney was the 1st FSSG chief of staff, however, given the large expansion of the FSSG's forces, General Usher thought it was appropriate to implement the position of a deputy commander.

point when 1st FSSG recognized that its own combat operations center needed to be reshaped to better manage the combat service support operations on the ground. Colonel Darrell L. Moore, 1st FSSG's chief of staff, described the new design:

> We flattened the [Forward] organization and pulled the MLC rep [Marine Logistics Command representative], air rep [air wing representative], CSSG reps [Combat Service Support Group representatives], and the 1st FSSG Fwd commodity managers (fuel, food, ammo, spare parts) into a "killer U" designed by Lieutenant Colonel Aaron T. Amey. Inside the "U," we then had all the levers right at arm's length for the final couple of weeks of active combat. We found that to be a nimble and responsive approach. Every rep seated at the "U" was right on at the same time as to decisions being made and emphasis being shifted.[16]

This new setup mirrored the function of a combat service support operations center and allowed the FSSG to be more responsive to the priorities of the commanders on the battlefield.[17] As a result, the direct and general support elements in place could be more effective. In the days ahead, however, 1st FSSG would experience an even greater stretch to their logistics chain, ultimately testing a capability that had become known as its center of gravity—distribution.

Transportation—Security, Intelligence, and Maintenance

Although the Transportation Support Group had planned on utilizing their robust distribution capability to support long-haul sustainment runs, they quickly found that their large fleet of vehicles had been greatly depleted by requirements to move the three engineer battalions and their equipment forward on the battlefield. Drivers and equipment were already overworked, but even longer hours became necessary to support the ever extending lines of communications and support. One critical requirement, the movement of fuel, was aided greatly by the Army's 319th Petroleum, Oil, and Lubricants Company. With their fleet of fuel tankers, they were able to transport twice as much fuel as Marine Corps assets were capable of in a single convoy.[18]

Lieutenant Colonel Jorge Ascunce, officer in charge of 1st FSSG's Logistics Movement and Engineering Coordination Center described the movement as the farthest inland in Marine Corps history. He commented that it was often ugly and conducted with brute force, but the performance of the individ-

Lack of Line Haul Transportation

With three battalions of tanks, four battalions of amphibious assault vehicles, and ample heavy engineer equipment, the line haul transportation requirement or the ability to transport heavy vehicles and equipment with large tractor trailers, exceeded the FSSGs' capabilities. Even within three major commands—1st FSSG, the Marine Logistics Command, and 4th FSSG—this capability simply did not exist. Reliance on the pledged support from the U.S. Army's 377th Theater Support Command to handle the line haul transportation of heavy equipment, which did not materialize, resulted in a shortfall that had to be filled by civilian contracted vehicles. Unfortunately, these vehicles were not suited to the desert environment, and many of these tractor trailers and lowboys got stuck in the sand along the main supply routes. In an interview, General Lehnert commented on the Marine Corps' shortage of line haul transportation. "The Marine Corps has zero ability to move one single tank. The reason that the tanks today are sitting at 34 percent readiness is that we did not have the same access to super HETs [heavy equipment transporter] and tank haulers that the U.S. Army did, so we drove them 600 to 1,000 miles and we drove the tracks right off them."[19]

Lieutenant Colonel Jorge Ascunce, the officer-in-charge of 1st FSSG's Logistics Movement and Engineering Coordination Center, also recognized the need for line haul transportation assets, a capability he felt the Marine Corps should have, possibly in the reserves, to pull out and use during operations such as this one. Similarly, he discussed the shortage of petroleum, oil, and lubricants trucks that forced the Marines to rely on the Army. Overall, they faced daily challenges with the non-availability of vehicle assets to cover so much ground and so many missions and the organization and communication capabilities. At times, several days would pass with no available vehicles in Transportation Support Group's lot. When asked about lessons learned, Colonel Ascunce jokingly commented that bringing more trucks would have helped.[20]

ual Marines allowed them to accomplish their missions. He specifically complimented the drivers and their conduct during the operations. One of the most inspirational moments of the war for the colonel was the second night of the war, when he went from truck to truck to speak to the Marines, most of whom had been up for days and were driving on less than four hours of sleep. Not a single Marine complained about his or her job or the conditions in which they were working. Their perseverance and dedication were significant, even though their contribution often went unnoticed.[21]

With forces spread out across hundreds of miles of desert, both 1st FSSG and the Marine Logistics Command (MLC) were heavily engaged in distribution efforts. This collaboration between the two commands may not have been detailed in the original operations plan, but with the campaign's exceptional speed and distance, all available distribution assets were required to accomplish the mission. General Usher discussed the need to share the distribution burden during an interview in early April 2003.

> Transportation Support Group's mission has become so broad; both in terms of the area in which they operate and the depth in volume of what we have to push forward, that how we synchronize efforts between the Transportation Support Group and the supporting MLC distribution push, is an area that we're refining now, but certainly was a little more demanding than I had envisioned. . . . we're working to kind of sort out that division of labor.[22]

Similarly, the MLC came to recognize that their role in distribution, which had been somewhat minimized during the original planning with I MEF, would be much broader and extensive. In an interview conducted in early May 2003, General Lehnert, commander of the MLC, reflected on his command's original framework under which he was to develop a plan for his transportation assets. "It was described as 'Get it to the Kuwaiti border, perhaps as much as 50 miles inland . . .' and by 50 miles inland meaning 50 miles into Iraq '. . . and we'll take it from there.'"[23]

Doctrinally, this had been a correct assumption. As the war unfolded, however, everything changed. By the end of March, the Marine Logistics Command Support Detachment-1, which was largely responsible for managing the contracted third country national vehicles and drivers at Camp Coyote in Kuwait, was conducting convoys into Iraq, and 2d Transportation Support Battalion (2d TSB) was routinely sent to Logistics Support Area Viper and beyond. On 31 March, Captain James R. Grooms, executive officer of 2d TSB's Company B, and the battalion operations officer, Major Patrick N. Kelleher, led a convoy carrying critical Health Services Battalion personnel and equipment to Support Area Anderson. There, a critical field medical facility was established to support I MEF forces on the forward edge of the battlefield. Upon arrival at SA Anderson, the battalion's convoy was quickly tasked with a return mission of carrying 128 enemy prisoners back to LSA Viper for interrogation. During the three-day period that the convoy was on the road, it covered a distance of more than 500 miles.

The rapid pace of operations required that quick and decisive actions be taken to ensure that supplies could reach forces in a timely manner. General Lehnert and his transportation commanders conducted continuous mission analysis and altered their original plans to best employ their precious distribution assets.

> We thought a lot about our culminating point. Initially when we were doing our planning, we thought that [it] would be [LSA] Viper, but then later on we moved that . . . point about—and I'd have to check the map—about 100 or 120 miles north of [SA] Anderson. Then the MEF asked us again if we could move further north. We moved the culminating point all the way to [SA] Chesty.[24]

By the first week of April, 2d TSB had moved to LSA Viper and began conducting operational level sustainment and resupply convoys to I MEF units at Anderson, Chesty, Geiger, Edson, and Forward Operating Base Fenway. Far exceeding their originally agreed upon responsibilities, 2d TSB logged nearly 1.2 million miles during the first 30 days of conflict, reaching more than 300 miles further into Iraq than originally planned.

One of the many innovations developed during Operation Iraqi Freedom came from Captain Michael F. Olness of 2d Transportation Support Battalion. He developed an innovative web-based application to track the battalion personnel, vehicles, fueling assets, communications, and critical information requirements.[25] The "Big Board," as it was known, provided the commander with a capacity readout of his battlefield distribution capabilities. At a glance, he and the higher headquarters of the Marine Logistics Command could not only view their asset availability, but also monitor the progress of convoys across time.[26]

With both 1st FSSG and the Marine Logistics Command conducting numerous large convoys across

Photo by MSgt Edward D. Kniery, USMC

Light armored vehicles are staged in preparation for providing security to a combat service support convoy in Iraq.

great distances, security had to be taken seriously. I MEF's focus on operational momentum had resulted in 1st Marine Division's concentrated efforts to rapidly close in on Baghdad, often breaking contact with smaller elements of enemy forces along the way. While these company- or smaller-sized enemy units were not a major threat to I MEF's overall operation, they caused problems for rear areas and harassed slow-moving convoys. From the commencement of hostilities in March, convoys routinely came under sniper fire, as well as small, organized attacks from enemy forces. In 1st FSSG, the Transportation Support Group (TSG) mitigated this problem by establishing a convoy control company, specifically designed to manage the security, as well as the command and control, of all convoy movement. From receipt of the mission order to completion of the movement, the convoy control elements—ranging from team to platoon size—managed the traffic. The drivers from 6th Motor Transport Battalion were responsible for the administration of the convoy loads, but it was the convoy control team that focused its efforts on suppressing any hostile actions to ensure the convoy's safe arrival at its destination. One of the benefits of this concept was the continuity of convoy commanders and teams. Despite this, though, they faced many challenges in their mission, to include a shortage of communications assets, civilian contracted vehicles not equipped to keep up with Marine convoys, and numerous weather and distance factors.[27]

Similar to the TSG's concept of using convoy control teams, the Marine Logistics Command convoys were augmented with additional security elements of the 2d Military Police (MP) Battalion. Reconfiguring their equipment and personnel to support the convoy security requirements, the members of the MP Battalion escorted more than 1,400 convoys, coordinating with both U.S. Army and British military police to maintain the overall security of main supply routes in both Kuwait and Iraq and sustain operational throughput in especially congested and unstable areas.[28]

In the first week of the war, 2d TSB's headquarters and service company commander Captain Marta M. DeVries had been tasked to lead a route reconnaissance in search of an alternate road bypassing Safwan. There had been continuous low-level threats from civilians who laid minor obstacles in the road in an effort to stall the convoys and steal from the vehicles. The route reconnaissance took two days and ultimately resulted in a safer bypass route that Coalition forces continued to use throughout the war. The MLC's intelligence section recognized that useful intelligence data could be gathered, not only during

Photo by MSgt Edward D. Kniery, USMC
A KC-130 taxies at Jalibah Airfield, LSA Viper, Iraq.

route reconnaissance missions, but also during convoys. Seeking to address security challenges as well as enhance intelligence gathering, the section implemented an intelligence collection and reporting system that employed truck drivers, military police Marines, convoy commanders, and other members of the MLC. This system was appropriately named "TruckInt." Modeled after the aviation community's pilot briefing and debriefing process, this intelligence tool was incorporated into the mission planning and standard operating procedures of all 2d FSSG units conducting convoys. There were two main components in the process. First, prior to a convoy mission, drivers and passengers would receive a briefing from an intelligence analyst, consisting of weather forecasts, weather effects analysis, an updated enemy activity report, and a trafficability assessment of primary and alternate routes. In addition to this standard briefing, convoy members would also be given intelligence requirements to include in their subsequent debriefing upon their return. The second component was the extensive debrief. Through their observations, interactions with locals, and contact with any enemy forces, convoy members would provide information to intelligence analysts, who would in turn, create formal intelligence reports. These reports were submitted to all units within the MLC, as well as the headquarters of Marine Forces Central Command, I Marine Expeditionary Force, the 377th Theater Support Command, and the Coalition Forces Land Component Command. As a result of these reports, the Marine Logistics Command was able to divert convoys to alternate routes when necessary, fine-tune its convoy defense posture, and continuously ensure that resupply missions were successfully executed.[29]

With the nonstop stream of convoys traveling hundreds of miles through harsh desert conditions, vehicles, equipment, and personnel were all pushed to their limits. General Lehnert noted though, that while Marines, particularly young 22- to 25-year-old Marines, were extraordinarily resilient, he was more worried about the ability of the equipment to hold up during the high operational tempo.[30] As a result, continuous and effective maintenance was never more critical. Throughout Operation Iraqi Freedom, the MLC exercised a program of maintenance to maximize timely response and full-range repair capability. At the unit level, Task Force Pegasus implemented a system that had a team of mechanics execute bumper-to-bumper maintenance while drivers slept between frequent convoy operations. This approach, which involved extensive corrective as well as preventive maintenance, kept the MLC readiness rate over 90 percent throughout the war.

Hantush: The Attack Resumes

As 1st FSSG continued to stretch its arc of sustainment across the battlefield, Combat Service Support Group 11 concentrated its efforts on supporting 1st Marine Division's immediate needs. While the majority of CSSG-11 and Combat Service Support Battalion 10 remained at Repair and Replenishment Point 24 until 1 April, the battalion's tactical command post and CSSG-11 forward departed on 31 March to conduct a leader's reconnaissance to the north near the town of Hantush. This site had been identified by both CSSG-11 and Marine Wing Support Group 37 during planning for a potential highway runway, and just south of Highway 17, Repair and Replenishment Point 25 was established. As they arrived in the area, Marines from CSSG-11 and CSSB-10 assumed the responsibility for security in the Hantush area. As a result, Colonel Pomfret received the nickname "Mayor of Hantush."[31] Elements of MWSG-37 and 1st Marine Division were nearby, converting a portion of the highway into a runway that would be used for both fixed- and rotary-wing aircraft. Using armored earthmovers, the division's combat engineers knocked down light poles and swept out guardrails to allow for the use of the highway as a runway. This would be the first opportunity for logistical resupply by air. With limited space, CSSB-10 used creativity and flexibility to fit most of its combat service support capability in this "lakeside property," marked by numerous stagnant irrigation ponds.[32]

On 2 April, as 1st Marine Division resumed its attack after the operational pause, CSSG-11 was positioned at Hantush to support the division's fight against the Baghdad Infantry Division. Combat Service Support Company 111 moved north on Highway 7, south of al-Hayy and continued to resupply Regimental Combat Team 1 in al-Kut. Combat Service Support Company 115, the lead element for Regimental Combat Team 5 (RCT-5) logistics, moved

Courtesy of 8th ESB

Marines from Bridge Companies A and C of 8th Engineer Support Battalion construct an improved ribbon bridge across the Tigris River to enable 5th Marine Regiment's movement toward Baghdad.

northeast along Highway 27 toward the Saddam Canal, where it set up a hasty repair and replenishment point.[33] As RCT-5 continued its attack toward an-Numaniyah, it became apparent that the single-lane bridge crossing on the Saddam Canal would not be sufficient for the regiment's lengthy convoys. Combat Service Support Company 117 moved north past ad-Diwaniyah, continuing to resupply Regimental Combat Team 7, and later that night, arrived at a location near an-Numaniyah Airfield, just south of the Tigris River. The next day, following directly behind RCT-7, the company crossed the river.[34]

8th Engineer Support Battalion's (8th ESB) Crossing Area Engineer-1, led by Major Timothy B. Seamon, worked with elements of RCT-5 to find a site suitable for constructing an alternate crossing. Late in the day, Bridge Company A built an improved ribbon, or assault float bridge across the Saddam Canal. It was built at night against light enemy opposition, but the greater challenge for the engineers was maneuvering their heavy equipment over steep entrance and exit banks. Almost simultaneous to the construction of the alternate crossing on the Saddam Canal, another bridging requirement emerged. The very next day, 8th ESB was called upon to construct a bridge across the Tigris west of an-Numaniyah. This crossing supported elements of 5th Marine Regiment and served as an alternate crossing site for the remainder of 1st Marine Division in the event existing bridges in an-Numaniyah were destroyed by enemy forces. Still fatigued from the previous night's bridge emplacement, Bridge Company A initiated the building of a 508-foot improved ribbon bridge and was later reinforced by Bridge Company C, which completed the bridge emplacement that night.[35]

In the early hours on 3 April, after the division units had cleared an-Numaniyah, CSSB-10 packed up and departed Repair and Replenishment Point 25. Just west of an-Numaniyah, the battalion established Repair and Replenishment Point 19, a Quick Mart–type roadside stop to provide fuel and other needed supplies to passing units. An otherwise routine and uneventful operation for CSSB-10, which had been moving and setting up at unparalleled rates of speed, Repair and Replenishment Point 19 would be remembered by most as the location where they heard the news about the death of one of their own. Private First Class Chad E. Bales died and several Marines were injured when a troop-carrying MK48 logistics vehicle system collided with a seven-ton truck. Although CSSB-10 left the area less than 24 hours later, a small detachment, led by CSSB-10 executive officer, Major Michael C. Varicak, remained to continue conducting the critical refueling mission. This repair and replenishment point was later designated Support Area Chesty, one of the two main support areas providing general logistical sustainment to all of I MEF. Elements of CSSB-10 were now spread between Repair and Replenishment Points 19, 24, and 25 due to continuing requirements to support elements of 1st Marine Division and turnover issues with CSSB-12 at Support Area Anderson.[36]

Chapter 6

Taking Baghdad and Tikrit (4–22 April 2003)

By 3 April, Regimental Combat Teams 1 (RCT-1) and 7 (RCT-7) had defeated the Baghdad Republican Guard Division at al-Kut and waited on the northern bank of the Tigris River for the order to attack into Baghdad. Meanwhile, Regimental Combat Team 5 (RCT-5) continued to attack west to a town on the southern bank of the Tigris River called al-Aziziyah. In addition to housing the headquarters of the II Republican Guard Corp's Anti-Armor Regiment, the town held bridges, which were key logistics points for the enemy. The enemy resistance was fierce, but the combination of 2d Tank Battalion's overwhelming firepower and 3d Battalion, 5th Marines' tenacity in clearing the town gradually wore the enemy down.[1]

Meanwhile, the support companies in Combat Service Support Group 11 (CSSG-11) focused their efforts on resupplying their regimental combat teams for the imminent attack into Baghdad. Combat Service Support Company 111 obtained fuel, water, and rations from Combat Service Support Battalion 12 at Support Area Anderson, after offloading Iraqi prisoners. They proceeded through an-Numaniyah and established a repair and replenishment point to support RCT-1. Combat Service Support Company 115 crossed the Tigris River and traveled up Highway 6 to establish a roadside refueling station. The following night, they displaced further north, but were held up after just 20 miles due to resistance along the route. Combat Service Support Company 117 continued to follow in trace of RCT-7 along Highway 6.[2]

While elements of Combat Service Support Battalion 10 (CSSB-10) continued to provide support at Repair and Replenishment Points 19 and 25, the remainder of Lieutenant Colonel Robert K. Weinkle's battalion moved north, passing through RCT-7's vehicles parked along both sides of Highway 6. Near the city of al-Aziziyah, where RCT-5 had just cleared out enemy forces, CSSB-10 established another repair and replenishment point, this time in an urban environment. Just north of the Tigris River, Repair and Replenishment Point 22 was set up in an abandoned service station along the highway. There were many remnants of the fighting that had occurred less than 24 hours prior to the establishment of the facility, including burning buildings, destroyed equipment, abandoned weapons, and curious civilians. In the meantime, the Marines located and collected large quantities of ordnance, which included mortar tubes and rounds, recoilless rifles, grenades, and large caches of small arms. These were identified to follow-on elements for destruction.

Despite the fact that his battalion was now spread across multiple repair and replenishment points, Colonel Weinkle's Marines managed to provide much needed support of rations, fuel, and ammunition to several division units. Often, this resupply occurred "just in time." Additionally, during the four days at Repair and Replenishment Point 22, maintenance

The Marines of CSSB-10 labor to establish a repair and replenishment point outside of Baghdad.
Courtesy of CSSB-10

Support Area Chesty, a vast area of barren desert, is located outside the city of An Numaniyah, Iraq.

contact teams executed risky recovery missions with minimal security. One team was even able to secure and retrieve a damaged M1A1 Abrams tank. In another operation, military police and mortuary affairs teams deployed to recover remains from an AH-1 Cobra helicopter crash, which occurred in close proximity to CSSB-10 vehicles.[3]

On 5 April, CSSG-11 followed the main element of 1st Marine Division to a suburb east of Baghdad and conducted reconnaissance of an area in the vicinity of Sarabadi Airfield and Highway 6. CSSB-10 also moved to this area, west of al-Aziziyah, and established Repair and Replenishment Point 23 in an agricultural complex previously used as an Iraqi military command post. After clearing Iraqi looters from the complex, they occupied the numerous abandoned houses and buildings for several different functions, including a military police operations center, post office, Iraqi prisoner holding facility, ammunition supply point, maintenance bays, and a motor pool. In addition to their combat service support functions, the battalion liaised with the local civilian populace. Members of the 3d Civil Affairs Group, who were attached to CSSB-10, interacted with local civilians in an effort to identify local resources such as diesel fuel. The civilians were also forthcoming about enemy activity and reported a warehouse that supposedly stored antiaircraft guns among several other types of weapons. After this report was confirmed, the civil affairs team secured the building and awaited the arrival of explosive ordnance disposal Marines, who destroyed the cache.[4]

Buildup of Support Area Chesty

On 4 April, Combat Service Support Battalion 12's (CSSB-12) command element, advanced party, and Combat Service Support Company 121 ended their stay at Support Area Anderson and departed for Support Area (SA) Chesty, near the town of an-Numaniyah. The location, just over 100 miles outside of Baghdad, was chosen during a leader's reconnaissance the previous day, in which Lieutenant Colonel Adrian W. Burke took a small team to look at a couple of sites near Repair and Replenishment Point 19 and 1st Marine Division's headquarters. Centrally located between the 1st Marine Division's main axis of advance on Baghdad and the Task Force Tarawa area of operations along Highway 7, the site chosen for SA Chesty provided the much-needed general support to sustain operations in and around the capital city. Where SA Chesty's geographic location was an advantage, its environmental features presented a major challenge. The support area was largely a vast area of barren land, with scarce infrastructure. The lack of buildings and pavement, coupled with continuously blowing sand and dirt, challenged the Marines in their efforts to establish large lots and staging areas, as well as manage the nonstop flow of convoys in and out of the area.

Also located at SA Chesty, Forward Resuscitative

Photo by MSgt Edward D. Kniery, USMC

A convoy of seven-ton trucks moves ammunition to forward units near Baghdad.

Surgical System 2 and Shock Trauma Platoon 8, which were now attached to CSSB-12, set up their equipment to provide level-two medical support to incoming casualties. Additionally, a detachment of over 300 engineers congregated at SA Chesty to perform a variety of engineering missions. Compiled from several engineer units and led by Major Todd D. Hook of 6th Engineer Support Battalion, this group, internally known as Task Force Hook, accomplished several critical tasks over the course of several days, which included building a 1.2-million-gallon fuel storage facility and a 200,000-gallon water production and storage site.[5] Just as Combat Service Support Battalion 18 had set up Logistics Support Area Viper to support I MEF's initial push through southern Iraq, CSSB-12 now established SA Chesty, a position 300 miles from its origin in Kuwait, to support operations near Baghdad. This would be the northernmost support area established to provide general support for I MEF and would greatly impact 1st Marine Division's fight in Baghdad.*

Midnight Run to Baghdad

On 5 April, on its first full day at Support Area Chesty, Combat Service Support Battalion 12 was tasked with an emergency resupply of more than 1,000 artillery projectiles, powder, and fuses to support a recent change in 11th Marines' fire support requirements in and around Baghdad. The regiment's mission changed from an open terrain fight where dual-purpose improved conventional munitions would have a greater impact on area targets to an urban fight that required the more precise high-explosive rounds. Because of the dispersion of transportaion assets across the battlefield, CSSB-12 recognized that they would have to form a convoy using their own organic assets.[6] In essence, CSSB-12, a general support organization, would assemble and execute a direct support resupply convoy. The destination for delivery was over 110 miles away, through what still remained uncleared enemy territory. Enemy regular and Fedayeen forces were reported to have been bypassed and were operating in the area. Colonel Burke led the convoy himself.

> With our own assets, without being really plugged into [CSSB] 10 yet, because they were so far-leaning as well, we were able to put together our own convoy [and] a security package inside of an hour, and then travel the 110 miles from this site to where the artillery battalions were firing from inside of six hours, through "Indian country." We put 40 Marines, 15 vehicles, and 1,000 artillery rounds at risk to make that run to meet a division "no kidding, we need it now" requirement. . . . We took fuses, powder, and round mixes so they could put the stuff right on the gun line.[7]

At 0400 the next morning, Colonel Burke's convoy reached its destination, just eight miles outside of Baghdad. CSSB-12's mantra during this operation was to "lean forward."[8] Doing exactly that, the battalion conducted a "just-in-time" delivery of munitions that

---

* Support Area Daly, which was located further north and closer to Baghdad, was planned but never occupied by a sizeable combat service support force

proved to be critical for regimental fire missions the next morning.

Maintenance and Ingenuity

Originally located at Camp Coyote in Kuwait, Combat Service Support Battalion 12's Maintenance Company, commanded by Major Ronald W. Sablan, had begun preparing to move weeks before the start of the war, and as that time got closer, they had systematically started shutting down their capabilities. As the company's convoys moved from Kuwait to Logistics Support Area Viper and eventually Support Area Anderson, the maintenance Marines continued to fix equipment. At Support Area Anderson for just a few days, they were given the order to move to Support Area Chesty. En route to their destination, Major Sablan's 91-vehicle convoy, which was escorted by light armored reconnaissance vehicles, was ambushed at two locations in the vicinity of the Saddam Canal. The Saddam Canal Bridge, a natural chokepoint along Route 27, caused the convoy to slow down and left some vehicles in the kill zone. Taking enemy fire from both sides of the road, members of the convoy returned fire and maneuvered through the ambush as quickly as possible. Sustaining minor vehicle damage only, the CSSB-12 convoy arrived at its destination with no casualties.

Once they arrived at SA Chesty, the maintenance company focused on equipment retrieval and providing service through contact teams. The MEF had designed an approach to handle unserviceable equipment. Designated maintenance collection points were set up for units to leave broken equipment behind, but unfortunately, these locations were not used, and most broken vehicles and equipment were left on the side of the road. The maintenance company did not have enough retrieval equipment to spread across the battlefield. Another major challenge the unit faced in sending out contact teams centered on security issues; their approach was to deploy with heavy security and intimidate or deter the enemy from attacking by showing an overwhelming amount of firepower.[9]

Similar to the maintenance companies within 1st FSSG, 2d Maintenance Battalion had immediately begun providing intermediate level maintenance support once they arrived in theater. The battalion was led by Lieutenant Colonel Brent P. Goddard, a former Field Supply Maintenance Analysis Office leader and executive officer of the combat service support element during Operation Uphold Democracy in Haiti. Through both camp-based maintenance support and mobile contact teams, they attempted to repair equipment as close to the customer as possible. As a result of this customer-focused approach, Colonel Goddard's Marines eventually dispatched nearly 1,200 maintenance contact teams throughout the Iraqi theater of operations. This forward concept of operations and the battalion's philosophy of "maintain" versus "repair" enabled the maintenance Marines to overcome a variety of challenges, which included poor communications, limited system support, lack of field maintenance facilities, and a shortage of repair parts.[10] With only half the personnel during OIF compared to peacetime operations, 2d Maintenance Battalion attained higher repair rates, closing more than 5,500 work orders on nearly 7,000 principle end items. Additionally, repair cycle times were shortened by nearly 200 percent from garrison metrics.[11]

Even as the operational tempo reached its peak during the war, the Marines continued to demonstrate creativity and ingenuity. In one instance, they used a stripped humvee to test engines, transmissions, and drive trains; in another, they built a dunk tank to test radiators and tires.[12] Ultimately, the maintenance Marines understood that while not glamorous in the traditional warfighting sense, their roles were critical in supporting the overall mission. Major Devon C. Young, executive officer of the battalion, described what most commanders in a support organization recognize in their Marines at one time or another. "All the Marines wanted to be up on the frontlines; they wanted to be up north, storming Baghdad. . . . I think the majority of them realized their role here was just as important as the Marines up front. Because everybody has their little piece of the puzzle they have to do."[13]

'Please Don't Let Me Run Out'

From the start of the war, there was perhaps no type of supply more critical than ammunition. Without it, the amazing speed and momentum accomplished by ground forces would have been pointless. Even before the war started, the criticality of ammunition was evident to all, down to the individual Marine rifleman. One Marine in particular, when asked by the I MEF ammunition officer if he needed anything else, simply said, "Sir, please don't let me run out." The ammunition detachment of Combat Service Support Battalion 12, led by Chief Warrant Officer–2 Bradley S. Baggiano, heard this story and adopted the Marine's plea as a constant reminder to his own Marines of their critical mission.[14] Doctrinally, their mission was to build up ammunition supply points, stock and issue ammunition to units on the ground.

Execution of this fairly straightforward mission, however, was met with numerous challenges. Poor weather conditions, continuously changing requirements, and limited communications, material handling, and transportation assets all made their job more difficult. Eventually ending up at Support Area Chesty, the detachment continued 24-hour operations to overcome these challenges and fulfill their mission. More importantly, though, they worked tirelessly to ensure that every Marine rifleman never ran out.

While CSSB-12's ammunition detachment dealt with tactical challenges, the ammunition detachment within Marine Logistics Command faced a whole set of other problems. Working at the wholesale level, Chief Warrant Officer–2 Terry G. Norris, the Marine Logistics Command's ammunition officer, had the responsibility of getting the ammunition to all of the 1st FSSG support areas. Relying heavily on the Army for support, he faced a shortage of ammunition, both in quantity and type, even before the war began. Original planning had estimated a requirement of supplying only two regimental combat teams. This grew into four regimental combat teams, and was increased by a number of unanticipated units, such as three engineer support battalions and several Marine wing support squadrons. These units, like elements of 1st Marine Division and Task Force Tarawa, would be near the front lines and moving far forward on the battlefield. Once the war started, poor visibility of battlefield distribution and limited reporting left Chief Warrant Officer Norris and his Marines in the dark on what they should be pushing forward. In the end, there was enough ammunition; as many individuals had often described other aspects of logistics support during Operation Iraqi Freedom, "it wasn't pretty," but the mission was accomplished and no Marine went without.

A Bridge Under Fire

On the eve of 1st Marine Division's imminent attack into Baghdad, 8th Engineer Support Battalion (8th ESB) was tasked to locate possible bridge crossings on the Diyala River. Lieutenant Colonel Niel E. Nelson, commanding officer of 8th ESB and force crossing engineer for 1st Marine Division, directed the efforts of his Marines, as well as reconnaissance elements from both Regimental Combat Teams 1 and 5, to locate all potential crossing points to the northeast of Baghdad. However, after 24 hours of intense route reconnaissance, no suitable approaches to the crossing sites had been found. All of the bridges crossing the Diyala River to the eastern side of Baghdad had been damaged to some extent. If these bridges were not fixed or suitable alternative routes built, elements of 1st Marine Division would have had to travel 35 kilometers north to another crossing (provided that the bridge there was still intact), cross into Baghdad and then travel in from the north. Colonel Nelson determined five locations for bridge emplacements to the southeast of Baghdad, just north of the confluence of the Diyala and Tigris Rivers, and it was decided that three crossings would be completed. One medium girder bridge would be placed overtop a bridge on Highway 6 that had been destroyed by the enemy earlier in the week, and two improved ribbon or assault float bridges would be put in place to cross military traffic only.[16] Major Thomas M. Pratt, operations officer for 8th ESB commented on the challenges the engineers faced at this particular crossing site:

> Doctrinally it says, "the RCT crosses the water obstacle and secures the bridgehead line." That was not able to happen because of the banks on the other side of the river; the tracks couldn't swim. So essentially, we had to build the bridges with two dismounted companies providing security for us. It's something that you always think you might do [but] you

Streamlined Ordering

At the tactical level, CSSG-11 had developed a system in coordination with the 1st Marine Division ammunition officer to streamline and simplify on-call emergency resupplies of ammunition. A detailed listing of common ammunition requirements was compiled and broken down into pallet-sized groupings. Each set of items, whether for an artillery battalion, an infantry company, or a particular weapons section, was then assigned a specific name, such as "sledgehammer" or "cannonball." When a unit needed a resupply of ammunition, it could pass its requirement through radio transmission with a simple call, such as "two cannonballs" or "three sledgehammers." CSSG-11 would immediately know what was requested and had the pre-palletized items ready to deliver. Additionally, the list of these ammunition packages was provided to both CSSB-12 and CSSB-18, which were able to use them to reduce their preparation time.[15]

84   COMBAT SERVICE SUPPORT

Photo by MSgt Edward D. Kniery, USMC

A medium girder bridge, built by Marines of the 8th Engineer Support Battalion, spans the Diyala River. The original bridge leading into Baghdad, had been destroyed by Iraqi forces.

The commanding general of 1st FSSG, BGen Edward G. Usher III (left), and the commanding officer of 8th Engineer Support Battalion, Col Niel E. Nelson, stand near the medium girder bridge that the battalion built crossing into Baghdad.

Photo by LtCol Melissa D. Mihocko, USMCR

really aren't prepared to go out there and build bridges by hand, under . . . direct and indirect fire.[17]

Once the crossing locations were determined, Colonel Nelson and his assistant force crossing engineer, Captain Brian E. Gard, split the remaining bridge assets and personnel into three bridge crossing units, supported by engineer maintenance assets under the commands of CAE-1 and CAE-5. The force crossing engineer command element coordinated the complicated maneuver of allocating assets and personnel, and coordinating their night movements for simultaneous bridge emplacements. The three bridges that 8th ESB's Bridge Company C, elements of Bridge Company A, and the Army's 459th Multi-Role Bridge Company emplaced across the Diyala River were completed within 36 hours and enabled two regimental combat teams, Regimental Combat Team 1 and 7, to cross into Baghdad. This southeastern approach into the capital city was critical to sustaining the momentum of 1st Marine Division's attack on Baghdad.[18]

Miraculously, the engineers suffered no fatalities during the building of these bridges. One Army soldier, however, was injured from a close-range explosion of an enemy artillery shell, suffering a concussion and some temporary hearing loss.

Taking the Capital

On 6 April, Combat Service Support Group 11 units were positioned to support the 1st Marine Division's cordoning of Baghdad. Combat Service Support Company 115 (CSSC-115) moved to a location known as "The General's Crossroads." Two dead Iraqis had been found at this site; one was later identified as the chief of staff of the Special Republican Guard. While setting up a repair and replenishment point, CSSC-115 received incoming mortar fire. Meanwhile, Combat Service Support Company 117 (CSSC-117) established their position at a former Saddam Fedayeen training camp, where they uncovered large arms caches. At this time, all CSSG-11 trucks were dispatched to Support Area Chesty to support an emergency resupply of artillery ammunition for 11th Marine Regiment.[19]

The next day, as 1st Marine Division was entering Baghdad, the Marines of Combat Service Support Battalion 10 once again departed for their next location, leaving just a small contingent at Repair and Replenishment Point 23. As the regimental combat teams continued to secure the city and surrounding

Marines of 8th Engineer Support Battalion built an assault float bridge across the Diyala River while under enemy fire. The engineers first built a pontoon bridge, then used bridging equipment to connect the remnants of the original bridge, which had been destroyed by enemy forces.

Courtesy of 8th ESB

Courtesy of CSSB-10

Several combat service support elements set up at CSSB-10's Repair and Replenishment Point 26, just on the outskirts of Baghdad. Previously a Republican Guard maintenance facility, the existing buildings provided ample space for the battalion's operations center, as well as maintenance and supply bays.

areas, CSSB-10 established Repair and Replenishment Point 26 in a Republican Guard maintenance facility. Located just on the outskirts of Baghdad, this proved to be a much more efficient combat service support location, as it provided ideal access to the city while remaining distant enough to avoid its congestion and associated force protection concerns. Elements of 6th Engineer Support Battalion and the Seabees also chose to set up at this location, which eventually became Support Area Daly. Unlike previous repair and replenishment points, where units were forced to set up in the sand, this site had ample concrete surfaces for maintenance bays and supply storage. It offered several existing buildings in which elements of the battalion were able to operate. The main building provided an excellent structure to house the combat service support operations center and company command posts. The Materiel Readiness Company, which included both supply and maintenance, was able to set up in actual maintenance bays.

A nearby landing strip, Salman Pak, which had just been abandoned by Iraqi forces earlier in the morning, provided the Marines a much-needed capability to have supplies flown in by KC-130s and helicopters. Piles of dirt and debris that had been strewn across the runway in an effort to prohibit the runway's use by Coalition forces, were quickly cleared by CSSG-11. Given the name Repair and Replenishment Point 26A, the runway was only 30 minutes away from the main repair and replenishment point. It was maintained by a small element of Marines from both CSSG-11 and CSSB-10. Post exchange supplies and a disbursing capability were brought forward to Repair and Replenishment Point 26, allowing the Marines in 1st Marine Division their first opportunity for much needed health and comfort items, as well as a welcome resupply of mail, sundry packs, meal enhancements, and fruit.

The facility was located just outside Baghdad, the center of fighting, and CSSB-10 experienced nightly attacks by enemy sniper fire. Despite this, the atmosphere at Repair and Replenishment Point 26 was much more permissive than previous repair and replenishment points, and focus began to shift to supporting the impending security and stabilization mission. While maintaining their ongoing combat service support mission, the Marines also sought out opportunities to conduct civil-military operations. Out in town, civil affairs Marines searched for new and innovative ways to draw captured fuel out of abandoned tankers, while maintenance contact teams were busy recovering more than 30 of 1st Marine Division's abandoned tracked and wheeled vehicles. At the same time, the battalion shared water produced by its reverse osmosis water purification units with Iraqi civilians. Prisoners continued to flow into the custody of the military police, including several high-ranking Iraqi military officials. Medical personnel in the battalion put their skills to good use, treating both Marine casualties and the seemingly endless numbers of Iraqi civilians seeking medical care.[20]

CSSG-11's forward command post set up with 1st Marine Division Forward command post in the stadium within Baghdad's Al Rasheed Airfield. Interestingly, the stadium scoreboard read "Iraq–0, USA–2." Also, in a museum at the airfield, displays showed mannequins dressed as U.S. soldiers surrendering; uniforms and equipment displayed were from the Vietnam era.[21] For three days while the small contingent of CSSG-11 forward was located inside the capital city, the combat service support companies conducted resupply convoys from outside the city. Initially, the crossings on the Diyala River did not allow for their large convoys to pass, but by 10 April, CSSC-111, CSSC-115, and CSSC-117 had moved and established repair and replenishment points inside Baghdad. The following day, CSSG-11's main element relocated to the center of Baghdad and established itself at an Iraqi security compound.[22]

Meanwhile, during the first week of April, Combat Service Support Battalion 22 (CSSB-22) moved from an-Nasiriyah to ad-Diwaniyah. On 7 April, Task Force Tarawa was given a mission to attack east from Qalat Sikar to al-Amarah in order to destroy the Iraqi 10th Armored Division. CSSB-22 split into two elements. The forward element moved to support units at Qalat Sikar; the rear remained at ad-Diwaniyah. Two days later, it was apparent that the Iraqis vacated their positions, and the attack was called off. The following day, when several units within Task Force Tarawa moved to an-Numaniyah, the battalion's rear element followed suit. On 11 April, its forward element joined the remainder of the battalion at SA Chesty.[23]

Increasing Fuel Demands

The demand for fuel grew daily as the war waged on. To accommodate this need, 6th Engineer Support Battalion (6th ESB) was tasked to install a second hose-reel system from Logistics Support Area Viper to Logistics Support Area Cedar, an Army fuel base in Iraq. This job, requiring an additional 27 miles of hose reel and eight booster stations, would not only supplement Marine forces, but all Coalition forces fighting in Iraq. By 10 April, the second tactical fuel system was completed and operational. The Army was so grateful for the additional support that in return they loaned two companies to move fuel for Marine forces. Their own Inland Petroleum Distribution System, which was based on rigid metallic pipe, had required extensive engineering work and more time to implement. In a conversation with some Army engineers, the battalion commander, Lieutenant Colonel Roger R. Machut, was told that even the civilian contractor from the company who built the system thought that the Army would be better off replacing their system with that of the Marine Corps'.[24]

After the second hose reel's installation, Marines from 6th ESB continued north to establish bulk liquid storage and production at Repair and Replenishment Point 26, which had been designated as Support Area Daly. Major Hook, who had completed ground engineering requirements for bulk liquid operations at Support Area Chesty, advanced to Repair and Replenishment Point 26, where he and his Marines built a 300,000-gallon fuel site and a 100,000-gallon water site. In addition, the engineers constructed a 48-man shower facility within the city limits of Baghdad that was used to provide showers for Marine Corps ground combat units.[25]

Recovery at An-Nasiriyah

Throughout the war, maintenance units conducted numerous recovery operations, repeatedly hauling disabled and damaged equipment from the battlefield to safety. No recovery mission was more arduous than the recovery of vehicles, equipment, and human remains from an-Nasiriyah on 10 April. Three weeks earlier, the Coalition had suffered its deadliest battle of the war thus far, and the emotional trauma was still fresh in everyone's mind. To perform this difficult task, a maintenance recovery team from Combat Service Support Company 121 (CSSC-121) linked up with a mortuary affairs team from Logistics Support Area Viper. Led by Captain Timothy M. Cooley, the maintenance team was tasked with the dangerous recovery of the damaged vehicles and equipment from the site of an amphibious assault vehicle explosion. "We had to pry the MK19 out of the turret weapons station and as we're doing that the round that was halfway down the barrel actually came out, lucky for us it did not explode and EOD came and retrieved the grenade."[26] Meanwhile, the mortuary affairs Marines had the responsibility of searching for human remains or personal effects of the casualties. Sifting through the charred rubble, Marines searched desperately for anything that could help identify the victims of the tragedy. Crushed and broken dog tags, while not an absolute proof of identity, were considered a precious find. The mission took several days and was conducted under tense conditions, as mobs of local Iraqis were assembling nearby to watch. While the crowd was not initially

Photo by MSgt Edward D. Kniery, USMC

Maintenance Marines from CSSB-18 retrieve an AAV destroyed in the battle of An Nasiryah while mortuary affairs Marines search for evidence of human remains.

hostile toward the Marines, Lieutenant Colonel John M. Cassady, officer in charge of the mortuary affairs detachment, noted that some of the locals began throwing stones at them as they departed the area.*27

Shifting Focus: Beans, Bullets, and Band-Aids to Mail, Money, and Morale

As fighting began to decrease, the focus of combat service support began to shift. Food, water, fuel, and ammunition had been the main focus of effort during combat operations, but by the first week of April, 1st FSSG recognized that it could simultaneously push various "services" towards the frontlines. In past conflicts, post exchange and mail services had always been a "nice to have;" mission accomplishment had never been dependent on the success of providing such luxuries. During Operation Iraqi Freedom, however, this luxury was recognized as being value added. Chief Warrant Officer–2 Carlos L. Holt, the 1st FSSG post exchange officer, believed that providing exchange services to the Marines during operations should be viewed as a "force multiplier."28 They made supplies available to the troops that helped them perform their mission, and the impact of the PX support on the morale of the Marines was ten-fold, especially with the products in the area of health and hygiene.

On 5 April, 1st FSSG opened what was determined to be the "first PX in enemy territory" at Logistics Support Area Viper. Two approaches to providing exchange services were used. An actual exchange facility was established in the field and 1st FSSG warfighting express services teams, which in-

---
* Unlike the doctrine of U.S. Army mortuary affairs, which does not typically have its soldiers deploy to an area until it has been secured, Marine Corps mortuary affairs executed recoveries in both permissive and hostile environments. Timeliness was critical for several reasons, but perhaps the most personally motivated reason was the idea of protecting the remains of fallen Marines from being desecrated at the hands of enemy forces. (LtCol John M. Cassady, USMCR, Maj Jefferson L. Kaster, USMCR, and CWO-4 Cheryl G. Ites, USMCR, "Caring for the Fallen–Mortuary Affairs in Operation Iraqi Freedom," *Proceedings* Apr04, 38)

Photo by MSgt Edward D. Kniery, USMC
1st Force Service Support Group opens the first PX in Iraq at LSA Viper.

cluded exchange, postal, legal, and disbursing services were also dispatched to the frontlines. These teams were sent out in response to a commander's request during an operational pause or to areas that were just slightly to the rear of combat operations.[29]

As exchange services emerged in various locations across the battlefield, it was obvious that 1st FSSG would need to provide another resource to Marines in the field—money. In the rear, the FSSG's disbursing units were able to set up banks, affording Marines the opportunity to obtain cash. During the war, however, disbursing agents did not have the luxury of setting up a stationary facility to which Marines could come; they literally had to reach out across the battlefield to their customers. One disbursing agent, Sergeant Monica E. Eroh, was based at Support Area Chesty where a post exchange and postal facility were located, but she spent a good deal of her time going out to various units in the field. On these frequent and often dangerous excursions, she carried the money on her body, using either moneybags or safes. Although the sergeant appeared as any typical Marine carrying a backpack full of gear, she often had up to $250,000 in cash strapped to her back. Armed and extremely cautious, Sergeant Eroh had to be escorted by a Marine guard wherever she went. During the war, millions of dollars were paid to Marines in I MEF, and the process of accountability was impeccable.[30]

Extended Operations: Stretching the Logistics Chain to Tikrit

On 11 April, 1st Marine Division organized a task force to secure Tikrit, the hometown of Saddam Hussein. Tucked up in the northern area of Iraq, this city was thought to be a key area for fleeing Iraqi military officials, and the task force's goal was to eliminate the city as a possible place of refuge for Saddam loyalists, as well as a source of instability. Similar to Second Lieutenant Presley N. O'Bannon's epic desert journey in 1805, Task Force Tripoli would stretch Marine forces another 112 miles beyond Baghdad. Comprised of elements from three light armored reconnaissance battalions, an artillery battalion (5th Battalion, 11th Marines), a force reconnaissance company, and the division forward command post, the task force, commanded by Brigadier General John F. Kelly, was built for speed.

With the majority of Combat Service Support Group 11 and its combat service support companies located in Baghdad and being resupplied by Combat Service Support Battalion 10 at nearby Repair and Replenishment Point 26, the provision of combat service support for 1st Marine Division was now in place. For Task Force Tripoli, CSSG-11 had to construct a new company capable of providing combat service support to a task force of 1,300 Marines and sailors. Led by Major Michael J. Callanan, CSSG-11's operations officer, this group of Marines from the group headquarters and CSSB-10 was assembled from across several locations in and around Baghdad and was ready to go within 12 hours of notification. After driving all night, Combat Service Support Company 101 (CSSC-101), also known as CSSC Tripoli, initially provided combat service support to the task force at its hastily established tactical assembly area in the northern outskirts of the city, and then followed in trace, as Task Force Tripoli moved north to secure one of the last serious strongholds of the war.

By the time CSSC Tripoli arrived in Tikrit, the majority of Marines and sailors had not slept in three days. Regardless, they set up Repair and Replenishment Point 29 on the Tikrit South Airfield* and focused their efforts on providing food, water, petroleum, oil and lubricants, and ammunition to the

---
* A massive fence line enclosed the Tikrit South Airfield and the field's lush woods had been stocked with exotic hunting game for the pleasure of Saddam Hussein and his sons. The first night they arrived, many Marines enjoyed a dinner of wild game. (Maj Michael J. Callanan comments on draft)

Major Michael Callanan, commander of CSSC-Tripoli, speaks to his Marines prior to stepping off for Tikrit.

1,300 Marines in the task force. Although they carried only four days of supply due to limited lift capabilities, the reliable reverse osmosis water purification units they carried were able to produce an unlimited supply of fresh water. This not only sustained the Marines, but also provided a good will offering to returning Tikriti civilians in dire need of water. On 14 April, just 56 hours after they had stepped off, CSSC-Tripoli began taking rounds of indirect fire in close proximity to the company's command post and steps away from the airfield itself. While reporting the incoming rounds to the division forward, Major Callanan concluded that an Iraqi mortar position was set up just outside of his company's position, shooting at the adjacent artillery positions of 5th Battalion, 11th Marines. This action caused the artillery Marines in 5/11 to return fire within close range of Major Callanan's repair and replenishment point. Realizing the potential danger in this situation, Major Callanan immediately took action to neutralize this threat. He and a few of his Marines quickly jumped in their vehicles and headed in the direction of the suspected enemy position. With two AH-1 Cobras flying above, they apprehended two Iraqi vehicles speeding away from the area. They detained 10 Iraqis, and although no weapons were found, they never came under fire again in Tikrit.

During their eight days there, CSSC-Tripoli not only provided combat service support to the Marines on the ground, but also performed numerous humanitarian operations, helping to secure the support and good will of the local Iraqis. They repaired a generator, donated medical supplies, and offered the shock trauma platoon and forward resuscitative surgical system's medical services to help reopen the city's main hospital. Additionally, while the Task Force Tripoli commander Brigadier General John F. Kelly met with many prominent groups in Tikrit to establish their post-Saddam existence, members of CSSC-Tripoli helped destroy a statue of Saddam Hus-

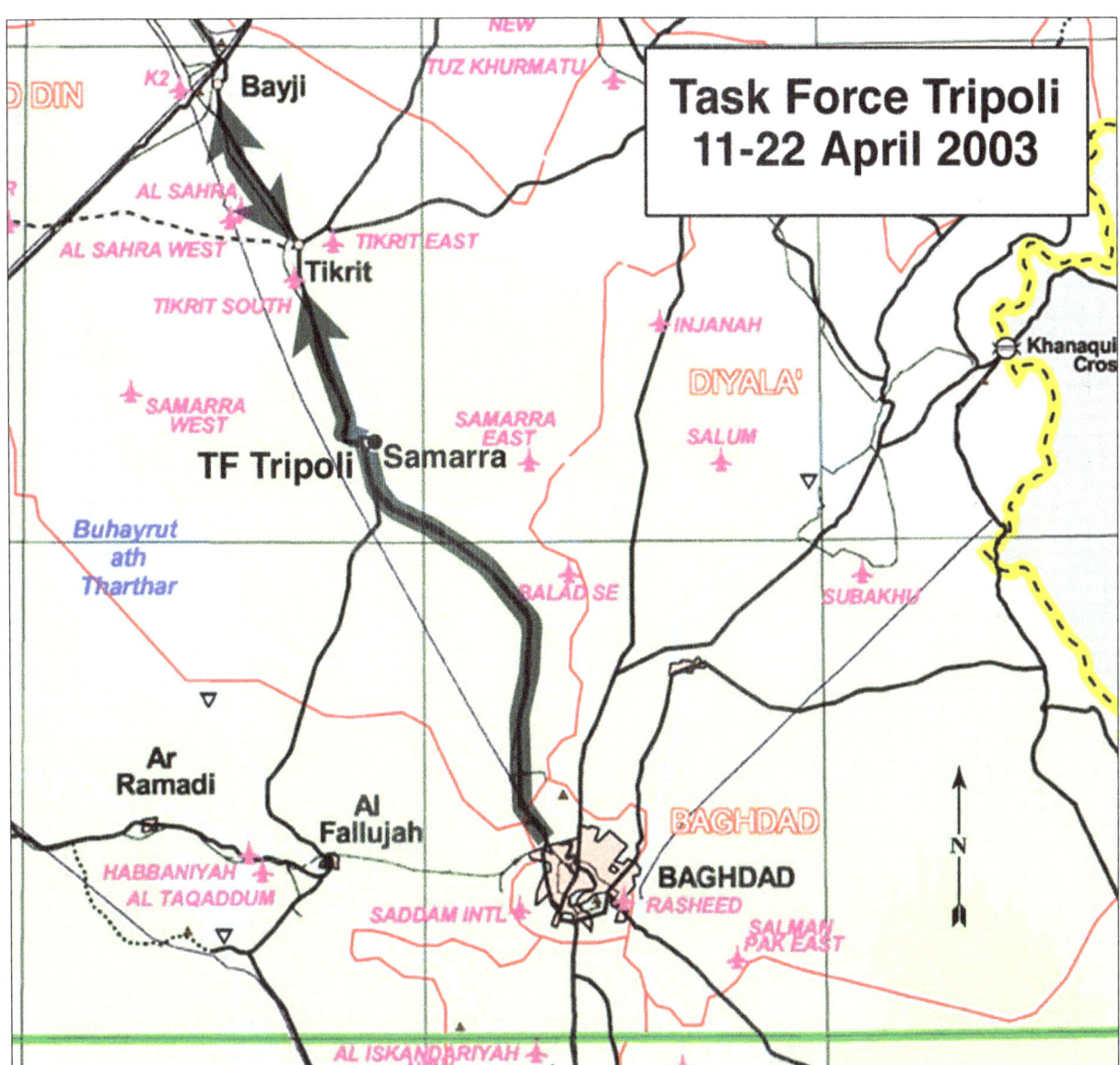

sein* that stood in the city's main square as well as all images of Saddam Hussein throughout the city. The unit also took possession of more than 150,000 small arms discovered hidden in a single hospital, and seized a number of French-made surface-to-surface missiles. At the nearby airfield, engineers from Marine Wing Support Group 37 conducted critical rapid runway repairs, much like the effective work they had done on multiple occasions throughout the 1st Marine Division's assault in Iraq. These repairs allowed the arrival of KC-130 Hercules aircraft just 48 hours after their initial arrival and opened the doors for continuous supply support. The initial Marine flight landing at the airfield, on which Lieutenant General James T. Conway traveled, delivered critical light armored vehicle repair parts and symbolized the overwhelming triumph of Task Force Tripoli in Tikrit.

At the conclusion of his stay in Tikrit, with just 10 minutes notice, Major Callanan was ordered by the Task Force Tripoli command post, which was setup outside of Saddam Hussein's palace, to intercept the U.S. Army's 4th Infantry Division, which had bypassed the task force's screen to the south and was rapidly moving to contact north toward Tikrit. The intent was to stop the division from attacking into the city and get the planned linkup back on track. There had been no communication with the 4th Infantry Division, and they were firing directly into the Task

---

* This statue was later melted down and used to build a memorial for U.S. Army 4th Infantry Division soldiers lost during OIF.

Force Tripoli zone in multiple areas with their close air support. From his position, Major Callanan raced in his vehicle into the path of the oncoming column of M2A3 Bradley fighting vehicles and M1A2 Abrams main battle tanks just outside the main gate to the city. In a one-on-one, heated confrontation with the commanding officer of Brigade Combat Team 1's lead battalion, Major Callanan maintained his composure while convincing the overzealous commander, who was ready to continue the attack into the city that the fight was over. The Marines had already secured Tikrit, and the situation was well in hand.[31]

Chapter 7

Security and Stabilization Operations

After fighting its way to Baghdad and stretching beyond its operational plan to secure Tikrit, 1st Marine Division settled into Phase IV of Operations Plan 1003V—security and stabilization operations. The Coalition forces had effectively defeated the enemy, pushing its battlefield successes all the way to Baghdad and beyond. Their role was now focused on securing and stabilizing a country whose recent loss of a longtime dictator created a severe power vacuum. They would still be responsible for rooting out the bad guys, but in many ways, the situation would be more complex. In large part, enemy forces not captured or killed had blended back into the civilian population, and a state of looting, crime, and general lawlessness prevailed. To make matters more complicated, the Marines now faced a situation where their assigned battlespace had no clear front or rear.

The Governates

On 18 April, 1st Marine Division's relief in place in Baghdad, with elements of the Army's 3d Infantry Division began. By 20 April, 1st Marine Division had reorganized and relocated to seven governates in southern Iraq: al-Qadisiyah, Babil, al-Muthanna, Karbala, an-Najaf, Wasit, and Dhi Qar. One infantry battalion was assigned to cover each governate, locating its headquarters in the appropriate capital city. These areas, which together accounted for half of Iraq's population, had their share of challenges. With an overwhelming Shia population, these regions had suffered the most during the three decades of Saddam Hussein's regime. In most areas, the infrastructure was extremely outdated, the result of willful neglect by the dictator and deterioration from years of UN sanctions. Other infrastructure had been destroyed in recent combat operations. Basic services, such as water, power, and sanitation, were scarce, and the security situation was deteriorating as each day passed. Taking a decentralized approach to the problem, 1st Marine Division distributed the control of each governate to the battalion commander assigned. Among the commander's immediate responsibilities was an assessment of the area's infrastructure and identification of threats to peace and good order, as well as local authorities that could help suppress the ongoing chaos. Setting up checkpoints to regulate movement and conducting patrols to promote good will, the Marines maintained a careful balance between maintaining a friendly presence on the streets and preserving a level of vigilance to react at any given moment to violent uprisings. 1st Marine Division's motto—No Better Friend, No Worse Enemy—was more fitting than ever. The battalions continued their search for the "bad guys" and their weapons and ammunition caches, while also initiating more permanent solutions to help rebuild the Iraqi infrastructure. Some projects included reconstituting the police force, repairing or installing electricity, and reestablishing some semblance of local government.[1]

Support Area Edson

By the time Task Force Tripoli had successfully secured its objective in Tikrit, it became obvious that Logistics Support Area Viper was no longer the best location for Brigadier General Usher and the 1st FSSG Forward to control the combat service support operations of its many units across the battlefield. Through much analysis and several site surveys led by the chief of staff, Colonel Moore, General Usher determined that the town of ad-Diwaniyah would be the optimal position on the battlefield for his headquarters. Straddling one of I MEF's main supply routes, ad-Diwaniyah not only gave 1st FSSG a central location within the I MEF area of responsibility, but also offered ample opportunities for humanitarian assistance operations. Al Qadisiyah University, a private Sunni institution, which lay in the outskirts of the town, was chosen as the site for the 1st FSSG headquarters' final support area, Edson. The FSSG forward moved from Viper to its new location on 19 April. A modest campus that had been looted during recent fighting, the university provided adequate structures and facilities for the Marines.

Soon after 1st FSSG forward established Support Area Edson, Combat Service Support Group 11 (CSSG-11) and Combat Service Support Battalion 10 (CSSB-10) began moving south to ad-Diwaniyah from Baghdad to set up their final repair and re-

Photo by MSgt Edward D. Kniery, USMC

1st Force Service Support Group headquarters moves onto the Al Qadisiya University campus near Ad Diyaniyah. Support Area Edson became the home for several FSSG units by late April, 2003.

plenishment point prior to redeployment. Combat Service Support Company Tripoli also returned from Tikrit to rejoin CSSG-11 in ad-Diwaniyah. Co-located with the 1st FSSG headquarters, CSSG-11 and CSSB-10 set up Repair and Replenishment Point 30 on the university campus to support the movement of all MEF units from the north to tactical assembly areas south of Baghdad. Numerous other 1st FSSG battalions, including 6th Engineer Support Battalion, which established a 150,000-gallon fuel farm and eight water purification units, 7th Engineer Support Battalion, and the Army's 716th Military Police Battalion, had already moved onto the campus, leaving minimal space for CSSB-10 to establish its site. As a result, Lieutenant Colonel Robert K. Weinkle's Marines launched another nearby location, designated Repair and Replenishment Point 30A, as their primary resupply point.[2]

As combat transitioned into security and stabilization operations, Al Qadisiyah University became the focal point of 1st FSSG's humanitarian efforts. Colonel Moore, the FSSG's chief of staff, led efforts to outline a series of projects to repair and improve the university campus. Closed shortly before the commencement of the war, the science and technology school fell victim to looters who stormed it shortly after the fall of Baghdad, destroying or stealing anything of value, to include doors, windows, and electric wiring. The campus was left in ruins. With the hope that the reopening of the school would help the Iraqi citizens gain back a sense of normalcy, Colonel Moore and several of his staff planned and coordinated with local contractors to repair and rebuild the school. Nearly $130,000 in captured Iraqi regime funds was obligated toward these contractors, not only to enable the school's opening, but also to boost the local economy by hiring unemployed and displaced workers.[3]

Support Area Geiger

In mid-April, Company C, 7th Engineer Support Battalion, departed Support Area Chesty for al-Kut Airfield, where they linked up with Task Force Tarawa. They rapidly repaired the 6,000-foot KC-130-capable runway by filling numerous craters, removing 40 dismantled vehicles, and clearing 30 other obstacles and debris from the airfield. Other missions included identifying and clearing ammunition caches and unexploded ordnance, conducting reconnaissance for a water production site, stockpiling engineering equipment, repairing bridges and schools, demilitarizing weapon systems and ordnance, establishing blocking positions, and constructing field hygiene facilities. Company C provided direct support to Task Force Tarawa's explosive ordnance disposal section in the collection and destruction of 1,188 rocket-propelled grenades, 35 SA-7 shoulder-fired surface-to-air missiles, 536 60mm mortars, 1,700 var-

Photo by MSgt Edward D. Kniery, USMC

Iraqi workers sign contracts with the 1st FSSG headquarters to repair damage at Al Qadisiyah University. The campus was looted and destroyed during fighting near Ad Diwaniyah.

ious artillery shells, and 30,000 pounds of P4 explosives. While sweeping three schools in al-Kut, they located and collected more than 300 60mm mortar rounds from a children's soccer field. They further swept 250 fighting positions, vehicle emplacements, and bunkers along Highway 7, east of al-Kut. In one location along Highway 1, they destroyed an enemy T-54/55 tank with two bangalore torpedoes, typically used to clear wire and antipersonnel mines. Company C recovered seven vehicles for Task Force Tarawa and completed the reconnaissance of one bridge, four schools, and two water points.

With a majority of its bridging missions complete, 8th Engineer Support Battalion (8th ESB) took on other engineering assignments, as well as a new role. 1st FSSG was stretched thin with truck assets and faced the continued forward expansion of the 1st Marine Division zone. It directed the battalion to convert from its assigned mission of bridging to one of long-haul support. Colonel Nelson reformed the battalion, reverted back to the operational control of 1st FSSG, and formed a contingency bridging element to sup-

Marines of the 8th ESB unload bridging equipment to convert their transport vehicles into much needed long-haul assets. Three companies within the battalion supported 1st FSSG between SA Chesty and Baghdad for ten days.

Photo by Courtesy of 8th ESB

96   COMBAT SERVICE SUPPORT

Courtesy of 8th ESB

Marines from 8th ESB worked with 2d Combat Engineer Battalion to remove and destroy unexploded ordnance throughout Baghdad. Shown here is two days worth of captured munitions.

Marines from 8th ESB work with Navy Seabees to repair the airfield at Al Kut.

Courtesy of 8th ESB

Courtesy of 8th ESB

Working on a goodwill project with Task Force Tarawa, Marines from 8th ESB cleaned and restored a British World War I cemetery in Al Kut.

port any future bridging missions. Upon returning to Support Area Chesty, the battalion unloaded its remaining bridge assets and formed three of its former bridge companies into long-haul transport companies. These provided direct support to 1st FSSG between Chesty and the vicinity of Baghdad for ten days.

While located at Support Area Chesty, elements of 8th ESB took on additional engineering assignments while simultaneously conducting logistics transportation operations. Teams of engineers worked with 2d Combat Engineer Battalion to remove and destroy unexploded ordnance throughout Baghdad. Engineer Support Company located and hauled more than 50,000 cubic yards of gravel to stem the dust on the roadways and stabilize many of the work areas at SA Chesty. On 17 April, the battalion redeployed to Support Area Geiger, where it supported Task Force Tarawa by performing unexploded ordnance removal and captured enemy ammunition operations, as well as airfield damage repair and general engineering missions. Additionally, during the month of April, the Marines in 8th ESB took on several humanitarian engineering projects. Platoons were dispatched to areas in and around al-Kut to repair playgrounds, determine military load classifications for area bridges, and maintain local runways. As a gesture of support and friendship, the battalion took part in a project with Marines from Task Force Tarawa to clean up and restore the British World War I cemetery located there. This weeklong project, which involved extensive trash cleanup and the piecing together of 50 headstones, ended in a symbolic ceremony between UK forces and U.S. Marines where the Union Jack was once again raised over the cemetery. 8th ESB's motto, Whatever It Takes, characterized its commitment during post-combat operations.[4]

On 20 April, 7th ESB's Company C conducted a relief in place with 8th ESB and moved to Support Area Edson near ad-Diwaniyah.[5] Three days later, the company was tasked to provide direct general engineering support to Regimental Combat Team 1 and 1st Battalion, 4th Marines at al-Hillah. Company C, in a humanitarian assistance effort, constructed 30 portable commodes, ten portable shower systems, 25 hygiene tables, and four dumpsters at the site of a collapsed jailhouse. They also welded 30 barrels and completed other metal work, recovered two armored combat earthmovers, conducted reconnaissance of soccer fields, schools, and two ammunition supply points for potential enemy munitions, and constructed 150 markers which they used to delineate a 250-acre minefield outside the city.[6]

When 7th ESB departed al-Kut, Combat Service Support Battalion 12 (CSSB-12) prepared to move in and establish Support Area Geiger, a decision that had been made during the preparation for Phase IV. The battalion began to downsize its capabilities at Support Area Chesty and sent an advanced party to

Photo by MSgt Edward D. Kniery, USMC

It was not all work for the 7th ESB Marines who repaired amusement park equipment that was damaged during fighting in An Numaniyah. They later had an opportunity to "test" their handiwork.

its final destination. While these Marines began establishing the new support area, CSSB-12's explosive ordnance disposal section was extremely busy in surrounding towns. In nearby al-Muwafaqiya and al-Hayy, the section recovered and destroyed hundreds of mortar rounds and rocket-propelled grenades that had been stored in local schools. Additionally, to further promote good will among the local population, they cleared known areas containing hazardous unexploded ordnance. The engineers from 6th Engineer Support Battalion joined CSSB-12 at al-Kut Airfield and established a water production and storage site with eight reverse osmosis water purification units as well as a fuel farm with 300,000-gallons of fuel storage. These were used to support Task Force Tarawa. On 25 April, the remainder of Colonel Burke's battalion began the move from Support Area Chesty to Support Area Geiger. It took five days to move the battalion, which included more than 354 loads of equipment and personnel. Support Area Geiger was CSSB-12's final support area prior to its return south, and the location from which it provided combat service support to all forces in central Iraq, including 1st Marine Division, Task Force Tarawa, 3d Marine Air Wing, the I MEF Engineer Group, and 1st FSSG.[7]

Reorganizing Combat Service Support Forces

By late May, Marines began the process of redeploying to their home bases in the United States. While several battalions had been reassigned as battalion task forces throughout regions south of Baghdad, nearly one half of 1st Marine Division began the trip home. Task Force Tarawa, which had sailed into theater four months earlier, reboarded amphibious ships for their month-long journey back to North Carolina, and elements of 1st FSSG began redeploying to Camp Pendleton. Throughout the end of May and June, the engineer support battalions, the transportation support group and Combat Service Support Group 15 returned to the United States. The majority of Combat Service Support 10 redeployed to Twentynine Palms, California, to prepare for the deployment of 7th Marine Regiment and other I MEF units at the Marine Corps Air Ground Combat Center.

Meanwhile, Combat Service Support Group 11, which had been the first unit of 1st FSSG in theater, reorganized and transformed itself to support the new security and stabilization operations mission. It would be the last unit of 1st FSSG out of theater. Gaining tactical control of Combat Service Support Battalion 12 in al-Kut and Combat Service Support Battalion 22 in an-Nasiriyah, as well as the remaining personnel and resources from CSSB-10, CSSG-11 was temporarily designated as Brigade Service Support Group 1 (BSSG-1) and then, as the sole 1st FSSG element remaining in Iraq for Phase IV, provided all direct and general combat service support to I MEF forces in country. Other units that attached to BSSG-1 included Charlie Company, 7th Engineer Support Battalion, the Army's 716th Military Police Battalion, a civil affairs team, and a new mortuary affairs team.*

The three combat service support companies that had supported their assigned regimental combat teams throughout the war were reassigned to new areas of responsibility: Combat Service Support Company 111 (CSSC-111) relocated to Tallil, where it supported 2d Battalion, 25th Marines, in an-Nasiriyah

---

* Prior to the war, CSSG-11 had received a mortuary affairs team as part of its table of organization. This team was dropped off to Camp Bougainville in Kuwait 48 hours prior to CSSG-11 crossing the line of departure. With limited equipment, these individuals were still able to perform their mission in an exemplary manner. On an interesting note, CSSG-11 also received two U.S. Army chemical platoons about 72 hours prior to crossing the line of departure. Because one of the platoons had no trucks and no NBC gear, they had to reorganize and redistribute the Marine Corps' NBC equipment. In some cases, Marines were literally sitting on one another's laps.

Photo by MSgt Edward D. Kniery, USMC
EOD Marines in 7th ESB prepare demolitions to destroy captured Iraqi weapons and munitions near Al Kut.

and 2d Battalion, 5th Marines in as-Samawah. Combat Service Support Company 117 (CSSC-117) was tasked to provide general combat service support to 3d Battalion, 7th Marines, in Karbala; 1st Battalion, 7th Marines, in an-Najaf; and 1st Battalion, 4th Marines, in al-Hillah. Combat Service Support Company 115 (CSSC-115) was assigned to support 3d Battalion, 5th Marines, in ad-Diwaniyah and 3d Battalion, 23d Marines, in al-Kut.

Additionally, three companies were created to support CSSG-11's new mission during the security and stabilization operations phase. With this mission, the group faced new hurdles, including long distances for transporting supplies and added difficulty in maintaining an already complex command and control scheme. Operating in ad-Diwaniyah and pulling support from CSSC-111 in Tallil, Combat Service Support Company 101, commanded by Captain Alonzo J. Jones III, was tasked to provide general support to all three companies. Between mid-May and mid-June, two more companies were created. Combat Service Support Company 102, commanded by First Lieutenant Ryan L. Miller, largely grew out of CSSC-115's capabilities and was specifically tasked to support 3d MAW elements, 3d Battalion, 23d Marines, and 4th Light Armored Reconnaissance Battalion operating in the vicinity of al-Kut. Combat Service Support Company 103, commanded by Second Lieutenant Alan J. Solis, grew out of CSSC-117 and took over Combat Service Support Company 151, which remained in place as a liaison cell to the I MEF headquarters group located at al-Hillah.

By summertime, international forces began to arrive in Iraq to relieve several battalions within 1st Marine Division. In July 2003, as 2d Battalion, 25th Marines, and 2d Battalion, 5th Marines, were relieved in an-Nasiriyah and as-Samawah by Italian and Dutch troops, CSSC-111 downsized and split into Combat Service Support Company 104 (CSSC-104) and Combat Service Support Company 105 (CSSC-105). These two smaller companies enabled portions of CSSC-111 to redeploy back to the United States, while maintaining the necessary level of support. CSSC-104, commanded by First Lieutenant Minh D. Tran, provided bulk fuel storage, combat service support to 2d Battalion, 25th Marines, an in-stride refueling point to returning I MEF convoys, an arrival/departure air control group, and liaison with the Army's 171st Area Support Group. Meanwhile, CSSC-105, which had relocated to Kuwait, expedited the procurement and distribution of high priority supplies and monitored the redeployment of Marines back home.

Once 2d Battalion, 5th Marines, conducted a relief in place with the Dutch, CSSC-115 moved south to Kuwait, in order to establish CSSG-11's retrograde control element. In this capacity, it facilitated the turn-in and redeployment of all organic and MPF equipment. When CSSC-115 moved back to Kuwait, CSSC-101 assumed the support missions of 3d Battalion, 5th Marines, and Combat Service Support Company 102 (CSSC-102). In addition, it continued to provide motor transport and heavy equipment assets. This served a critical need in both the delivery of humanitarian supplies, as well as the return of CSSG-11's equipment and personnel. In the meantime, CSSC-117 continued to support a large number of battalions still spread out in an-Najaf, al-Hillah, Babylon, and Karbala.

Photo by MSgt Edward D. Kniery, USMC
BGen Edward G. Usher III, center, with his commanders at Support Area Edson.

1st FSSG Commanders

On 11 July 2003, Brigadier General Usher relinquished command of the 1st FSSG to Brigadier General Richard S. Kramlich. Following his two-year command of 1st FSSG, General Usher was assigned as the Assistant Deputy Commandant for Installations and Logistics at Headquarters U.S. Marine Corps. In a change-of-command ceremony held back at Camp Pendleton, California, General Usher spoke of the challenges that 1st FSSG faced while serving in Kuwait and Iraq. He noted that the key to their success was "the basic grit and determination of the individual Marine and sailor who embraced the mission, embraced their jobs, leaned forward, and never leaned back."

During this period, while still providing combat service support to all of the Coalition forces in the I MEF area of operations, CSSG-11 also accomplished several non-combat service support tasks. In July, it supported the establishment of the military stipend payment program in ad-Diwaniyah and an-Nasiriyah. Through this program, captured Iraqi funds were used to pay former Iraqi military personnel, so that they could feed their families without turning to crime or joining the insurgency. Additionally, elements of CSSG-11 worked tirelessly to obtain AK-47 rifles and ammunition from Combined Joint Task Force 7,* for the purpose of outfitting newly developed police departments throughout the MEF's area of responsibility. The Marines successfully acquired over 10,000 AK-47s, 1,700 pistols, and one million rounds of ammunition, ultimately distributed to the Marine infantry battalions to properly train and stand up the Iraqi police forces. Several engineering and clean-up projects also kept CSSG-11 busy. In August, CSSG-11's Engineer Company, commanded by Navy Lieutenant Michael P. Leonard*, completed force protection work on a bank in downtown ad-Diwaniyah by building rebar fencing and emplacing a concrete curb and driveway. Additionally, they destroyed a mural of Saddam Hussein at the entrance of the Al Qadisiya University, replacing it with an old Iraqi school bell, which they helped refurbish along with the entire university grounds, prior to turning it over to the Iraqi Ministry of Education in October 2003.

---

* Combined Joint Task Force 7, commanded by LtGen Ricardo S. Sanchez, replaced Coalition forces Land Component Command (CFLCC) on 14 June 2003 as the command controlling all military ground forces, U.S. and non-U.S., deployed in occupied Iraq. Their mission was to conduct offensive operations to defeat remaining noncompliant forces and neutralize destabilizing influences in the area of operations (AO), to create a secure environment in direct support of the Coalition Provisional Authority, and concurrently conduct stability operations which support the establishment of government and economic development to set the conditions for a transfer of operations to designated follow on military or civilian authorities.

---

* With the turnover of several personnel, Lt Leonard, a Navy Seabee who had been on exchange to the Marines of 7th ESB, was transferred to CSSG-11 and given the opportunity to command a Marine company.

Chapter 8

The Special Purpose MAGTF

Initial planning for the reconstitution, regeneration, and re-embarkation (R3) of maritime prepositioning force (MPF) equipment began before troops were even on the ground in the fall of 2002. Throughout the offensive campaign in March and April of 2003, planners continued to prepare for the imminent retrograde operations that would occur at the conclusion of the war, and even as they continued to sustain I MEF with logistical support, the Marine Logistics Command (MLC) began to shift its focus to the mission of redeployment. The scope of MPF R3 operations included the reloading of 11 MPF ships with more than 450,000 individual items, 6,000 loaded containers, and 5,000 principle end items. To assist in the handling of such an expansive task, Headquarters Marine Corps (HQMC) task-organized a reconstitution liaison support team (RLST) of approximately 20 to 25 military and civilian personnel. This team was on-hand to assist the Marine Forces Central Command in planning and coordinating R3 operations, as well as acting as HQMC's liaison to resolve problems with MPF R3 policies and processes.

As the executive agent for MPF retrograde operations, 2d FSSG, which had been previously reorganized and renamed the Marine Logistics Command (MLC), again worked for Marine Forces Central Command, but this time redesignated as the Special Purpose Marine Air Ground Task Force (MAGTF). The Special Purpose MAGTF formed to re-embark all assets used by Marines in Kuwait and Iraq during Operation Iraqi Freedom. Three Maritime Prepositioned Ships Squadrons, consisting of 11 ships, needed to be reconstituted with this equipment and restored to the highest mission capable status in preparation for future operations.

On 15 June, the Marine Logisitics Command offi-

Maritime prepositioned force ships docked at Kuwait's Port of Ash Shuayba. Eleven MPF ships were reloaded between July and November of 2003.

Photo by CNA

USMC Photo

Prior to assuming command of the Special Purpose MAGTF in June 2003, BGen Ronald S. Coleman served as the assistant deputy commandant for Installation and Logistics.

cially became the MPF Special Purpose MAGTF, consisting of 2,470 Marines, sailors, and contractors. One week later, Brigadier General Ronald S. Coleman arrived in Kuwait and assumed command of the Special Purpose MAGTF from Brigadier General Lehnert on 25 June. Having served a tour with the Navy in Vietnam, General Coleman spent his 30-year Marine Corps career in a variety of supply and logistics billets, including commanding officer of both 2d Maintenance and 2d Supply Battalions. During an interview conducted in 2004 while he commanded 2d FSSG's operations in Port-Au-Prince Haiti, General Coleman talked about the FSSG's turnover during OIF-I; initially, the time and location of the turnover was unknown.

> We had both—I shouldn't say we both—he (General Lehnert) hoped it'd be in Lejeune, so he could bring them back. Quite honestly, I'd hoped we'd be in Kuwait, so I could get over there. But it was his command, and I honestly believe that it should have been; I would love to have seen him bring them back home. You take somebody to war, you want to bring them home from war. It did not work out that way. [It was decided by higher authority that] . . . our special purpose MAGTF would be formed for the regeneration of the MPF equipment.[1]

Limited guidance or doctrine existed to help form the Special Purpose MAGTF, and similar to the MLC, there was no model on which to base its organization. The core of the MAGTF came from 2d FSSG and was augmented by personnel from 1st FSSG, Marine Force Reserve, and Blount Island Command.[*] The organization of the Special Purpose MAGTF consisted of five major subordinate organizations, including area commander, supply battalion, maintenance battalion detachment, transportation support battalion, and MP/security battalion.

With a small staff, the area commander, Lieutenant Colonel David M. Smith, had the overall responsibility for maintaining Camp Fox, the primary location for retrograde operations. Perhaps the most remote and desolate of all the camps set up in Kuwait, Fox, which was located southwest of Kuwait City, possessed both poor roadways and uncooperative terrain. As a result, a large investment had been made in improving the camp's infrastructure to support the Marine Logistics Command's operations, making it an ideal location to base retrograde operations. Colonel Smith's mission broke down into four main areas: designing and organizing a plan for Camp Fox; serving as primary contract manager for all life-support services, equipment, and materials; serving as project manager for installation, operation, and maintenance of non-organic/non-tactical structures and mechanical systems; and providing a camp fire department.[2]

Supply Battalion was comprised of four companies—ammunition; packing, preservation, and packaging; medical logistics; and supply. Commanded by Colonel Peter J. Talleri, the battalion had two main missions during retrograde operations: receiving, storing, and accounting for the MPF equipment and supplies being returned to the Special Purpose MAGTF; and ordering, tracking, and delivering supplies, equipment, and parts needed for the reconstitution and regeneration portions of the entire operation. The battalion required an extensive infrastructure on Camp Fox to hold and maintain the supplies needed for containerized storage on each ship, as well as the repair parts required by the maintenance sections to repair equipment in theater.[3]

---

[*] As the Commandant of the Marine Corps' Executive Agent for Marine Corps Prepositioning Programs, Blount Island Command, located in Jacksonville, Florida, plans, coordinates, and executes the logistics efforts in support of maritime prepositioning ships.

The maintenance battalion detachment, led by Major Don A. Mills, reorganized from its general support maintenance structure in the Marine Logistics Command to a new four-section organization: ordnance, motor transport, utilities, and engineer maintenance. Each maintenance area had its own focus, but generally, the detachment's mission was to perform second, third, and fourth echelon maintenance on all returning MPF equipment. Additionally, the detachment was tasked to provide maintenance contact teams as required, prioritize the repair of incoming equipment, and build and prepare ship containers and blocks to store and transport large equipment.[4]

As a follow-on organization from the MLC's transportation support battalion, a transportation detachment was created to support the MPF reconstitution, regeneration, and re-embarkation. This detachment, led by Lieutenant Colonel Charles G. Chiarotti, was organized to manage command and control of transportation capabilities, physical assets to move personnel and equipment, and personnel to support all transportation operations. Consisting of four main sections—aerial port, port operations, theater distribution center, and the third country national liaison section—the detachment's missions included port staging and ship loading of equipment, closing and inspection of equipment and containers for MPF loading and retrograde movement, and port and aircraft loading operations at the aerial port of embarkation.[5]

The military police battalion, led by Major Eric J. Eldred, was responsible for assessing antiterrorist and force protection requirements at the various retrograde sites throughout Kuwait and supervising the implementation of security procedures and assets. In addition to the five main areas of the Special Purpose MAGTF, there was also an engineering detachment that assisted in fuel system preparations, operated the wash-down and staging facility, coordinated agricultural and customs inspections, and provided material handling equipment operators, a communications element, a medical element, and a headquarters and service battalion element to provide personnel and administrative support.

Daily sandstorms at Camp Fox intensified the already harsh desert conditions during the SPMAGTF's reconstitution and regeneration of MPF equipment.

Photo by CNA

By the summer of 2003, it was common knowledge that Marine forces might be called back to serve in Iraq during 2004. In a conversation with Brigadier General Coleman, Major General James N. Mattis, commanding general of 1st Marine Division, stated point blank that they would be back in the February or March timeframe and would need the reconstituted MPF equipment for their follow-on operations. The original R3 plan called for an eight-month timeline to repair equipment in theater and load 11 ships. Brigadier General Coleman, however, proposed an alternate course of action where the majority of equipment would be loaded onto MPF ships immediately and returned to Blount Island Command for repairs. He knew that desert conditions were not ideal for the type of operations his Marines would be performing.

Now it's 125, we're in the sand, you can expect a sandstorm every day. The long supply line. At this point, when I first got there, it wasn't opened yet, but there was one building being built, so they could work inside. All the repairs, regeneration was being done outside, under tents. Brutal, brutal conditions. Between that and the supply line, I called my people together and I said, "OK, let's look into this." Is there any value added in loading up the ships as best we can, fixing what we have, but in the meantime, looking into, rather than ordering a part, and having parts shipped over here, fix it, and send it back. Are there any items, since most of the ships had to go to Blount Island anyway, is there any validity in, ordering a part, LTI [limited technical inspection], have the part sent to Blount Island, put the gear on board the ship, send it back to Blount Island, and it gets fixed there. Because the first order of business was to get the ships that we thought may come back to war right away, get those fixed. Those were the ships that we thought General Mattis would use again and he is, in fact, using them.[6]

At Blount Island Command, not only were conditions much more conducive to working on broken equipment, but much-needed repair parts were more accessible. This alternative approach cut the timeline down by three months. From an operational per-

Marines of the SPMAGTF clean equipment at the Nestle Washdown Site, one of three locations in Kuwait designated for this purpose.

Photo by CNA

Photo by CNA

Vehicles are embarked in the lower hold of the MPF ship USNS PFC James Anderson Jr. *(T-AK-3002) to be shipped back to Blount Island Command for necessary repair.*

spective, the benefits of this plan included leveraging both locations, lowering overseas costs, and ultimately decreasing the amount of time required to get the MPF back to full capability. From a personnel perspective, General Coleman saw this course of action as benefiting the Marines. Not only would it minimize their exposure to the harsh desert conditions, but it would get them home quicker.[7]

By mid-July, the commanding general issued a letter of instruction providing detailed guidance to each operational area. Retrograde operations consisted of three phases. Phase I, sourcing and preparation, which occurred at Camp Fox, al-Jaber, and Ali al-Salem, included receiving equipment, conducting maintenance, inventorying and requisitioning required supplies, ensuring quality assurance, accepting and transporting the equipment. During Phase II, movement and staging, the SPMAGTF moved equipment to wash-down facilities, conducted agricultural and customs inspections, and set up staging for further movement to the port facilities. Three sites used during this phase were the Kuwait Naval Base and Nestle wash-down sites, and the Kuwait Public Transportation Center Bus Terminal. Phase III, embarkation, included loading the equipment onto the MPF ships and took place primarily at Kuwait's Port of Ash Shuaybah.[8]

Reconstitution, regeneration, and re-embarkation (R3) operations required the movement of thousands of truckloads of vehicles, equipment, containers, and supplies. The Special Purpose MAGTF's logistics movement control center (LMCC) scheduled and coordinated the movement of more than 200 trucks per day. The control center, which was part of the SP-MAGTF's G-3 current operations section, used transportation assets from 2d FSSG and the Army's 377th Theater Support Command, but largely depended on locally contracted transport equipment with third country national drivers.[9]

In early September 2003, General Coleman massed the troops to commend them on their hard work and tell them that they would likely be home by Thanksgiving. This was a major morale boost, as the majority of these Marines had been in theater since the fall of 2002, and earlier estimates had pushed their return date as late as March of 2004. Having an end in sight was an immeasurable relief. A week later, in a private meeting with Lieutenant General Conway, the I MEF Commanding General, Brigadier General Coleman revealed that he in fact planned to have the troops home in time for the Marine Corps Birthday Ball in early November. After the meeting, as he spoke to the troops of the Special Purpose MAGTF, General Conway candidly broke the good news by announcing that they would likely be home in time for the ball.[10] General Coleman later commented that in his almost 30 years of Marine Corps service, the special purpose MAGTF was "the most satisfying operation he had ever participated in." In large part, this was due to the sheer magnitude of their mission and the unparalleled dedication shown by his Marines.

> We had Marines, because it was so hot, that wore gloves to fix gear so they didn't burn their hands. And you go out and talk to those Marines, and they're just as happy as they can be. We went down in the well of one of the ships we were loading, the weatherman takes his thermometer in the well of the ship, and it was 151. The Marines were just working.[11]

In the end, between 7 July and 4 November, the Special Purpose MAGTF successfully loaded 11 MPF ships to either full combat support capable status or a status such that they could support combat operations immediately if the identified shortfalls in their loadouts could be provided from CONUS. During this period, the Marines of the SPMAGTF also continued to provide support to I MEF forces remaining in Iraq. In the end, the mission was completed in approximately 190 days, well ahead of the original timeline of 240 days.[12] The majority of 2d FSSG, including General Coleman, was back in Camp Lejeune, North Carolina, on 8 November, and the final planeload of the Special Purpose MAGTF Marines landed in CONUS the next day. As promised, they were all home before the Marine Corps' birthday on 10 November 2003.[13]

Epilogue

The Future for the FSSGs

One of the most significant aspects of combat service support during Operation Iraqi Freedom was the reorganization of both 1st and 2d FSSG. While similar concepts were implemented throughout Desert Shield/Desert Storm, during Operation Iraqi Freedom-I, the FSSGs stretched beyond traditional doctrine and reached a new level of achievement. Whether their actions were necessitated by factors such as speed, maneuver, and distance or inspired by the sheer adrenaline of accomplishing the mission, the FSSGs pushed every boundary and limitation within the logistics arena. The future for the FSSGs, however, remains uncertain. Several commanders, including Brigadier General Usher, Commanding General of 1st FSSG, recognized this fact:

> I think we have some soul-searching to do, and I think we have some realities we have to just look at and address in a realistic manner. As we leave this theater here, we've worked on a notional return organizational structure that we're going to redeploy as we deployed over here. To start switching people around now would just turn it into total chaos. . . . I just think that's something we're going to have to address, both as 1st FSSG and I MEF, but in a larger sense sort of some guidelines from the logistics leadership of the Marine Corps on how we structure ourselves for the next ten years.[1]

Brigadier General Lehnert, Commanding General of 2d FSSG, commented on the broader picture of both 1st and 2d FSSG:

> Perhaps the FSSGs need to sit back for a minute and say it isn't a matter of "they have to look alike." One of them is going to have a wholesale function, and one of them is going to have a retail function; and if you accept that and that you're going to go to war as one big MEF, and you're going to travel long distances, then one of the FSSGs is probably going to have a tactical CSS function and the other one is going to have an operational CSS function.[2]

It is a given that as warfare changes, the approach to supporting the warfighter also needs to change. Shortfalls in certain areas, such as communications and line-haul transportation will need to be addressed. The organization of the FSSGs may be different the next go-around. The general wholesale and retail assignments may shift between East Coast and West Coast FSSGs, but there is one constant that will always remain—the innate ability of Marines to adapt and overcome any circumstance through hard work, ingenuity, and sheer drive.

What will be remembered about combat service support during Operation Iraqi Freedom may well depend on who you ask in the future. Perhaps the infantryman will remember that on certain days of his three-week march to Baghdad, he only ate one MRE in case replenishment was nowhere nearby; or the supply officer will remember his frustration with not knowing when a critical part would arrive at his position. Perhaps though, the truck driver will remember his amazement when fuel was delivered to him through a six-inch hose from 60 miles away, the doctor will remember her satisfaction in knowing that she saved the life of every Marine that entered her tent, or the artilleryman will recall his relief at the sight of a convoy carrying ammunition just as his unit began to run low on the gun line. Individual memories may be anecdotal; some positive, some negative. The big picture of Marine logistics in Operation Iraqi Freedom is that they conducted a historic operation far exceeding expectations of distance, speed, and overall tenacity. In the end, despite all the obstacles and challenges, the logistics came through and supported the maneuver units. Through innovations at the highest staff levels and dogged determination by the most junior Marine, the logisticians always found a way to make it happen.

Notes

Chapter 1

[1] Commanders and Staff of 1st FSSG, "Brute Force Combat Service Support: 1st Force Service Support Group in Operation Iraqi Freedom," *Marine Corps Gazette* Aug03, 34; hereafter Commanders and Staff of 1st FSSG article.

[2] Transcript of President George W. Bush Commencement Speech at West Point, New York, 1 June 2002, Office of the Press Secretary (http://www.whitehouse.gov/news/releases/2002/06/20020601-3.html).

[3] LtCol Adrian W. Burke, intvw, 13Mar03, (Oral HistColl), Quantico, VA; hereafter Burke intvw, 13Mar03.

[4] Maj Steven M. Zimmeck, (Ret.), *US Marines in the Persian Gulf, 1990-1991 Combat Service Support in Desert Shield and Desert Storm*, (Washington, D.C.: Hist&MusDiv, 1999), 67.

[5] Burke intvw, 13Mar03.

[6] BGen Edward G. Usher, intvw, 19Mar03, (Oral HistColl), Quantico, VA; hereafter Usher intvw, 19Mar03.

[7] Usher intvw, 19Mar03.

[8] Burke intvw, 13Mar03.

[9] Usher intvw, 19Mar03.

[10] Col Darrell L. Moore, intvw, 29Mar03, (Oral HistColl), Quantico, VA; hereafter Moore intvw.

[11] Col John J. Pomfret, intvw, 5Mar03, USMC (Oral HistColl), Quantico, VA; hereafter Pomfret intvw, 5Mar03.

[12] Pomfret intvw, 5Mar03.

[13] LtCol John J. Broadmeadow, "Logistics Support to 1st Marine Division During Operation Iraqi Freedom," *Marine Corps Gazette* Aug03, 44-45.

[14] Pomfret intvw, 5Mar03.

[15] Lt Robert K. Weinkle Jr., intvw, 6Mar03, (Oral HistColl), Quantico, VA; hereafter Weinkle intvw, 6Mar03.

[16] Combat Service Support Group–11 ComdC, 1Jan.03–30Apr03; hereafter CSSG-11 ComdC.

[17] Weinkle intvw, 6Mar03.

[18] BGen Edward G. Usher, intvw, 4Apr04, (Oral HistColl), Quantico, VA; hereafter Usher intvw, 4Apr03.

[19] LtCol Michael D. Malone, intvw, 7May03, (Oral HistColl) Quantico, VA; hereafter Malone intvw.

[20] Malone intvw.

[21] Col Bruce E. Bissett, intvw, 27Apr03, (Oral HistColl), Quantico, VA.

[22] Combat Service Support Group 15 ComdC, 1Jan03–30Jun03; hereafter CSSG-15 ComdC.

[23] LtCol Robert W. Higbee, intvw, 7Mar03, (Oral HistColl), Quantico, VA.

[24] 2d MEB ComdC, 1Jan–30Jun03.

[25] Lt Thomas N. Goben, intvw, 27Apr03, (Oral HistColl), Quantico, VA; hereafter Goben intvw.

[26] Col John L. Sweeney Jr., intvw, 21Mar03, (Oral HistColl), Quantico, VA; hereafter Sweeney intvw.

[27] Transportation Support Group ComdC, 1Jan03–30Jun03; hereafter TSG ComdC.

[28] Col David G. Reist, intvw, 10Mar03, (Oral HistColl), Quantico, VA; hereafter Reist intvw.

[29] LtCol Patrick J. Hermesmann, intvw, 10Mar03, (Oral HistColl), Quantico, VA.

[30] Reist intvw.

[31] LtCol Adrian W. Burke, comments on draft, n.d. [Aug05]. Author's files.

[32] LtCol Jorge Ascunce, intvw, 24Apr03, (Oral HistColl), Quantico, VA; hereafter Ascunce intvw.

[33] Ascunce intvw.

[34] Usher intvw, 19Mar03.

[35] LtCol Roger R. Machut, intvw, 8Apr03, (Oral HistColl) Quantico, VA; hereafter Machut intvw, 8Apr03.

[36] LtCol Niel E. Nelson, intvw, 6Mar03, (Oral HistColl), Quantico, VA; hereafter Nelson intvw.

[37] Cdr Gregory M. Huet, USN intvw, 10Mar03, Oral HistColl), Quantico, VA; hereafter Huet intvw.

[38] Commanders and Staff of 1st FSSG article, 35.

[39] Capt Eric C. McDonald, USN intvw, 3May03, (Oral HistColl), Quantico, VA.

[40] Cdr Miguel A. Cubano, USN intvw, 2May03, (Oral HistColl), Quantico, VA.

[41] Huet intvw.

[42] LtCol Kim S. Orlando, USA intvw, 23Apr03, (Oral HistColl), Quantico, VA; hereafter Orlando intvw.

[43] Orlando intvw.

[44] BGen Edward G. Usher, intvw, 11May03, (Oral HistColl), Quantico, VA; hereafter Usher intvw, 11May03.

[45] Orlando intvw.

[46] Ibid.

[47] Combat Service Support Battalion 19 ComdC, 1Jan–30Jun03.

[48] Col James P. Sheahan, intvw, 22Mar03, (Oral HistColl), Quantico, VA.
[49] Moore intvw.
[50] Usher intvw, 19Mar03.
[51] Ibid.
[52] LCpl Joseph J. Klan, intvw, 4May03, (Oral HistColl), Quantico, VA.
[53] BGen Michael R. Lehnert, intvw, 8May03, (Oral HistColl), Quantico, VA; hereafter Lehnert intvw.
[54] Usher intvw, 19Mar03.
[55] Lehnert intvw.
[56] Lehnert intvw.
[57] BGen Michael R. Lehnert and Col John E. Wissler, "MLC: Sustaining Tempo on the 21st Century Battlefield," *Marine Corps Gazette* Aug03, 30.
[58] Dr. Joseph Miciewicz, Center for Naval Analyses, comments on draft, 1Sep05, author's files; hereafter Miciewicz comments.
[59] Col Russell A. Eve, intvw, 5May03, (Oral HistColl), Quantico, VA.
[60] Headquarters and Service Battalion, 2d FSSG, ComdC, 1Jan03–30Jun03.
[61] Col John Wissler, intvw, 25Apr03, (Oral HistColl), Quantico, VA; hereafter Wissler intvw.
[62] LtCol Christopher B. Martin, intvw, 29Apr03, (Oral HistColl), Quantico, VA.
[63] Capt Stephen M. Pachuta, USN, intvw, 30Apr03, (Oral HistColl), Quantico, VA.
[64] Col Tracy L. Mork, intvw, 27Feb03, (Oral HistColl), Quantico, VA; Col John T. Larson, intvw, 25Feb03, (Oral HistColl) Quantico, VA.

Chapter 2

[1] 2d FSSG Narrative Final
[2] Col Stephen W. Otto intvw, 6May03, (Oral HistColl), Quantico, VA; hereafter Otto intvw.
[3] 2d FSSG Narrative Final
[4] Otto intvw; Maj Arthur J. Pasagian intvw, 2May03, (Oral HistColl), Quantico, VA; Maj Steve A. Plato intvw, 6May03, (Oral HistColl), Quantico, VA; 2d FSSG (Fwd) ComdC, 1Jan03–30Jun03.
[5] Sgt Colin Wyers, "1st FSSG Custom-Tailors Units in Kuwaiti Desert" *Marine Corps News* 23Jan03.
[6] LtCol David M. McMiller, intvw, 25Apr03, (Oral HistColl), Quantico, VA.
[7] Capt Charles A. Graybeal, and 2dLt Afinju O. McDowell, "Camp Bougainville," *CSSB-10 Cruisebook*, 9.
[8] Maj David V. Raimo, intvw, 3Mar03, (Oral HistColl), Quantico, VA.
[9] Capt Charles A. Graybeal, and 2dLt Afinju O. McDowell, "Camp Bougainville," *CSSB-10 Cruisebook*, 9.
[10] Author's Journal. 24Feb03–19May03. Author's files; hereafter Author's journal.
[11] 2dLt Jason C. Brezler, intvw, 30Apr03, (Oral HistColl), Quantico, VA; Lt Timothy A. Wallace, USN intvw, 30Apr03, (Oral HistColl), Quantico, VA.
[12] Col Niel E. Nelson Notes, 5Sept07, author's files; hereafter Nelson notes.
[13] MLC Narrative Final, n.d., author's files; Meier intvw; Maj Kevin P. Reilly, intvw, 1May03, (Oral HistColl), Quantico, VA.
[14] Col William A. Meier, intvw, 29Apr03, (Oral HistColl), Quantico, VA; hereafter Meier intvw.
[15] BGen Edward G. Usher, *Testimony to the House Armed Services Committee*, 30Mar04.
[16] Usher intvw, 11May03.
[17] Maj Emily J. Elder, intvw, 7May03, (Oral HistColl), Quantico, VA; Maj Brandon D. McGowan Award Narrative
[18] Lehnert intvw.
[19] Lehnert intvw.
[20] Lehnert intvw.
[21] 2d FSSG Narrative Final; MLC Support Detachment 1 ComdC 10Mar03–15Apr03; Lehnert intvw.
[22] LtCol Roarke L. Anderson, intvw, 3May03, (Oral HistColl), Quantico, VA.
[23] Maj Julie L. Nethercot, intvw, 3May03, (Oral HistColl), Quantico, VA; hereafter Nethercot intvw.
[24] LtCol Kenneth S. Helfrich, intvw, 3May03, (Oral HistColl), Quantico, VA.
[25] Nethercot intvw.
[26] Author's journal.
[27] Pomfret intvw, 5Mar03.
[28] CSSG–11 ComdC.
[29] Weinkle intvw, 6Mar03.
[30] Combat Service Support Battalion 22 ComdC, 1Jan03–30Jun03; Goben intvw.
[31] Goben intvw.
[32] CSSG-15 ComdC.
[33] LtCol Kathleen M. Murney, intvw, 4Mar03, (Oral HistColl), Quantico, VA.
[34] LtCol Roger R. Machut, intvw, 4Mar03, (Oral HistColl), Quantico, VA; hereafter Machut intvw, 4Mar03.
[35] 6th Engineer Support Battalion ComdC, 1Jan03–30Jun03; hereafter 6th ESB ComdC.
[36] 7th Engineer Support Battalion ComdC, 1Jan03–30Jun03; hereafter 7th ESB ComdC.
[37] LtCol Niel E. Nelson, and Maj Joseph J. Klocek, "8th Engineer Support Battalion's Support of Operation Iraqi Freedom" *Marine Corps Gazette* Dec03, 39; hereafter Nelson and Klocek article.
[38] Nelson and Klocek article.
[39] Nelson notes.
[40] TSG ComdC, 6th Motor Transport Battalion

ComdC, 1Jan03–30Jun03.

[41] TSG ComdC.

[42] Author's journal.

Chapter 3

[1] I Marine Expeditionary Force Operations Plan 1003V (Unclassified).

[2] Capt Alonzo J. Jones, "RRP-1" *CSSB-10 Cruisebook*, 25.

[3] Combat Service Support Battalion 10 ComdC, 1Jan03–30Jun03; hereafter CSSB-10 ComdC.

[4] Lindsay Murdoch, "Slaughter at Safwan Hill," *Sydney Morning Herald*, 22Mar03.

[5] Author's journal.

[6] Steven Komarow, David J. Lynch and John Diamond, "Fine-Tuned On the Fly, War Plan Prevails," *USA TODAY*, 16Apr03.

[7] LtGen James Conway, intvw, "The Invasion of Iraq," *PBS Frontline* 26Feb04.

[8] Capt Suzan F. Thompson, intvw, 9May03, (Oral HistColl), Quantico, VA; hereafter Thompson intvw.

[9] Usher intvw, 19Mar03.

[10] *CSSB-10 Cruisebook*; CSSG-11 ComdC; CSSB-10 ComdC.

[11] Lt Michael P. Leonard, USN intvw, 16Apr03, (Oral HistColl), Quantico, VA; 7th ComdC.

[12] Capt Kevin P. Coughlin, intvw, 31Mar03, (Oral HistColl), Quantico, VA.

[13] 1st Marine Division (Reinforced) Cruisebook, *No Better Friend, No Worse Enemy*.

[14] LtCol Robert K. Weinkle Jr., intvw, 25Apr03, (Oral HistColl), Quantico, VA.

[15] Capt Alonzo J. Jones, "RRP-3" *CSSB-10 Cruisebook*, 27.

[16] Nelson notes.

[17] Cpl Jeff Hawk, "Profile: US Marine Corps Chief Warrant Officer–4 Tom Cierley–Bulk Fueler Brings Bulk of Experience to Iraq," *Defend America News* 5Jan05 (http://www.defendamerica.mil/profiles/june2003/pr060203a.html).

[18] Machut intvw, 8Apr03.

[19] 6th ESB ComdC.

[20] 7th ESB ComdC.

[21] Maj Emily J. Elder, intvw, 7May03, (Oral HistColl), Quantico, VA.

[22] Maj Ronald W. Sablan, intvw, 14Apr03, (Oral HistColl), Quantico, VA; hereafter Sablan intvw.

[23] Capt Mark F. Birk, intvw, 30Mar03, (Oral HistColl), Quantico, VA.

[24] 2d Transportation Support Battalion ComdC, 1Jan03–30Jun03.

[25] CSSB-10 ComdC.

[26] LtCol Valerie E. Thomas, intvw, 12Apr03, (Oral HistColl), Quantico, VA.

Chapter 4

[1] Goben intvw.

[2] Goben intvw.

[3] LtCol John M. Cassady, and CWO-4 Cheryl G. Ites, intvw, 9May03, (Oral HistColl), Quantico, VA; hereafter Cassady and Ites intvw.

[4] Author's journal.

[5] LtCol John M. Cassady, Maj Jefferson L. Kaster, and CWO-4 Cheryl G. Ites, "Caring for the Fallen–Mortuary Affairs in Operation Iraqi Freedom," *Proceedings* Apr04, 36-40; hereafter Cassady, Kaster, and Ites article.

[6] LtCol John M. Cassady, intvw, 13Mar03, (Oral HistColl), Quantico, VA; Cassady, Kaster, and Ites article.

[7] 1st Marine Division (Reinforced) Cruisebook, *No Better Friend, No Worse Enemy*, ch. 5 summary.

[8] CSSB-10 ComdC. *CSSB-10 Cruisebook*.

[9] 2dLt Sarah M. Stokes, "RRP-10," *CSSB-10 Cruisebook*, 33.

[10] 2d TSB ComdC; 2d FSSG sig events; Maj Matthew S. Cooke, e-mail, 7Jan05; Maj Michael J. Callanan, comments on draft, n.d. [Aug05], author's files; hereafter Callanan comments.

[11] Callanan comments.

[12] CSSB-10 ComdC.

[13] Maj Edward P. Wojnaroski, "RRPs 2, 4, and 7; Sandstorm Stop: The Ride of the RRP4 Opening Package," *CSSB-10 Cruisebook*, 31.

[14] James Meek, " US Advance Grinds to Halt in Teeth of Storm," *The Guardian* 26Mar03.

[15] Combat Service Support Battalion 22 ComdC, 1Jan03–30Jun03; Goben intvw; Williamson Murray and Robert H. Scales, *The Iraq War: A Military History* (Cambridge: Belknap Press, 2003),110.

[16] Machut intvw, 8Apr03.

[17] Machut intvw, 8Apr03.

[18] Machut intvw, 8Apr03.

[19] Maj Michael P. McCarthy, intvw, 6May03, (Oral HistColl), Quantico, VA.

[20] 6th ESB ComdC.

[21] Cdr James P. Flint, USNR, intvw, 5Apr03, (Oral HistColl), Quantico, VA; hereafter Flint Intvw.

[22] Author's journal.

[23] Flint intvw; Capt Kenneth E. Nixon, USN, intvw, 29Mar03, (Oral HistColl), Quantico, VA.

[24] Capt Glen M. Goldberg, USN, Cdr Patrick H. Bowers, USN, and Lt Denisha L. Robbins, USN, intvw, 31 Mar03, (Oral HistColl), Quantico, VA.

[25] Goldberg, Bowers, Robbins intvw.

[26] Capt Peter F. O'Connor, USN, intvw, 9Apr03, (Oral

HistColl), Quantico, VA.
[27] Al Bloom, "Fleet Hospital 3 Changes Navy Medicine," *Navy Newsstand,* 9Apr03.
[28] Al Bloom, "Fleet Hospital 3–Best Care in Iraq," *Navy Newsstand,* 30Apr03.
[29] Nelson notes.
[30] Nelson and Klocek article.
[31] Nelson intvw.
[32] Nelson and Klocek article, 41.
[33] CSSB-10 ComdC; *CSSB-10 Cruisebook.*
[34] 7th ESB ComdC.

Chapter 5

[1] LtCol Thomas N. Collins, intvw, 6Mar03, (Oral HistColl), Quantico, VA.
[2] Lehnert intvw.
[3] Usher intvw, 11May03.
[4] Lehnert intvw.
[5] Combat Service Support Battalion 12 ComdC, 1Jan03–30Jun03; Combat Service Support Group 15 ComdC 1Jan03–30Jun03; Capt Patryck J. Durham, intvw, 9Jul04, (Oral HistColl), Quantico, VA; hereafter Durham intvw.
[6] Thompson intvw.
[7] Usher intvw, 4Apr03.
[8] LtCol Adrian W. Burke, intvw, 16Apr03, (Oral HistColl), Quantico, VA; hereafter Burke intvw, 16Apr03.
[9] Maj John E. Vincent, intvw, 15Apr03, (Oral HistColl), Quantico, VA; hereafter Vincent intvw.
[10] GySt Melba L. Garza, intvw, 26May03, (Oral HistColl), Quantico, VA.
[11] MWSS 371 ComdC, 1Jan03–30Jun03.
[12] CSSG-15 ComdC.
[13] Vincent intvw.
[14] Durham intvw.
[15] Usher intvw, 19Mar03.
[16] Col Darrell L. Moore, e-mail, 9Feb06, author's files.
[17] Miciewicz comments.
[18] 1st TSG ComdC.
[19] Lehnert intvw.
[20] Ascunce intvw.
[21] Ascunce intvw.
[22] Usher intvw, 4Apr03.
[23] Lehnert intvw.
[24] Lehnert intvw.
[25] 2d TSB ComdC.
[26] Wissler intvw.
[27] Capt Brook W. Barbour, and 1stLt Christopher D. Waters, intvw, 1Apr03, (Oral HistColl), Quantico, VA.
[28] 2d FSSG Narrative Final.
[29] 2d FSSG Narrative Final.
[30] Lehnert intvw.
[31] Pomfret intvw, 7May03.

[32] Callanan comments.
[33] CSSG-11 ComdC.
[34] CSSG-11 ComdC.
[35] Nelson and Klocek article.
[36] CSSB-10 ComdC.

Chapter 6

[1] 1st MarDiv ComdC, 1Jan03–30Jun03.
[2] CSSG-11 ComdC.
[3] CSSB-10 ComdC.
[4] *CSSB-10 Cruisebook.*
[5] Maj Todd D. Hook Award Summary of Action; hereafter Hook Award.
[6] Burke intvw, 16Apr03.
[7] Burke intvw, 16Apr03.
[8] Burke intvw, 16Apr03.
[9] Sablan intvw.
[10] Marine Logistics Command Historical Interviews, (Oral HistColl), Quantico, VA.
[11] 2d FSSG Narrative Final.
[12] SgtMaj Richard R. Rawling, intvw, 27Apr03, (Oral HistColl), Quantico, VA.
[13] Maj Devin C. Young, intvw, 27Apr03, (Oral HistColl), Quantico, VA.
[14] Chief Warrant Office-2 Bradley S. Baggiano, and Chief Warrant Office-2 David Stevens, intvw, 16Apr03, USMC (Oral HistColl), Quantico, VA.
[15] 1st Force Service Support Group Historical Interviews, (Oral HistColl), Quantico, VA.
[16] Nelson notes.
[17] Nelson notes; Maj Thomas M. Pratt, intvw, 16Apr03, (Oral HistColl), Quantico, VA; hereafter Pratt intvw.
[18] Nelson notes; Pratt intvw; Capt Brian E. Gard, intvw, 16Apr03, (Oral HistColl), Quantico, VA; Capt Timothy A. Vandeborne, USA intvw, 15Apr03, (Oral HistColl), Quantico, VA; Nelson and Klocek article, 42.
[19] CSSG-11 ComdC.
[20] CSSB-10 ComdC; *CSSB-10 Cruisebook.*
[21] Callanan comments.
[22] CSSG-11 ComdC.
[23] CSSB-22 ComdC.
[24] Machut intvw, 8Apr03.
[25] Hook Award.
[26] Capt Timothy M. Cooley, e-mail, 21Oct04, (Oral HistColl), Quantico, VA.
[27] Cassady and Ites intvw, 9May03.
[28] CWO-2 Carlos L. Holt, intvw, 5Apr03, (Oral HistColl), Quantico, VA; hereafter Holt intvw.
[29] Holt intvw; LtCol Anthony E. Poletti, intvw, 8Apr03, (Oral HistColl), Quantico, VA.
[30] GySgt Terry L. Austin, and Sgt Monica E. Eroh,

intvw, 8May03, (Oral History Collection, Quantico, VA.

[31] Maj Michael J. Callanan, Intvw, 7May03, (Oral HistColl), Quantico, VA; Callanan comments.

Chapter 7

[1] 1st Marine Division (Reinforced) Cruisebook, *No Better Friend, No Worse Enemy*, Ch. 8.
[2] CSSB-10 ComdC.
[3] Cpl Jeremy M. Vought, "FSSG Marine Help Iraqis Repair Looted, Damaged University," *Marine Corps News*, 13May03.
[4] Nelson and Klocek article, 43-44.
[5] 7th ESB ComdC.
[6] 7th ESB ComdC.
[7] CSSG-15 ComdC; CSSB-12 ComdC.
[8] Cpl Jeremy M. Vought, "Usher Relinquishes Command to Kramlich," *Marine Corps News* 17Jul03.

Chapter 8

[1] BGen Ronald S. Coleman, intvw, 20Apr04, (Oral HistColl), Quantico, VA; hereafter Coleman intvw.
[2] John Reynolds, CNA Report CIM D0009987.A2/Final, *A Description of Operation Iraqi Freedom Maritime Prepositioned Force Reconstruction, Regeneration, and Re-embarkation* (OIF MPF R3), Jun. 2004, The CNA Corporation; hereafter Reynolds Report.
[3] Reynolds Report.
[4] Reynolds Report.
[5] Reynolds Report.
[6] Coleman intvw.
[7] Coleman intvw.
[8] Coleman intvw.
[9] Reynolds Report.
[10] Coleman intvw.
[11] Coleman intvw.
[12] Reynolds Report.
[13] Coleman intvw.

Epilogue

[1] Usher intvw, 11May03.
[2] Lehnert intvw.

Appendix A

Chronology of Significant Events

2001

11 September	Al-Qaeda terrorists attack the World Trade Center and the Pentagon.
25 November	Marines of Task Force 58 land in Afghanistan as part of the operation to deprive al-Qaeda of its base in that country.

2002

January	Marine Forces, Pacific orders I Marine Expeditionary Force (I MEF) to focus on preparing for contingencies in the U.S. CentCom theater; MEF planners begin over a year of work on plans to invade Iraq.
11 October	The Pentagon orders I MEF to deploy its headquarters staff to Kuwait for service with Coalition Forces Land Component Command (CFLCC) under Army LtGen David D. McKiernan.
15 November	I MEF headquarters deploys to Kuwait; newly appointed I MEF Commander LtGen James T. Conway deploys with his headquarters.
24 November	CFLCC exercise to test command and control links with I MEF and other commands, "Lucky Warrior 03-1," begins.
9 December	CentCom exercise "Internal Look," based on the current version of the plan for the invasion of Iraq, begins.

2003

2 January	Pentagon issues Deployment Order 177A, soon to be followed by 177B, which orders the wholesale deployment of I MEF forces to theater.
5 January	2d FSSG Forward stands up to become the Landing Force Support Party establishing Camp Fox, the sea port of debarkation (SPOD), and the aerial port of debarkation in Kuwait.
13 January	Gen Michael W. Hagee becomes the 33d Commandant of the Marine Corps.
14 January	1st FSSG establishes its Combat Operations Center at Tactical Assembly Area (TAA) Coyote.
15 January	Amphibious Task Force (ATF) East departs Morehead City, North Carolina, for Kuwait; the first of 11 MPSRON ships arrive at the SPOD in Kuwait; offloading and transport of equipment to several locations in Kuwait begin.

17 January	Amphibious Task Force (ATF) West departs San Diego, California, for Kuwait.
7 February	The offload of the 11 MPSRON ships is completed in record time.
8 February	CFLCC exercise "Lucky Warrior 03-2," labeled "a dress rehearsal" for war, begins with MEF participation.
16 February	The 2d Marine Expeditionary Brigade (2d MEB) with ATF East begins to go ashore in Kuwait to reinforce I MEF; its aviation elements transfer to 3d MAW control and the ground elements are redesignated Task Force Tarawa.
24 February	Amphibious Task Force West begins offloading its west-coast Marine units in Kuwait; most other Marines follow by air.
9 March	First leaflets dropped in Baghdad urging non-interference with Coalition operations and soliciting support from Iraqi people.
17 March	President Bush issues an ultimatum to Saddam Hussein to leave Iraq within 48 hours.
18 March	Operation Southern Watch aircraft conduct airstrikes against Iraqi early warning radars and command-and-control capabilities; Marine forces are ordered to staging areas.
Night of 19-20 March	U.S. Air Force aircraft and Navy vessels conduct unplanned attack against Saddam Hussein and other Iraqi leadership targets in what becomes popularly known as the "decapitation strike," which does not succeed but does initiate hostilities.
20 March	Iraq retaliates by firing surface-to-surface missiles against Coalition troops in Kuwait; ground combat operations begin in the night; I MEF is supporting attack of Army's V Corps; Regimental Combat Team 5 is leading Marine unit.
21 March	Marines capture the Rumaylah oil fields, a key objective of the campaign; Marines and British forces secure the port of Umm Qasr before moving on the city of Basrah, their most important objective.
23 March	Task Force Tarawa begins to secure the city of an-Nasiriyah and its key bridges over the Euphrates River and the Saddam Canal; heavy fighting ensues; friendly fire incident occurs at bridge over canal; II MEF commander MajGen Henry P. Osman deploys to northern Iraq to establish the Military Coordination and Liaison Command (MCLC) under operational control of CentCom in order to maintain political stability.
Night of 24-25 March	"Mother of all sandstorms" begins, slowing operational tempo for approximately two days.
24-27 March	1st Marine Division continues to advance up Routes 1 and 7 toward Baghdad.
25 March	6th Engineer Support Battalion completes their 57-mile hose-reel tactical

	fuel system, capable of pumping fuel from the Kuwait-Iraq border to Logistics Support Area Viper.
27 March	"Operational pause" begins to consolidate supply lines and address threats by irregular Iraqi formations on the ground; 3d MAW air offensive continues unimpeded, rendering many Iraqi combat units ineffective.
29 March	1st Force Service Support Group (FSSG) Forward assumes command and control at Logistics Support Area Viper near Jalibah, Iraq.
1 April	Division resumes progress toward Baghdad; FSSG continues to perform resupply with cooperation of Wing and Marine Logistics Command.
6-7 April	8th Engineer Support Battalion constructs three bridges across the Narh Diyala River, allowing elements of 1st Marine Division to cross into Baghdad.
7 April	Regimental Combat Team (RCT)-7 crosses the Diyala River and moves on outskirts of Baghdad from the east; Army conducts second "Thunder Run" into capital.
9 April	Marines of 3d Battalion, 4th Marine Regiment, part of RCT 7, assist Iraqi civilians in toppling a large statue of Saddam Hussein in Firdos Square in Marine area of operations (AO), Eastern Baghdad.
10 April	RCT-5 engaged in heavy fighting at Almilyah Palace and Abu Hanifah mosque in Baghdad; looting begins as fighting tapers off; Marines begin post-combat operations
13 April	1st FSSG Forward assumes command and control at Support Area Edson near ad-Diwaniyah, Iraq.
13-14 April	Task Force Tripoli, out of 1st Marine Division, takes control of Tikrit, Saddam Hussein's hometown
20 April	Relief in place with U.S. Army in eastern Baghdad is complete; MEF redeploys its forces to the southern third of Iraq; mission is now security, humanitarian assistance, and reconstruction; focus of effort is seven infantry battalions from 1st Marine Division in seven governates (or districts).
20 April	The offload of all "black-bottom" ships is completed.
1 May	Under a banner reading "Mission Accomplished," President Bush announces that major combat operations are over.
12 May	Ambassador L. Paul Bremer III takes over as civil administrator in Iraq, replacing Jay M. Garner. Bremer's Coalition Provisional Authority soon replaces Garner's Office of Reconstruction and Humanitarian Assistance.
19 May	2d Transportation Support Battalion completes the re-embarkation of ATF East at Kuwait Naval Base.

26 May	2d Transportation Support Battalion completes the re-embarkation of ATF West at Kuwait Naval Base.
3 June	2d FSSG Forward is relieved of duties as the Landing Force Support Party; redeploys to Camp Lejeune, North Carolina.
15 June	2d FSSG stands down as the Marine Logistics Command and stands up the Maritime Prepositioning Forces Special Purpose Marine Air Ground Task Force (MPF SPMAGTF); BGen Ronald S. Coleman assumes command of the SPMAGTF.
22 July	Saddam Hussein's sons Uday and Qusay are killed in firefight with U.S. Army in Mosul.
19 August	A truck bomb explodes at the UN headquarters in Baghdad, killing 20 people, including the UN High Commissioner for Human Rights.
3 September	At Camp Babylon, I MEF conducts a transfer of authority to a Polish-led international Coalition force; most remaining Marines return to the United States.
13 October	CSSG-11 is the last unit within 1st FSSG to leave theater.
10 November	Marines of Special Purpose MAGTF celebrate the Marine Corps Birthday in CONUS after completing the work of repatriating all Marine Corps equipment from theater.

Appendix B

Command and Staff List

1st Force Service Support Group

Commanding General	BGen Edward G. Usher III (to 10 July 03)
	BGen Richard S. Kramlich (from 10 July 03)
Deputy Commander	Col John L. Sweeney Jr.
Chief of Staff	Col Darrell L. Moore
AC/S G-1	LtCol Frank L. Tapia Jr.
AC/S G-2	Maj Brian G. Fitzpatrick
AC/S G-3	Col Gregory R. Dunlap
AC/S G-4	LtCol Thomas M. Vilas
AC/S G-6	LtCol David W. Smith
Combat Service Support Group 16 Commanding Officer	LtCol Michael J. Taylor
Combat Service Support Group 11 Commanding Officer	Col John J. Pomfret (July 02–August 03)
	Col Charles L. Hudson (from August 03)
Combat Service Support Battalion 10 Commanding Officer	LtCol Robert K. Weinkle Jr.
Combat Service Support Company 111 Commanding Officer	Capt Grant R. Shottenkirk
Combat Service Support Company 115 Commanding Officer	Capt Suzan F. Thompson
Combat Service Support Company 117 Commanding Officer	Capt Andrew J. Bergen
Combat Service Support Company Tripoli Commanding Officer	Maj Michael J. Callanan
Combat Service Support Battalion 22 Commanding Officer	LtCol Thomas N. Goben
Combat Service Support Battalion 13 Commanding Officer	LtCol Michael D. Malone
Combat Service Support Company 133 Commanding Officer	Maj Robert D. Dasch Jr.

120 COMBAT SERVICE SUPPORT

Combat Service Support Company 134
Commanding Officer							Capt Henry K. Lyles

Combat Service Support Company 135
Commanding Officer							Maj Kenneth A. Evans

Combat Service Support Group 14
Commanding Officer:							Col John T. Larson

Combat Service Support Group 15
Commanding Officer:							Col Bruce E. Bissett

Combat Service Support Company 151
Commanding Officer							LtCol Robert W. Higbee

Combat Service Support Battalion 12
Commanding Officer							LtCol Kathleen M. Murney (to 27 March 03)
									LtCol Adrian W. Burke (from 27 March 03)

Combat Service Support Company 121
Commanding Officer							Maj Michael E. Bean

Combat Service Support Battalion 18
Commanding Officer							LtCol Thomas N. Collins

Combat Service Support Company 181
Commanding Officer							Capt Patryck J. Durham

Health Services Battalion
Commanding Officer							CDR Gregory M. Huet, USN

Transportation Support Group
Commanding Officer:							Col David G. Reist

6th Motor Transport Battalion
Commanding Officer							LtCol Patrick J. Hermesmann

6th Engineer Support Battalion
Commanding Officer							LtCol Roger R. Machut

7th Engineer Support Battalion
Commanding Officer							LtCol Scott H. Poindexter

8th Engineer Support Battalion
Commanding Officer							LtCol Niel E. Nelson

716th Military Police Battalion, USA
Commanding Officer							LTC Kim S. Orlando, USA

Combat Service Support Battalion 19
Commanding Officer							LtCol David M. Kluegel

Expeditionary Medical Facility 3
Commanding Officer   CAPT Peter F. O'Connor, USN

2d Force Service Support Group / Marine Logistics Command

Commanding General   BGen Michael R. Lehnert
Chief of Staff   Col Robert L. Songer
AC/S G-1   Maj Craig E. Stephens
AC/S G-2   Maj Timothy W. Nichols
AC/S G-3   Col Russell A. Eve
AC/S G-6   LtCol Kenneth S. Helfrich

2d Force Service Support Group Forward
Commanding Officer   Col Stephen W. Otto

Headquarters and Service Battalion (-)
Commanding Officer   LtCol Craig C. Crenshaw

2d Supply Battalion (-)
Commanding Officer   Col William F. Johnson

2d Maintenance Battalion (-)
Commanding Officer   LtCol Brent P. Goddard

2d Transportation Support Battalion (-)
Commanding Officer   Col John E. Wissler

Beach and Terminal Operations Company (-)
Commanding Officer   Maj Robert A. Kaminski

MLC Support Detachment 1
Commanding Officer   Maj Tyson Geisendorff

2d Military Police Battalion
Commanding Officer   LtCol Christopher B. Martin

8th Communications Battalion
Commanding Officer   LtCol Roarke L. Anderson

Marine Wing Communications Squadron 48
Commanding Officer   LtCol Kavin G. Kowis

Detachment, 8th Engineer Support Battalion
Officer-In-Charge   1stLt Jeremy N. Henwood

2d Medical Battalion
Commanding Officer   CDR Benjamin G. M. Feril, USN

Detachment, 2d Dental Battalion
Officer-In-Charge   CAPT Stephen J. Connelly, USN

Special Purpose MAGTF

Commanding General	BGen Ronald S. Coleman
Chief of Staff	Col Robert L. Songer
AC/S G-1	Capt Mark R. Schroeder
	Capt Rennie R. Givens (26Aug03)
AC/S G-2	Capt Ryan Janiczek
AC/S G-3	Col Dennis M. Arinello
AC/S G-6	Maj David Forrest

Detachment, Headquarters and Service Battalion
Officer-In-Charge   Maj Michael J. Prouty

2d Supply Battalion (-)
Commanding Officer   Col Peter J. Talleri

Detachment, 2d Maintenance Battalion
Officer-In-Charge   Maj Don A. Mills

Detachment, 2d Transportation Support Battalion
Officer-In-Charge   LtCol Charles G. Chiarotti

Detachment, 2d Military Police Battalion
Officer-In-Charge   Maj Eric J. Eldred

Detachment, 8th Engineer Support Battalion
Officer-In-Charge   1stLt Jeremy N. Henwood

Detachment, Marine Wing Communications Squadron 48
Officer-In-Charge   Maj Sean D. Parker

Detachment, 2d Medical and 2d Dental Battalion
Officer-In-Charge   Lt Ray Perez, USN

Appendix C

Unit List

1st Force Service Support Group [1st FSSG]

Combat Service Support Group 11 [CSSG-11]
    Combat Service Support Battalion 10 [CSSB-10]
        Combat Service Support Company 111 [CSSC-111]
        Combat Service Support Company 115 [CSSC-115]
        Combat Service Support Company 117 [CSSC-117]
    Combat Service Support Company Tripoli

    Combat Service Support Battalion 22 [CSSB-22]

    Combat Service Support Battalion 13 [CSSB-13]
        Combat Service Support Company 133 [CSSC-133]
        Combat Service Support Company 134 [CSSC-134]
        Combat Service Support Company 135 [CSSC-135]

Combat Service Support Group 14 [CSSG-14]

Combat Service Support Group 15 [CSSG-15]
    Combat Service Support Company 151 [CSSC-151]
    Combat Service Support Battalion 12 [CSSB-12]
        Combat Service Support Company 121 [CSSC-121]
    Combat Service Support Battalion 18 [CSSB-18]
        Combat Service Support Company 181 [CSSC-181]

Combat Service Support Group 16 [CSSG-16]

Health Services Battalion [H&SBn]

Transportation Support Group [TSG]
    6th Motor Transport Battalion [6th MTBn]

6th Engineer Support Battalion [6th ESB]
7th Engineer Support Battalion [7th ESB]
8th Engineer Support Battalion [8th ESB]
716th Military Police Battalion, USA [716th MPBn]
Combat Service Support Battalion 19 [CSSB-19]
Expeditionary Medical Facility 3 [EMF-3]

2d Force Service Support Group / Marine Logistics Command

2d Force Service Support Group Forward [2d FSSG]
Headquarters and Service Battalion (-) [H&S Bn]
2d Supply Battalion (-) [2d SupBn]
2d Maintenance Battalion (-) [2d MaintBn]

2d Transportation Support Battalion (-) [2d TSB]
                Beach and Terminal Operations Company (-) [Bch&TermOpsCo]
MLC Support Detachment 1 [MLC SuptDet]
2d Military Police Battalion [2d MPBn]
8th Communications Battalion [8th CommBn]
Marine Wing Communications Squadron 48 [MWCS-48]
Detachment, 8th Engineer Support Battalion [Det, 8th ESB]
Detachment, 2d Medical Battalion [Det, 2d MedBn]
Detachment, 2d Dental Battalion [Det, 2d DentBn]

Special Purpose MAGTF

Detachment, Headquarters and Service Battalion [Det, H&SBn]
2d Supply Battalion (-) [2d SupBn]
Detachment, 2d Maintenance Battalion [Det, 2d MaintBn]
Detachment, 2d Transportation Support Battalion [2d TSB]
Detachment, 2d Military Police Battalion [Det, 2d MPBn]
Detachment, 8th Engineer Support Battalion [Det, 8th JESB]
Detachment, Marine Wing Communications Squadron 48 [Det, MWCS-48]
Detachment, 2d Medical and 2d Dental Battalion, [Det 2d Med&2dDenBn]

Appendix D

Glossary of Terms and Abbreviations

AAV	Amphibious Assault Vehicle
AK-47	A Kalashnikov automatic rifle
AO	Area of Operations
ATLASS	Asset Tracking Logistics and Supply System
BAS	Battalion Aid Station
Blue Force Tracker	A satellite system that allowed commanders to see the locations of friendly units on a computer screen
BSSG	Brigade Service Support Group
CAE	Crossing Area Engineer: an engineer (bridging) company designated as a river crossing command and control unit, co-located with a supported regimental combat team headquarters to provide command and control over the bridge build and then control the crossing area as the regiments passed through the river crossing area
CENTCOM	U.S. Central Command, the joint (and sometimes combined) command responsible for the Middle East, headed by the combatant commander (formerly known as a regional commander-in-chief)
CFLCC	Coalition Forces Land Component Commander, a functional command under the combatant commander
CG	Commanding General
CA	Civil Affairs
CJTF	Commander, Joint Task Force or Combined–Joint Task Force
CNA	Center for Naval Analyses
CONUS	Continental United States
CSS	Combat Service Support
CSSA	Combat Service Support Area
CSSB	Combat Service Support Battalion
CSSC	Combat Service Support Company
CSSE	Combat Service Support Element

CSSG	Combat Service Support Group
CSSOC	Combat Service Support Operations Center
EMF	Expeditionary Medical Facility
ESB	Engineer Support Battalion
FCE	Force Crossing Engineer: the engineer (bridging) battalion commanding officer and his support staff, co-located with the division forward headquarters to provide over-arching command and control of all of the bridge assets assigned to the FSSG/Division
Fedayeen	Arabic word meaning "men of sacrifice," irregular fighters for Saddam Hussein
FOB	Forward Operating Base
FRSS	Forward Resuscitative Surgical System: a small, self-contained, and mobile team with surgical capabilities, designed to forward displace, to take care of those casualties who were not stable enough to survive a flight rearward to a surgical company
FSSG	Force Service Support Group
HMMWV	High-Mobility, Multipurpose Wheeled Vehicle (the jeep of this war, the humvee)
ID	Infantry Division: as in the U.S. Army's 3d ID
ILC	Integrated Logistics Capability
IRB	Improved Ribbon Bridge. A modular bridge with integral superstructure and floating supports, consisting of a ramp bay at each bank and the required number of interior bays to complete the span
LAR	Light Armored Reconnaissance
LAV	Light Armored Vehicle
LMECC	Logistics Movement and Engineering Coordination Center
LSA	Logistics Support Area
LSB	Landing Support Battalion
LVS	Logistics Vehicle System
MAGTF	Marine Air-Ground Task Force (the basic organization for committing Marines to combat, with command, air, ground, and support elements)
MAP	Medical Augmentation Program. A program that provides medical personnel to the operating forces during situations requiring medical personnel augmentation
MarCent	Marine Corps Forces Central Command

MAW	Marine Aircraft Wing: rough equivalent of a ground division in size
MEB	Marine Expeditionary Brigade: a detachable part of the MEF
MGB	Medium Girder Bridge. A hand-erectable, heavy-duty, prefabricated deck bridge consisting of high strength components, which can be assembled into bridges of varying lengths
MEF	Marine Expeditionary Force: a corps-level MAGTF
MEU(SOC)	Marine Expeditionary Unit (Special Operations Capable): a small MAGTF built around a battalion landing team
MLC	Marine Logistics Command: a theater-level component subordinate to MarCent
MOPP	Mission-Oriented Protective Posture: a state of readiness with respect to the threat of an NBC attack; levels run from 0 to IV and correspond to the amount of protective clothing worn
MOS	Military Occupational Specialty
MP	Military Police
MPF	Maritime Prepositioning Force (made up of MPS)
MPS	Maritime Prepositioning Ship (staged in strategic locations, carrying equipment for use in wartime contingencies)
MRBC	Multi-Role Bridge Company; a U.S. Army company of engineers, specifically trained and mobilized for the purpose of bridge building
MRE	Meals ready-to-eat
MSD	Marine Logistics Command Support Detachment
MSR	Main Supply Route
MSSG	Marine Expeditionary Unit Service Support Group
MT	Motor Transport
MTVR	Medium Tactical Vehicle Replacement; the mobile, high-performance, 7-ton truck purchased by the Marine Corps to replace their aging fleet of 5-ton trucks
MWSS	Marine Wing Support Squadron
NBC	Nuclear, Biological, Chemical (as in the "threat of an NBC attack," or "NBC protective gear")
OIC	Officer-In-Charge
OIF	Operation Iraqi Freedom

OPCON	Operational Control, command authority that is inherent in combatant command authority (which is exercised by the combatant commander) and which may be delegated. It is the authority to perform functions involving organizing and employing subordinate commands. Compare TaCon.
OPLAN	Operations Plan
OPORD	Operation Order
OSCC	Operation Systems Control Center
POG	Port Operations Group; a task-organized unit, located at the seaport of embarkation and/or debarkation under the control of the landing force support party and/or combat service support element, that assists and provides support in the loading and/or unloading and staging of personnel, supplies, and equipment from shipping
POL	Petroleum, Oil, and Lubricants
PX	Post Exchange
R3	Reconstitution, Regeneration, and Re-embarkation
RCT	Regimental Combat Team
RFF	Request for Forces
RIP	Relief in place. When one unit replaces another in a given area
ROC	Rehearsal of Concept
ROE	Rules of Engagement
ROWPU	Reverse Osmosis Water Purification Unit. A mechanical device that produces potable water from a variety of raw water sources
RRP	Repair and Replenishment Point
RSO&I	Reception, Staging, Onward Movement, and Integration: the phases which units pass through upon reached a combat theater between disembarking from their transport to being ready for combat
SA	Support Area
SASO	Security and Stabilization Operations
SEABEE	Navy engineer: from "CB" for construction battalion
SJA	Staff Judge Advocate
SPMAGTF	Special Purpose Marine Air-Ground Task Force

SPOD	Sea Port of Debarkation: a seaport designated in a theater of operations as the point of debarkation for forces arriving by sea
STP	Shock Trauma Platoon: a small, mobile medical unit similar to a forward deployed emergency room, whose functions center around stabilization, triage, and the holding of patients
TAA	Tactical Assembly Area
TACON	Tactical Control: detailed and local control of units, inherent in OpCon but may be delegated
T/E	Table of Equipment
TF	Task Force
T/O	Table of Organization
TPFDD	Time–Phased Force Deployment Data
TSB	Transportation Support Battalion
TSC	Theater Support Command
TSG	Transportation Support Group
TTP	Tactics, Techniques, and Procedures
USA	United States Army
USN	United States Navy
UXO	Unexploded Ordnance

Appendix E

Presidential Unit Citation

THE SECRETARY OF THE NAVY
WASHINGTON, D.C. 20350-1000
3 November 2003

The President of the United States takes pleasure in presenting the PRESIDENTIAL UNIT CITATION to

I MARINE EXPEDITIONARY FORCE

for service as set forth in the following

CITATION:

For extraordinary heroism and outstanding performance in action against enemy forces in support of Operation IRAQI FREEDOM from 21 March to 24 April 2003. During this period, I Marine Expeditionary Force (MEF) (REIN) conducted the **longest sequence** of coordinated combined arms overland attacks in the history of the Marine Corps. From the border between Kuwait and Iraq, to the culmination of hostilities north of Baghdad, I MEF advanced nearly 800 kilometers under sustained and heavy combat. Utilizing the devastating combat power of organic aviation assets, coupled with the awesome power resident in the ground combat elements, and maintaining momentum through the herculean efforts of combat service support elements, I MEF destroyed nine Iraqi Divisions. This awesome display of combat power was accomplished while simultaneously freeing the Iraqi people from more than 30 years of oppression and reestablishing basic infrastructure in the country. During the 33 days of combat, to the transition to civil-military operations, I MEF sustained a tempo of operations never before seen on the modern battlefield, conducting four major river crossings, maintaining the initiative, and sustaining forces. The ferocity and duration of the campaign was made possible through the skills and determination of the Soldiers, Sailors, Airmen, Marines, and Coalition Partners comprising I MEF at all levels, all echelons, and in all occupational fields. By their outstanding courage, aggressive fighting spirit, and untiring devotion to duty, the officers and enlisted personnel of I Marine Expeditionary Force (REIN) reflected great credit upon themselves and upheld the highest traditions of the Marine Corps and the United States Naval Service.

For the President,

[signature]

Secretary of the Navy

Appendix F

Navy Unit Commendation

2D FORCE SERVICE SUPPORT GROUP

For service as set forth in following

CITATION:

For exceptionally meritorious service during assigned mission in action against enemy forces in Operations ENDURING FREEDOM and IRAQI FREEDOM from 15 December 2001 to 1 June 2003. Throughout this period, 2d Force Service Support Group repeatedly demonstrated unprecedented operational flexibility, innovation, and tactical expertise during near-simultaneous operations in Cuba, Kuwait, and Iraq. Receiving urgent deployment orders to Guantanamo Bay, Cuba, 2d Force Service Support Group formed Joint Task Force 160, responsible for receiving and holding al-Qaida and Taliban terrorists for further intelligence exploitation and prosecution. In less than 96 hours after arrival, they constructed a holding capability for 100 detainees. Detainee population grew to 320 in less than a month. During Operation IRAQI FREEDOM, 2d Force Service Support Group again demonstrated its operational flexibility by becoming the Marine Logistics Command, an operational logistics enabling force. As one of the first Marine Forces in theater, it offloaded over 70,000 Marines and associated equipment four days ahead of schedule, making it the most expedient offload in Marine Corps History. During hostilities, the Marine Logistics Command delivered 4.2 million gallons of fuel, 10 million meals ready-to-eat, and 8,784 short tons of critical sustainment throughout a battlefield spanning over 430 square miles. The commanding general deployed his headquarters twice, amassing nearly nine months of combat service support in support of Operations ENDURING FREEDOM and IRAQI FREEDOM. By their truly distinctive achievements, extensive enthusiasm, and unfailing devotion to duty, the Marines and sailors of 2d Force Service Support Group reflected great credit upon themselves and upheld the highest traditions of the United States Naval Service.

Secretary of the Navy

Index

Ad-Diwaniyah, 53, 69,78, 87, 93-95, 97, 99, 100
Aircraft
    Bell AH-1 Cobra, 72, 80, 90
    Bell UH-1N Iroquois (Huey), 50
    Fairchild Republic A-10 Warthog, 53
    Lockheed KC-130 Hercules, 56, 77, 86, 91, 94
    Sikorsky CH-53 Sea Stallion, 10, 36, 50, 64
    Sikorsky UH-60 Black Hawk, 55
Air Force Units
    320th Expeditionary Aeromedical Evacuation Squadron, 33
    Aeromedical Evacuation Liaison Team, 33
    Mobile Air Staging Facility Team, 33
Al-Aziziyah, 79-80
Al-Emeri, Khuder, 51, 62
Al-Hayy, 77, 98
Al-Hillah, 97, 99
Ali Al Salem, 6, 21, 105
Ali Hassam, 62
Al-Jaber, 6, 21, 105
Al-Kut, 39, 53, 57, 70, 72, 77, 79, 94-95, 97-99
Al-Mu'aytyah, 67
Al-Muthanna, 93
Al-Qadisiyah University, 93-95, 100
Al-Rasheed Airfield, 87
Ambush Alley, 57
Amey, Lieutenant Colonel Aaron T., 74
Anderson, Lieutenant Colonel Roarke L., 28
An-Najaf, 93, 99
An-Nasiriyah, 46, 48-50, 53, 55, 57, 64-65, 67, 69, 71, 73, 87, 98-100
An-Numaniyah, 78-80, 87, 98
Army, U.S.
    V Corps, 27, 39
    3d Infantry Division, 34, 46, 48, 53, 64, 93
    4th Infantry Division, 91
    101st Airborne Division, 11, 73
    377th Theater Support Command, 15-16, 19, 29, 74, 77, 105
    63d Signal Battalion, 33
    83d Chemical Battalion, 33
    716th Military Police Battalion, 10-12, 94, 98
    7th Chemical Company
        7th Biological Integrated Detection System Platoon, 33
    51st Chemical Company, 33
    319th Petroleum, Oil, and Lubricants Company, 8, 74
    459th Multi-Role Bridge Company, 64, 66, 85
    507th Maintenance Company, 53
    574th Multi-Role Bridge Company, 64
Ar-Rifa, 71
Ascunce, Lieutenant Colonel Jorge, 8, 74
Ash Shatrah, 71
Ash Shuaybah, Port of, 20-21, 28, 33, 105
As-Samawah, 99
Asset tracking logistics and supply system (ATLASS), 26
Ba'ath Party, 51, 53
Babcock, Major William L., Jr., 22
Babil, 93
Babylon, 99
Baggiano, Chief Warrant Officer 2 Bradley S., 82
Baghdad, 8, 21, 36, 39-40, 42, 56, 59, 69, 73, 76-87, 89, 93-98, 107
Bales, Private First Class Chad E., 78
Bergen, Captain Andrew J., 4
Bergman, General John W., 13
Big Board, The, 75
Bilski, Lieutenant Commander Tracy R. (USN), 10
Bird, Captain Susan, 34, 44, 67
Birk, Captain Mark F., 49
Bissett, Colonel Bruce E., 6

Blount Island Command, 102, 104, 105
Bohman, Captain Harold R. (USN), 10
Boomer, Lieutenant General Walter E., 1
Bowers, Commander Patrick H. (USN), 63
Brabham, Brigadier General James A., 1, 2
Breach Point West, 33, 34, 37, 40, 44, 46-47, 49, 58, 69
Breach Point North, 44
bridging, 9, 10, 36-37, 46, 65, 67, 78, 85, 95, 97
British Units
    1 (UK) Armored Division, 21
    6th Supply Regiment, 25
    14th Geographic Squadron, 26
British WWI cemetery, 97
Broadmeadow, Lieutenant Colonel John J., 4
Burke, Lieutenant Colonel Adrian W., 2, 30, 71-72, 80-81, 98
Bush, President George W., 1, 39
Caley, Major James C., 31
Callanan, Major Michael J., 57, 89-92
Camps
    Arifjan, 19, 28
    Betio, 23, 34
    Bougainville, 23, 30, 32, 40, 98
    Commando, 21, 42
    Coyote, 22-24, 27, 30, 33-34, 36, 41-42, 47-48, 50, 54-55, 73, 75, 82
    Fox, 18, 24-25, 27-29, 41-42, 102-103, 105
    Guadalcanal, 23
    Guam, 23
    Iwo Jima, 23, 54-55, 73
    Lejeune, NC, 7, 9, 17-18, 24, 102, 106
    Matilda, 21
    Midway, 23, 29-30
    Okinawa, 23
    Peleliu, 23
    Pendleton, CA, 4, 7, 9, 11, 44, 73, 98, 100
    Ryan, 21, 31
    Saipan, 36
    Solomon Islands, 23, 33, 41
    Tarawa, 23, 27
    Wake Island, 22
Cassady, Lieutenant Colonel John M., 54-55, 88

Center for Naval Analyses, 14
Chiarotti, Lieutenant Colonel Charles G., 103
Cierley, Chief Warrant Officer 4 Thomas M., 46
civil affairs, 33, 50-52, 62, 80, 86, 98
classes of supply, 17, 25-26
Coalition Forces Land Component Commander (CFLCC), 15, 34, 39, 100
Coleman, Brigadier General Ronald S., 102, 104-106
Collins Lieutenant Colonel Thomas N., 6, 48, 69
combat stress, 61-63
Combined Joint Task Force 7, 100
Comfort (T-AH 20), 61
Connelly, Captain Stephen J. (USN), 18
convoys, 7-9, 11, 13, 17, 20, 26-27, 31-32, 34-36, 40, 42-45, 48-51, 53, 57-58, 67, 69-77, 80-82, 87, 99, 107
Conway, General James T., 1, 33, 39, 43, 91, 106
Cook, Major Matthew S., 37, 56
Cooley, Captain Timothy M., 87
Coughlin, Captain Kevin P., 23, 45, 47
Council of Colonels, 7
Crenshaw, Lieutenant Colonel Craig C., 16
Crossing Area Engineer (CAE), 64, 65, 78
Curtin, Sergeant Major Michael, 14
DeVries, Captain Marta M., 76
Dhi Qar, 93
direct support, 1-7, 14, 29-32, 39, 42, 44, 46-47, 53, 64, 69, 73, 81, 94, 97, 100
Diyala River, 36, 66, 83-85, 87
Durham, Captain Patrick J., 69, 73
Eldred, Major Eric J., 103
engineer support element (ESE), 8
engineering, 7-9, 34-35, 47, 67-69, 81, 87, 95, 97, 100
Eroh, Sergeant Monica E., 89
Euphrates River, 21, 39, 46, 49-50, 53, 55-57, 59, 64, 67
Exercises
    Combined Arms Exercises, 16
    Rolling Thunder, 26
    Unitas, 26
expeditionary medical facility (EMF), 48, 63, 64
Fedayeen, 53, 56, 67, 81, 85
Feril, Commander Benjamin G. M. (USN), 18
Flint, Commander James P. (USN), 61

Fort Campbell, Kentucky, 10
Fort Lewis, Washington, 5, 6
forward resuscitative surgical system (FRSS), 10, 34, 60, 63, 69, 71, 80, 90
Foss, Major Joseph J., 22
    Airfield, 54-55
Franks, General Tommy R. (USA), 1
friendly fire, 31, 53
Gard, Captain Brian E., 85
Garza, Gunnery Sergeant Melba L., 72
Geisendorff, Major Tyson B., 27, 42
general support, 1-4, 6, 15, 17, 32, 44, 71, 73-74, 80-81, 99, 103
Goben, Lieutenant Colonel Thomas N., 7, 32, 53
Goddard, Lieutenant Colonel Brent P., 17, 82
Goldberg, Captain Glenn M. (USN), 61
Golden Spike, 47
Grooms, Captain James R., 75
Guantanamo Bay, 14, 24
Haar, Captain Christopher M., 36
Habayeb, First Lieutenant Leith R., 45
Hagee, General Michael W., 33
Hailston, Lieutenant General Earl B., 33
Hantush, 56, 70, 77
Helfrich, Lieutenant Colonel Kenneth S., 28
Hermesmann, Lieutenant Colonel Patrick J., 8, 36
Higbee Lieutenant Colonel Robert W., 6
Highways
    Highway 1, 45-46, 53, 55-56, 64, 66-68, 70-71, 95
    Highway 6, 79-80, 83
    Highway 7, 46, 53, 64-65, 67, 71, 77, 80, 95
    Highway 8, 56
    Highway 17, 71, 77
    Highway 27, 56, 78
    Highway 80, 45
Holt, Chief Warrant Officer 2 Carlos L., 88
Hook, Major Todd D., 81, 87
hose reel system, 9, 33, 37, 46-47, 58, 67, 73, 87
Huet, Commander Gregory M. (USN), 10
Hussein, Saddam, 39, 51, 53, 89-91, 93, 100
inland petroleum distribution system (IPDS), 46, 87
integrated logistics capability (ILC), 15

Iraqi Units
    Republican Guard, 79, 85-86
    10th Armored Division, 87
Ites, Chief Warrant Officer 4 Cheryl G., 54, 88
Jalibah, 44, 46-47, 49-50, 57
    Airfield, 53-54, 58, 77
James, Corporal Evan T., 60
Johnson, Colonel William F., 17, 26
Joint Task Force Horn of Africa, 21, 26
Jones, Captain Alonzo J., III, 99
Jones, Captain Jamie, 45
Kaminski, Major Robert A., 42
Karbala, 12, 93, 99
Kelleher, Major Patrick N., 75
Kelly, Brigadier General John F., 89-90
Klan, Lance Corporal Joseph J., 14
Klocek, Major Joseph J., 64-65
Kluegel, Lieutenant Colonel David M., 13
Korthaus, Sergeant Bradley S., 60
Kramlich, Brigadier General Richard S., 100
Krulak, Brigadier General Charles C., 1, 2
Kuwait, 6, 9, 13, 15, 17-24, 27-37, 39-42, 44, 46-47, 50, 55-56, 62, 73, 75-76, 81-82, 98-104
Kuwait City, 102
Kuwait City International Airport, 20, 25, 28
Kuwait Naval Base, 20-21, 25, 28, 31, 105
Kuwait Public Transportation Center Bus Terminal III, 105
La Nouvelle Company, 22
Lehnert, Brigadier General Michael R., 14-15, 18-19, 24, 27-28, 70, 74-75, 77, 102, 107
Leonard, Lieutenant Michael P. (USN), 100
logistics movement and engineering coordination center (LMECC), 8-9
logistics movement control center (LMCC), 8, 56, 105
Logistics Support Area Fox. *See* Camp Fox
Logistics Support Area Viper, 12, 27, 36, 44-45, 47-50, 56, 58-63, 67, 69, 73, 75, 77, 81-82, 87-89, 93
Lopez, Captain Jose M., 47, 67
Lucas, Captain Christopher R., 13
Machut, Lieutenant Colonel Roger R., 9, 33-34, 46-47, 58, 60, 87
maintenance, 2-5, 7, 9, 15-17, 27, 33, 48-49, 56, 67,

69, 77, 80, 82, 86-88, 102-103, 105
Malone, Lieutenant Colonel Michael D., 5-6
Marine Corps, U.S.
    Birthday Ball, 106
    units (air)
        3d Marine Aircraft Wing, 5-6, 13, 21, 29, 60, 99
        Marine Wing Support Group 37, 77
        Marine Wing Communications Squadron 48, 29
        Marine Wing Support Squadron 371, 71
        Marine Wing Support Squadron 373, 67
    units (ground)
        Marine Forces, Central Command (MarCent), 2, 15-16, 18, 20-21, 29
        Marine Logistics Command, 2, 4, 14-18, 24-29, 35, 40, 42, 74-77, 101-103
        I Marine Expeditionary Force, 1-8, 10-11, 13-15, 18, 20-21, 26-27, 31, 33-34, 36, 39, 42-44, 47-48, 55, 63, 71-73, 75, 76, 78, 81-82, 89, 93, 98-101, 106-107
        II Marine Expeditionary Force, 17, 26, 28, 31
        I Marine Expeditionary Force Engineer Group, 21, 25, 68, 98
        2d Marine Expeditionary Brigade, 20, 21, 28
        1st Marine Division, 3-5, 7, 9, 12, 16, 21, 29-32, 35-36, 39-40, 43-48, 50, 53, 55-56, 60, 64-67, 69, 71, 73, 76-78, 80-81, 83, 85-87, 89, 91, 93, 95, 98, 104
        Regimental Combat Team 1, 4, 21, 45-46, 50, 53, 55, 57, 64-65, 67, 69, 72, 77, 79, 83, 85, 97
        Regimental Combat Team 2, 7, 31-32, 53, 58
        Regimental Combat Team 5, 4, 39-40, 43, 53, 55-56, 64-65, 70-71, 77-79
        Regimental Combat Team 7, 4, 40, 45, 53, 55, 64-65, 67, 70, 78-79
        4th Marines
            1st Battalion, 99
        5th Marines
            2d Battalion, 99
            3d Battalion, 99
        7th Marines
            1st Battalion, 99
            3d Battalion, 99
        11th Marines, 4, 34, 40, 44, 81, 85, 89, 90
        23d Marines
            3d Battalion, 99
        25th Marines
            2d Battalion, 98
        1st Force Service Support Group, 1-4, 6-9, 11-19, 21-24, 26-28, 30, 34-35, 37, 39-42, 44, 46-48, 51-52, 60, 62, 69, 71-77, 82-84, 88-89, 93-95, 97-98, 100, 102, 107
        2d Force Service Support Group, 1-2, 9, 14, 15-21, 24-29, 35, 46, 70, 77, 101-102, 105-107
        2d Force Service Support Group Forward, 19-21
        4th Force Service Support Group, 3, 5, 10, 12-14, 18, 74
        3d Civil Affairs Group, 52, 80
        Brigade Service Support Group 1, 3, 98
        Combat Service Support Group 1, 4-5
        Combat Service Support Group 11, 3-7, 23, 30-32, 39-40, 44, 46, 50, 56-57, 67, 69, 73, 77, 79-80, 83, 85-87, 89, 93-94, 98-100
        Combat Service Support Group 15, 3, 6-7, 10, 23, 32-33, 71, 98
        Combat Service Support Group 16, 3
        MEU Service Support Group 11, 13
        MEU Service Support Group 22, 7
        Transportation Support Group, 3, 7-8, 23, 36-37, 40, 49-51, 74-76, 98
        11th Marine Expeditionary Unit (Special Operations Capable), 13
        15th Marine Expeditionary Unit (Special Operations Capable), 20-21, 71, 73
        22d Marine Expeditionary Unit (Special Operations Capable), 7
        24th Marine Expeditionary Unit (Special Operations Capable), 20, 26, 72
        1st Combat Engineer Battalion, 35
        1st Tank Battalion, 67

Index

1st Transportation Support Battalion, 3, 4, 7, 35

2d Combat Engineer Battalion, 35, 96, 97

2d Dental Battalion, 16, 18

2d Maintenance Battalion, 15-17, 82, 102

2d Medical Battalion, 16, 18

2d Military Police Battalion, 16-17, 24, 76

2d Supply Battalion, 15-17, 26, 102

2d Transportation Support Battalion, 15-17, 20, 27, 41, 44, 49, 56, 75-76

3d Light Armored Reconnaissance Battalion, 34, 44, 55-56, 67

4th Landing Support Battalion, 5, 13

4th Light Armored Reconnaissance Battalion, 99

4th Maintenance Battalion, 18

4th Supply Battalion, 18

6th Communications Battalion, 14

6th Engineer Support Battalion, 3, 9-10, 13, 23, 33, 35, 37, 46-37, 50, 58-60, 73, 81, 86-87, 94, 98

6th Motor Transport Battalion, 3, 8-9, 35-36, 45, 49, 76

7th Engineer Support Battalion, 3, 9, 23, 33-35, 44, 47, 66-69, 71, 94, 97-100

8th Communications Battalion, 16, 28-29

8th Engineer Support Battalion, 3, 9, 15, 17, 23-24, 35-37, 40, 46, 64-67, 78, 83-85, 95-97

Combat Service Support Battalion 10, 3-5, 11, 31-32, 37, 39-40, 43, 45, 48, 50, 56-57, 59, 67, 69, 77-81, 85-86, 89, 93-94, 98

Combat Service Support Battalion 12, 3, 6-7, 33, 37, 40, 42, 47-48, 67, 71-73, 78-83, 97-98

Combat Service Support Battalion 13, 3, 5, 6

Combat Service Support Battalion 18, 3, 6-7, 26, 33, 37, 40, 42, 44, 47-49, 58, 69, 73, 81, 83, 88

Combat Service Support Battalion 19, 13

Combat Service Support Battalion 22, 3, 7, 31-32, 53, 57-58, 69, 87, 98

Headquarters and Service Battalion (1st FSSG), 3, 6, 35

Headquarters and Service Battalion (2d FSSG), 16, 25

Health Services Battalion, 3, 10, 18, 23, 33-34, 75

Beach and Terminal Operations Company, 42

Combat Service Support Company 101, 89, 99

Combat Service Support Company 102, 99

Combat Service Support Company 103, 99

Combat Service Support Company 104, 99

Combat Service Support Company 105, 99

Combat Service Support Company 111, 3-4, 40, 46, 67, 71, 77, 79, 98

Combat Service Support Company 115, 3-4, 43, 56, 67, 70, 77, 79, 85, 99

Combat Service Support Company 117, 3-4, 45, 67, 78-79, 85, 99

Combat Service Support Company 121, 80, 87

Combat Service Support Company 133, 3, 5, 6

Combat Service Support Company 134, 3, 5, 6

Combat Service Support Company 135, 3, 5, 6

Combat Service Support Company 151, 3, 6, 42, 99

Combat Service Support Company 181, 69

Combat Service Support Company 191, 13

Combat Service Support Company 222, 7

Combat Service Support Company

Tripoli, 89, 94
    Marine Logistics Command Support Detachment 1, 27, 42
    Warfighting Center, 55
Maritime Prepositioning Force (MPF), 17, 20, 29, 33, 99, 101-106
Maritime Prepositioning Ship Squadrons (MPSRONs), 19, 20
Martin, Lieutenant Colonel Christopher B., 17
Mattis, Major General James N., 32, 104
McCarthy, Major Michael P., 59-60
McGowan, Major Brandon D., 26
medical augmentation program (MAP), 18, 61
medical support, 2, 4, 7, 9-10, 16-18, 25-27, 30, 32-33, 37, 45, 48, 53-54, 60-61, 63-64, 71, 73, 75, 81, 87, 90
Meier, Colonel William A., 24
military police, 4, 10-12, 17-18, 24, 27, 43-45, 76-77, 80, 86, 103
Miller, First Lieutenant Ryan L., 99
Mills, Major Don A., 103
mission oriented protective posture (MOPP), 30-31
Moore, Colonel Darrell L., 4, 13, 44, 47, 74, 93-94
mortuary affairs, 33, 54-55, 80, 87-88, 98
motor transport, 4, 8-9, 17, 48, 69, 99, 103
Murney, Lieutenant Colonel Kathleen M., 6, 71
Natonski, Brigadier General Richard F., 53
Naval Hospital Jacksonville, 61
Navy Units
    Fleet Hospital Three, 63
    Navy Mobile Construction Battalion 4, 25
Nelson, Lieutenant Colonel Niel E., 9, 35, 46, 64-67, 83-85, 95
Nestle Washdown Site, 104
Nethercot, Major Julie L., 29
Norris, Chief Warrant Officer 2 Terry G., 83
O'Bannon, Second Lieutenant Presley N., 89
O'Connor, Captain Peter F. (USN), 63
Olness, Captain Michael F., 75
opening package, 39-40, 43, 45
Operations
    Desert Shield/Desert Storm, 1-2, 4, 6, 8, 55, 71, 107
    Desert Spear, 13
    Enduring Freedom, 10, 26
    Iraqi Freedom, 1-2, 4-10, 13, 17-19, 21, 26-29, 33, 35, 38-39, 50-51, 55, 63, 70, 73, 75, 77, 83, 88, 101, 107
    Just Cause, 14
    Sea Signal, 14
    Uphold Democracy, 82
Operations Plan 1003V, 13, 19, 28, 39, 93
operation systems control center (OSCC), 29
Orlando, Lieutenant Colonel Kim S. (USA), 11, 12
Otto, Colonel Stephen W., 19
Pachuta, Captain Stephen M. (USN), 18
Padilla-Ramirez, Sergeant Fernando, 72
Pasagian, Major Arthur J., 19
Persian Gulf War, 1-2, 4, 39
PFC James Anderson Jr. (T-AK-3002), 20, 105
Poindexter, Lieutenant Colonel Scott H., 9, 34
Pomfret, Colonel John J., 4, 30-31, 39, 46, 50, 77
Poole, Captain Forrest C., III, 45
post exchange (PX), 16, 22, 25, 33, 86, 88-89
Pratt, Major Thomas M., 65, 83
Qalat Sikar, 51, 67, 71-72, 87
Raimo, Major David V., 23
reconstitution, regeneration, and re-embarkation (R3), 101, 104-105
rehearsal of concept (ROC) drill, 29-30
Reist, Colonel David G., 3, 7-8, 36
Repair and Replenishment Points (RRPs)
    RRP1, 40, 41
    RRP2, 40, 41, 43
    RRP3, 39, 41, 45, 50
    RRP4, 39, 41, 43, 50
    RRP7, 41, 46, 50, 56, 67
    RRP10, 41, 56-57
    RRP14, 71
    RRP19, 41, 78-80
    RRP22, 41, 79
    RRP23, 41, 80, 85
    RRP 24, 41, 67, 69, 71, 77-78
    RRP25, 41, 77-79
    RRP26, 41, 86-87, 89
    RRP26A, 41, 86
    RRP29, 89

RRP30, 41, 94
RRP30A, 41, 94
reservists, 5-6, 8-11, 13-14, 17, 28, 52, 54, 60
reverse osmosis water purification units (ROWPUs), 50, 59-60, 86, 89, 98
Routes
    Dallas, 43
    Tampa, 43, 45-46
Rumaylah Oil Fields, 39, 43, 53
Sablan, Major Ronald W., 82
Saddam Canal, 53, 55, 58, 78, 82
Safwan Hill, 40
Saipan (LHA 2), 7, 31
Salman Pak, 86
Sanchez, Lieutenant General Ricardo S., 100
Sanchez, Sergeant Major Manual J., 37-38
sandstorm, 48, 55, 57-58, 60, 66-67, 69-70, 103-104
Sarabadi Airfield, 80
Seabees, U.S. Navy 17, 25, 60, 68, 86, 96, 100
Seamon, Major Timothy B., 64, 66, 78
Shane, Staff Sergeant Perry H., 67
Sheahan, Colonel James P., 12-13
Shia, 53, 93
shock trauma platoon (STP), 7, 10, 18, 30, 32, 45, 53, 58, 60, 63, 69, 71, 81, 90
Shottenkirk, Captain Grant R., 4
Smith, Lieutenant Colonel David M., 102
Solis, Second Lieutenant Alan J., 99
Special Purpose Marine Air Ground Task Force (SP-MAGTF), 101-103, 105-106
Stokes, Second Lieutenant Sarah M., 56
supply, 4-6, 15, 17, 25-26, 32, 69, 70, 82, 86, 89, 91, 102
Support Area (SA)
    Anderson, 67, 69, 72-73, 75, 79-80, 82
    Basilone, 67, 71-72
    Chesty, 40, 75, 78, 80-83, 85, 87, 89, 94-95, 97-98
    Daly, 81, 86, 87
    Edson, 75, 93-94, 97, 100
    Geiger, 75
Sweeney, Colonel John L., 4, 37-38, 73

Tactical Assembly Area (TAA) Coyote. *See* Camp Coyote.
Talleri, Colonel Peter J., 102
Task Forces
    Dirt Pig, 68
    Hook, 81
    Pegasus, 41, 49, 77
    Tarawa, 7, 21, 28, 31-32, 35, 44, 46-48, 53, 55, 57, 60, 64, 80, 83, 87, 94-95, 97-98
    Tripoli, 89-93
    Yankee, 13
third country national (TCN), 20, 27-28, 42, 75, 103, 105
Thomas, Lieutenant Colonel Valerie E., 52, 62
Thompson, Captain Suzan F., 4, 43-44, 70-71
Tigris River, 48, 67, 78-79, 83
Tikrit, 79, 89-94
Tran, First Lieutenant Minh D., 99
TruckInt, 77
Twentynine Palms, CA, 4-5, 16, 57, 98
Udairi Range, 32
Usher, Brigadier General Edward G. III, 2-5, 7-9, 11-14, 22, 26, 30, 35, 44, 48, 57, 70-71, 73, 75, 84, 93, 100, 107
U.S. Military Academy, West Point, 1
Varicak, Major Michael C., 78
Vasquez, First Sergeant Gonzalo A. "Butch", 40
vehicles
    amphibious assault vehicle (AAV), 49, 53, 74, 87-88
    seven-ton truck, 8, 40, 45, 56, 72, 78, 81
    heavy equipment transporter (HET), 74
    high mobility multipurpose wheeled vehicles (HMMWV), 10
    M1A1 Abrams tank, 48, 80
    M1A2 Abrams tank, 92
    M2A3 Bradley fighting vehicle, 92
    M88 Hercules tank, 67
    MK48 logistics vehicle system (LVS), 36, 78
Vietnam War, 17, 20, 56
Vincent, Major John E., 71-73
Wallace, Lieutenant Timothy A. (USN), 17

Walter Reed Army Institute of Research Land Combat Study Team, 63
Wasit, 93
Weapons
    60mm mortars, 94-95
    AK-47, 44, 100
    bangalore torpedoes, 95
    M240G, 67

SA-7 shoulder-fired surface-to-air missile, 94
Weinkle, Lieutenant Colonel Robert K., 4-5, 31, 39, 45, 57, 79, 94
Wentz, Gunnery Sergeant Wesley M., 23
Winthrop, Captain Andrew R., 44
Wissler, Colonel John E., 15-17, 41-42
Wojnaroski, Major Edward P., 43, 57
Young, Major Devon C., 82

www.ingramcontent.com/pod-product-compliance
Lightning Source LLC
Chambersburg PA
CBHW060254240426
43673CB00047B/1927